Our Roots Are
Still Alive

The Story of the
Palestinian People

Written by the Palestine Book Project:
Joy Bonds, Jimmy Emerman, Linda
John, Penny Johnson, Paul Rupert

Illustrations: Ron Weil of Gonna Rise
Again Graphics

Design: Leah Statman of Gonna Rise
Again Graphics

Layout: Joy Bonds and Leah Statman

Peoples Press

We wish to thank all the people who supported this book - especially those who read and criticized its several drafts. Special thanks to Hal Muskat and Harvey Bender who worked on the book in its earliest and most difficult stages.

We wish to extend special thanks to Milton Taam of Liberation News Service, whose photos appear on pages 81, 87, 124, 126, 130, 161, 170, 174, 176, 178.

Library of Congress Cataloging in Publication Data

Peoples Press. Palestine Book Project.
    Our roots are still alive.

    Bibliography: p.
    1. Jewish-Arab relations—1917-   I. Title.
DS 119.7.P44 1977   956.9   77-10952

Published and copyrighted by Peoples Press, 1977.

Single copies, $3.50. Discounts available for bulk and classroom orders. Permission to reprint parts of this book can be obtained from Peoples Press. For additional copies and a catalog of other materials, write:

                    Peoples Press
                    PO Box 40130
                    San Francisco, CA 94110
                    (415) 282-0856

To the people of Tal al Zaatar
Their resistance is a torch for all those struggling for freedom.

Middle East

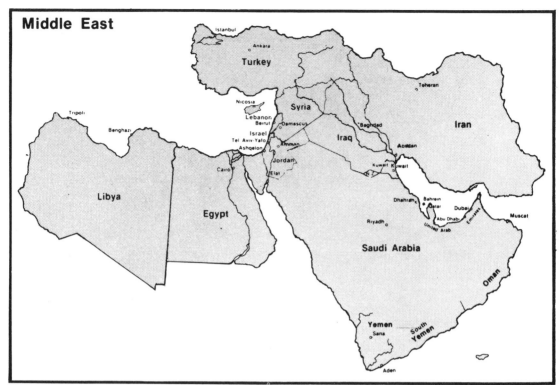

Istanbul
Ankara
Turkey
Teheran
Nicosia
Syria
Lebanon
Beirut
Damascus
Baghdad
Iran
Israel
Tel Aviv-Yafo
Amman
Iraq
Ashqelon
Abadan
Tripoli
Benghazi
Jordan
Kuwait Kuwait
Cairo
Elat
Libya
Egypt
Dhahran
Bahrein
Dubai
Qatar
Muscat
Riyadh
Abu Dhabi
United Arab
Emirates
Saudi Arabia
Oman
Yemen
Sana
South Yemen
Aden

Palestine

Lebanon
Damascus
GOLAN HEIGHTS
Haifa
Nazareth
Syria
Nablus
Tel Aviv
Jaffa (Yafo)
WEST BANK
Jordan River
Lydda
Jerusalem
Amman
Hebron
Gaza
Dead Sea
GAZA STRIP
Israel
Jordan
SINAI PENINSULA
Elat
Al 'Aqabah

Contents

Introduction

Our Roots Are Still Alive is a book about the Palestinian people. It is the story of a people uprooted by force of arms from their homeland, deprived of their means of existence, branded as refugees. Yet the Palestinians have survived, kept alive their history and culture, and have unceasingly sought to return to their homeland.

This is the story of a people who have faced immense difficulties. It is not a difficult story to understand, yet it is rarely told in the United States. Understanding what has happened to the Palestinians unlocks the history of the Middle East in this century: for the Palestinian people are at the heart of the conflict in the Middle East today.

This book is necessarily a story of war and conflict. It tells how powerful European countries fought to control the land, waterways and rich resources of the Middle East; how Jews from Russia and Europe, in a movement called Zionism, fought to establish the state of Israel on Palestinian soil; how the United States became involved in the Middle East, what its interests are, and how it uses every weapon at its command to protect those interests.

This book is also a story of the human spirit — its strength and vision. The Palestinians are not exceptional people. They share with people everywhere a most common and persistent longing: to live in peace, with the dignity possible only in a society that is free and just. Only their particular circumstances and history set them apart. It is here, in their story, that the spirit of sacrifice and determination emerges once again, as it does among all people who take their hopes and dreams in hand, to forge a better future for themselves and their children.

—July, 1977

Chronology

1517 - Ottoman Turks conquer Palestine.

1881 - Pogroms begin in Russia. First wave of Jewish immigration to Palestine.

1897 - First Zionist Congress, held in Basle, Switzerland, proclaims goal of a "national home in Palestine for the Jewish people."

1913 - Arab Congress in Paris demands self-government from Turkey. Anti-Zionist groups begin to form among Palestinians.

1916 - The Arab Revolt against the Turks begins. Britain promises the Arabs independence, but negotiates the secret Sykes-Picot treaty with France to colonize the Arab countries.

November, 1917 - Britain's Balfour Declaration promises a "national home" in Palestine to the Zionists.

1920 - World War I ends. Britain is granted a mandate over Palestine. Riots in Jerusalem.

1921 - 1929 - Series of Palestinian protests against British rule and increased Jewish immigration culminate in major incident at Wailing Wall in 1929.

1933 - Adolph Hitler comes to power in Germany. New influx of Jewish settlers to Palestine.

1936 - 1939 - Palestinian general strike and armed rebellion against the British Mandate government, demanding independence for Palestine. Heavy fighting throughout the country.

1939 - British issue White Paper restricting Jewish immigration to Palestine. World War II begins.

1942- 1946 - Zionists shift organizing focus to the U.S. and issue Biltmore Program in New York City calling for the formation of a Jewish State in Palestine. Open warfare flares between Britain and the Zionists.

November 1947 - The UN votes to partition Palestine. War begins in Palestine between Zionists and Palestinians.

May 15, 1948 - State of Israel proclaimed. Arab League troops intervene in Palestine on behalf of Palestinians.

January 1949 - Ceasefire. Israel occupies 80 percent of Palestine. Three-quarters of a million Palestinians made refugees.

1956 - President Nasser of Egypt nationalizes the Suez Canal. Israel, France and Britain invade Egypt. On the eve of the invasion, Israeli soldiers massacre 37 Palestinians at Kfar Kassem. Israel withdraws from Egypt after six months of occupation.

1958 - Fateh - the Palestine National Liberation Movement - is founded.

1964 - Palestine Liberation Organization founded in Cairo.

1965 - Palestinian guerrillas launch armed struggle against Israel.

June 5 - June 11, 1967 - War between Israel and the Arab states of Egypt, Syria and Jordan. Israel triples in size, occupying the rest of Palestine, as well as the Egyptian Sinai and the Syrian Golan.

March 1968 - Palestinian guerrillas hold off major Israeli attack at Karameh, Jordan.

February 1969 - Palestinian Resistance assumes control of the Palestine Liberation Organization. PLO adopts goal of a "democratic secular state" in all of Palestine.

September 1970 - King Hussein launches all-out attack against Palestinians in Jordan.

May 1973 - Palestinians and Lebanese supporters defend refugee camps against attack by Lebanese Army.

August 1973 - Palestine National Front formed in the Occupied Territories - the West Bank and Gaza Strip.

October 6, 1973 - Egypt and Syria start limited war against Israel. After the ceasefire, U.S. Secretary of State Henry Kissinger begins "shuttle diplomacy" to try to reach a settlement favorable to U.S. interests.

November 1974 - PLO Chairman Yasser Arafat addresses the United Nations. PLO granted observer status at UN. First General Uprising in the Occupied Territories.

April 1975 - Lebanese rightists begin civil war in an attempt to crush the Palestinian presence in Lebanon.

September 1975 - Kissinger engineers Israeli-Egyptian agreement.

November 1975 - UN condemns Zionism as a form of racism and recognizes the "national rights" of the Palestinians. Second General Uprising in the Occupied Territories.

January 1976 - Beginning of Third General Uprising in Occupied Territories when U.S. vetoes resolution supporting the national rights of the Palestinians in the UN Security Council.

May 31, 1976 - Syria invades Lebanon to tame Palestinians and prevent a leftist victory in the war.

August 12, 1976 - The refugee camp of Tal al Zaatar falls to the rightists after seven weeks of siege.

October, 1976 - Riyadh Summit Conference establishes an uneasy peace in Lebanon.

March 1977 - Palestine National Council affirms independence of the Palestinian movement and its goal of a democratic secular state.

1: Our Roots Are Entrenched Deep in the Earth

Here — we have a past
        a present
        a future.
Our roots are entrenched
Deep in the earth.
Like twenty impossibles
We shall remain.
—Tawfiq Zayyad

For centuries, the peasants of the Palestinian village, al-Yahudiyya, were a people wedded to their land. Their village rested in a valley among the hills of central Palestine, near the port city of Jaffa. Like other Palestinians in the thousand or so villages that dotted the countryside, they had painstakingly terraced many of the hills, converting them to usable land. Irrigation ditches built by their ancestors centuries before brought water to the land which yielded citrus, olives and grain. On the rocky hills bedouins — nomadic people — followed the spring grasses with their herds, and villagers tended sheep and cattle. The people of al-Yahudiyya used the nearby land for grazing their animals. In the late 1880s, two moneylenders gained formal ownership of this land as payment for village debts. As the peasants considered use of the land a God-given right, the passing of ownership did not worry them. But soon, these traditional assumptions and the villagers' way of life were challenged by newcomers to Palestine.

In 1878 Jewish settlers from Europe bought al-Yahudiyya's grazing land from the two moneylenders. They established an agricultural colony, Petah Tiqva, but remained aloof from the surrounding Palestinian villages. After several years the new settlers ordered the Palestinian peasants to stop using the pastures for grazing. However, the peasants continued to use the land, and tempers flared quickly on both sides. One day in March 1886, the Jewish settlers seized ten of the Palestinians' donkeys — an act which sparked an attack by fifty angry villagers from al-Yahudiyya. Turkish authorities, who ruled Palestine at the time, immediately sent soldiers to protect the settlers at Petah Tiqva. Two days later the Turks arrested thirty-one Palestinians from al-Yahudiyya and ordered them held for trial.[1]

The fighting at Petah Tiqva was the first skirmish in what has become a century-long battle between the Palestinian people and Jewish settlers from Europe for the land of Palestine. But the incident at Petah Tiqva was not the first time foreigners and Palestinians clashed for control of this small strip of land by the Mediterranean Sea. The history of Palestine is one of frequent invasion and repeated resistance.

Crossroads for Empire

Palestine lies at the crossroads of three continents — Europe, Asia and Africa — and is a holy land to three major religions — Islam, Christianity and Judaism. A succession of empires and conquerors have sought control of Palestine's port cities and trade routes, its land and people. Each newcomer eventually was either absorbed into the population or replaced by yet another conqueror. Since the seventh century, the people of Palestine have been Arab, with a common language and culture. Palestinian cities like Jerusalem were centers of Arab civilization where scholars, poets and scientists congregated. Over the centuries, most Palestinians became Moslems, although small communities of Jews and Christians maintained their faiths.

The Sultan of Turkey conquered Palestine for his Ottoman Empire in 1517. For the next four hundred years, the Turks ruled Palestine as part of an administrative area called Greater Syria — which was to become the countries of Palestine, Syria and Lebanon in the twentieth century. Although Palestine was not a precisely defined geographic area until that time, the people of Jerusalem, Jaffa, Haifa, Gaza and Nablus and the peasants in the surrounding countryside used the term *Filastin* or Palestine to describe their land.

Even under the rule of the Turks, and for as long as the villagers could remember, the land of Palestine belonged to those who worked it. The peasants had to pay heavy taxes on the land, and many lived their lives in debt to local merchants and tax collectors. Drought, locusts, bad harvests and occupying armies plagued their way of life. But as long as the peasants worked in the orchards and fields, buried their dead on the land and raised their children to till it, they believed no one would dare to take their land. Events outside of Palestine were soon to prove them wrong.

The Turkish Empire had weakened in the years since it captured Palestine, and the Sultan had been forced to grant many concessions to the rising empires of Europe. Britain was especially interested in gaining control of the Middle East. For over two centuries the ships and agents of the British Empire had roamed the world, plundering the wealth of Asia, Africa and the Americas. The slave trade from Africa and the seizure of gold, silver, cotton, spices and other goods had made Britain the most industrialized country in the world. As British factories produced more goods, Britain searched for new markets for its products. In 1838 Britain signed the Anglo-Turkish Treaty which allowed British merchants complete freedom to sell their goods in Arab markets. Over the next ten years, British exports to Greater Syria tripled. As Britain's economic stake in the area grew, it looked for a way to extend its political influence.

The British thought they could gain a foothold in Palestine by offering "protection" to one of its religious minorities. Other European powers had given protection to small Christian sects, granting them special privileges, including immunity from trial by Turkish courts and exemption from many taxes. In 1840 Britain set up a consulate in Jerusalem for the protection of the twenty thousand Jews who lived in religious communities in Palestine.

The protection of these Jews was only a first step. Once Britain had taken the Jews of Palestine under its wing, some British politicians began to envision a more powerful method of control — the founding of a *European* Jewish settler colony on Palestinian soil. In 1840 Lord Palmerston, a powerful British aristocrat, asked his government to give its official seal of approval to the immigration of European Jews to Palestine.[2] He argued that this scheme would serve the larger interests of the British Empire. The trade routes across Palestine were, as one official said, "the high road to India." India was Britain's richest colony, a major source of cotton for the flourishing British textile industry. A grateful and dependent community of Europeans in Palestine would make this strategic way-station between England and India friendlier to British interests.

In 1875 the British gained control of the newly built Suez Canal in Egypt. Now British merchant ships could sail from Europe to India in half the previous time. Securing Palestine would give the British a buffer zone to the east of the vital canal. The proposal for Jewish colonization of Palestine became more appealing to British ruling circles. Lord Shaftsbury argued its merits in 1876:

> Syria and Palestine will before long become very important. The country wants [lacks] capital and population. The Jews can give it both. And has not England a special interest in promoting such restoration? It would be a blow to England if either of her rivals should get a hold of Syria. Her Empire reaching from Canada in the West to Calcutta and Australia in the South East would be cut in two .... She must preserve Syria to herself .... To England then naturally belongs the role of favoring the settlement of the Jews in Palestine.[3]

European Settlers Come to Palestine

Palestinians in the port city of Jaffa took note of the first great influx of European settlers in the 1880s. During these years the Czar of Russia encouraged a series of attacks on Russian Jews. Under the banner of Zionism (which we will explore further in the next chapter) thousands of European Jews came to Palestine. Most of the new immigrants settled in Jerusalem or Jaffa. Many were anxious to find work or open shops in the cities; but others wanted to farm. Jewish settlers formed eight agricultural colonies in these first years. Since there was very little uncultivated land in Palestine, each land purchase by Jewish settlers displaced Palestinian peasants. As the incident at Petah Tiqva showed, the presence of European settlers caused friction from the very beginning. On a visit to Palestine in 1891, Ahad Ha'am, a famous Jewish writer, observed the high-handed manner of the settlers:

> [They] treat the Arabs with hostility and cruelty, deprive them of their rights, offend them without cause and even boast of these deeds; and nobody among us opposes this despicable inclination.[4]

Palestinians rebelled against such treatment and the loss of their lands. In addition to the attack on Petah Tiqva in 1886, there were minor incidents over the next several years at many of the Jewish settlements and a major attack on the colony at Rehovet in 1892. Some Palestinians began to demand that the Turks prohibit land sales to Europeans. In the towns and cities, too, there was growing unrest. Wealthy Palestinian families watched uneasily as control of trade in the cities passed slowly to Europeans. Many of these prominent Palestinian families had prospered under Turkish rule. Along with other powerful families in Greater Syria, they had often been able to pressure the Sultan on matters which affected them. But in the last years of the nineteenth century, their influence diminished as the Europeans gained more power over the Turkish Sultan.

British strength in particular continued to grow. In 1881, the same year the first Zionist settlers came to Palestine, the British conquered Egypt. During the next twenty years Britain frequently imposed its will on the Turkish Sultan. A test of Palestinian and British influence with the Turks came in 1903 when Zionists asked to establish the Anglo-Palestine Company in Jaffa. The Company was a bank designed to help Zionists buy land in Palestine. Palestinians in Jaffa demanded that the Sultan stop the bank, and at first he agreed. But when the British informed the Sultan that they backed the bank, he gave in. The Sultan's action angered Palestinians, and some of them began to sharply criticize Turkish rule over their country.

Palestinians became more hopeful in 1908 when the Young Turks, a group of Turkish military officers, overthrew the Sultan. The Young Turks promised equality for all peoples in the empire and convened a parliament with representatives from all the Arab provinces. In order to secure goodwill for the new government, the Young Turks lifted the censorship which had been imposed by the Sultan.

Throughout the Arab provinces, aboveground and underground movements emerged, demanding greater freedom for the Arab peoples. Most Arabs were not yet demanding complete independence from the Turks, hoping instead for reforms within the empire. Palestinians were part of this young Arab nationalist movement. As soon as the censorship ended, prominent families and intellectuals in Palestine began to publish newspapers — *Falastin* in Jaffa and *al-Karmel* in Haifa. Through these papers, Palestinians joined with other Arabs in calling for reforms, including the use of Arabic as an official language. The Palestinians also began to examine Zionist designs on Palestine, and called on the rest of the Arab peoples to learn about this movement of European settlers.

The Young Turks understood that the Arab nationalist movement was a threat to their empire. Soon they banned all political organizations which seemed to favor self-government for the Arabs, and restored a strict censorship. They made Turkish the only official language of the schools and government. Arrogant officials and Turkish intellectuals mocked Arab history and culture. This repression only sparked more Arab resistance. In 1911 seven Arab students in Paris created *al-Fatat,* the Young Arab Society. Organizing secretly in small cells, *al-Fatat* grew quickly to a membership of several hundred in the Arab provinces. It demanded total independence from the Turks.

In February 1913, the Committee of Reform in Beirut, an aboveground group, went beyond the limits allowed by the Turks and openly demanded self-government for the Arab provinces. Large demonstrations of support were held in Syria and Palestine. Telegrams calling for independence were sent to Constantinople, the Turkish capital. The Turks immediately dissolved the Committee and closed down its headquarters. Shops and businesses in Beirut shut down in protest. Newspapers appeared with black borders and printed as their only story the Turkish order to dissolve the Committee. Demonstrations swelled until the Turks withdrew their order. The Committee then joined with *al-Fatat* to hold the First Arab Congress in Paris in June, 1913. The Congress raised demands for an end to Turkish censorship, for the use of the Arabic language and for greater Arab self-government.

Palestinians supported these demands, but they criticized the Congress for failing to note the particular threat which Zionism posed to Palestinian Arabs. Only a few months earlier a large land sale to the Zionists had prompted *Filastin* to write:

> [I]f this state of affairs continues ... then the Zionists will gain mastery over our country, village by village, town by town; tomorrow the whole of Jerusalem will be sold and then Palestine in its entirety.[5]

For thirty years, Palestinians had witnessed Zionist settlers from Europe arriving to colonize their land. This experience prompted them to begin building an organized political movement that combined Arab nationalism with specific Palestinian issues. Increasingly the movement opposed both Turkish rule and Zionist colonization. In 1913 a Palestinian lawyer from Jaffa founded the National Party with the specific goal of fighting Zionism. Anti-Zionist societies formed in the Palestinian cities of Jerusalem and Nablus and in Egypt and Iraq as well. They tried to raise money to buy lands that might otherwise be sold to Zionist colonies. Palestinians rioted in Tiberias in 1914 when Zionists tried to buy the Hulah marshes and its rich mineral concessions from the Turks.

As the conflict between the Arab people of Palestine and the Zionist settlers intensified, more and more Palestinians began to study the Zionist movement carefully. Palestinian students translated Zionist documents from Europe and circulated them secretly in Palestine. These writings clearly proclaimed the Zionist goal — to build a Jewish state in Palestine.

Footnotes

1. Neville J. Mandell, *The Arabs and Zionism before World War I* (Berkeley, Calif.: 1976), pp. 35-36.
2. Cited by George Jabbour, *Settler Colonialism in Southern Africa and the Middle East* (Beirut: 1970), p. 22.
3. Ibid., p. 23.
4. "The Truth in Palestine," in Hans Kohn, ed., *Nationalism and the Jewish Ethic,* (New York: 1962), cited by Erskine Childers, "The Wordless Wish: From Citizens to Refugees," in Ibrahim Abu-Lughod, ed. *The Transformation of Palestine,* (Evanston, Ill.: 1971), pp. 166.
5. Mandell, pp. 139-40.

2: Zionism: The False Return

This land (Russia) where we have been living for many hundreds of years and to which we are bound by thousands of threads — this land is our home.
—Jewish Workers Organization (Bund) in Russia

Jewish settlers came to Palestine under the banner of a movement called Zionism. In the Zionist view, the history of Palestine ended with the Roman conquest of the Jewish Kingdom in 70 A.D. The intervening two thousand years of Palestinian history were brushed aside by the new immigrants, eager to colonize the region. In the eyes of the Zionists, Palestine was waiting for its rightful owners—the Jewish people—to return.[1]

The First Zionist Congress founded the World Zionist Organization at Basle, Switzerland, in 1897. The Congress proclaimed: "The aim of Zionism is to create for the Jewish people a home in Palestine secured by public law." The word "home" was a diplomatic way to say "state," as Theodore Herzl, the first president of the World Zionist Organization, confided in his diary. "No need to worry," Herzl wrote, "the people will read it as Jewish State."[2] Zionists adopted Herzl's book, *The Jewish State,* as the unofficial manifesto of their movement.

The Czar Orders Pogroms

The Zionist movement to build a Jewish state in Palestine was born in response to the vicious attacks on Jews that were sweeping Russia. Economic crisis plagued the decaying feudal system of Russia in the late 1800s. The increasing misery of the Russian people led to acts of rebellion against the Czar, or king, of Russia. He organized and encouraged pogroms — mass attacks on Jews — to divert his starving subjects' anger away from the real source of their problems: his rule. The Czar's agents exploited the racism and Jew-hating that had smoldered in Christian Europe and Russia for centuries, and had flared up into anti-Semitic movements in times of crisis. Czarist newspapers and secret police provoked the desperate, landless peasants to attack the equally-starving Jews.

The pogroms forced many Jews to leave Russia. Societies known as "Lovers of Zion," which were forerunners of the Zionist organization, convinced some of the frightened emigrants to go to Palestine. There, they argued, Jews would rebuild the ancient Jewish "Kingdom of David and Solomon." Most Russian Jews ignored their appeal and fled to Europe and the United States. By 1900, almost a million Jews had settled in the United States alone.

In that same year, a new round of economic disasters struck Russia. Between 1901 and 1903, three thousand businesses shut down. Over a hundred thousand workers were thrown out into the streets, jobless and hungry. Wages were cut sharply. In the large cities, strikers confronted the police. In the countryside, the Czar's troops shot peasants who were demanding land.

By 1903, a growing revolutionary movement threatened the Czar's throne with demands for a democratic government. Czar Nicholas III and his Interior Minister, Wenzel Von Plehve, desperately ordered a new wave of pogroms. On April 6, 1903, Czarist police stood by with folded arms while a mob attacked Jewish homes and stores in the town of Kishinev. The mob was inflamed by articles in the province's only newspaper, which was funded by Von Plehve. In two days of rioting, forty-six Jews were killed and eighty-six were left wounded or crippled. Eyewitnesses told of Jews being torn in two and babies beaten to death on the street.[3] The news of Kishinev rallied people to protest across Europe and in America. Large demonstrations were held in New York, Philadelphia and Baltimore.

In the Jewish ghettos of Russia, members of the newly founded Zionist Organization clashed with organizers of Russia's growing revolutionary movement over the best way to put an end to the pogroms. Zionists controlled the only legal newspaper in Yiddish — the language which most Russian and Eastern European Jews spoke. All other Yiddish publications were banned. Interior Minister Von Plehve had given his blessing to the Zionist paper earlier in 1903. For despite their differences, Zionists and the Czar's government shared one basic assumption: both believed Jews did not belong in Russia. The paper portrayed Jews as eternal "aliens" in Russia and concluded: "Only one ray of light remains in Jewish life. That is Zionism which calls people to their old home."[4]

Revolutionary organizers attacked the Zionist viewpoint in illegal newspapers, smuggled into shops or passed secretly in the crowded streets of the ghetto. The

Russian workers demanding jobs confront the Czar

Bund, an all-Jewish socialist organization, vigorously protested Zionism's fundamental idea of Jews as "aliens." The Bund's newspaper argued:

> [O]ur ancestors came as peaceful dwellers, and in the course of a thousand years, together with the surrounding population, aided in the cultural development of the land, watering it with their sweat, soaking it with their blood, and covering it with their bones .... The land where we have been living for many hundreds of years and to which we are bound by thousands of threads, this land is our home.[5]

The Bund's Fifth Congress called for a revolutionary solution to anti-Semitism. "Only the common struggle of the proletariat [working class] of all nationalities will destroy those conditions that give rise to such events as the pogrom at Kishinev."[6] All revolutionary parties insisted that only social revolution could put an end to the conditions which fostered anti-Semitism and all forms of racism. V.I. Lenin, the

Russian Jews in Pinsk organized for self-defense against pogroms.

head of the Bolshevik Party, organized against anti-Semitism, pointing out the hand of the Czar in the rioting:

> The Czarist police, in alliance with the landowners and the capitalists, organized pogroms against the Jews. The landowners and capitalists tried to divert the hatred of the workers and peasants who were tortured by want against the Jews .... It is not the Jews who are the enemies of the working people. The enemies of the workers are the capitalists of all countries.[7]

Revolutionary groups won over an increasing number of Russian Jews. In 1903, Chaim Weizmann, a Russian Zionist, sent a report to Theodore Herzl:

> The Zionist movement failed here since it did not succeed in attracting the best of Jewish youth. The lion's share of youth is anti-Zionist, not from an assimilationist point of view as in Western Europe, but rather as a result of their revolutionary mood .... Almost the entire Jewish student body stands firmly behind the revolutionary camp.[8]

A month after the Kishinev pogrom, in May of 1903, Theodore Herzl arrived in Russia as a representative of the World Zionist Organization. He came to meet with Interior Minister Von Plehve, the man who engineered the pogroms. Herzl could have condemned Von Plehve for his crimes against Jews, but he did not come to Russia to discuss pogroms. He wanted Von Plehve's help. The Turkish Sultan had slowed down Zionist immigration to Palestine and Herzl believed the Russian Czar could intervene on the Zionists' behalf. If the Czar did intervene, Herzl would return the favor. At the upcoming Zionist Congress, Herzl would cut off any attacks on the Czar. Herzl recorded in his diary:

> For I had understood all along that he [Von Plehve] attached much importance to the forthcoming Zionist Congress, obviously because he saw that the Kishinev business was bound to come up there for a frank airing. When that happens, I could be in the position of doing him a service by cutting the thing short.[9]

Herzl did as he promised. The Sixth Zionist Congress did not attack anti-Semitism in Russia. Herzl believed that this silence helped the Zionist movement. But it clearly was not in the interests of the beseiged Russian Jews. The questions arise: *In whose interest was Zionism? Whom did it serve?* Although Zionism claimed to be in the interest of poor and working-class Jews, it actually served the needs of middle-class European Jews and the European powers.

Class Base of Zionism

A look at Herzl's own life suggests how Zionism served middle-class Jews. His background was typical of many prosperous Jews in Western Europe at the time. Many held comfortable positions in the professions, trade and finance. They felt assimilated into European society. In the 1880s, economic depression hit all of Europe. The steady stream of penniless Jewish immigrants escaping the Russian pogroms alarmed middle-class Jews. Their security seemed threatened by the new immigrants' poverty, strange accents and distinct customs. Middle-class Jews began to look for their own solution to the problems that anti-Semitism created for them.

Theodore Herzl belonged to this middle class. From his student days, he was aware of the growing anti-Semitism in Austria, where he lived. As a lawyer, before he became a journalist, he had resented being barred as a Jew from the higher positions in the Austrian civil service. But he was not a Jewish activist. He maintained his distance from the plight of Jews until a major Vienna newspaper made him its correspondent in Paris. There he was to become a Zionist.

In January 1895, Herzl began covering the trial of Colonel Alfred Dreyfus, a Jewish officer in the French Army who was charged with spying. The French right wing, in an attempt to wrest control of the army from the liberal forces in the government, launched a vicious campaign against Dreyfus and his liberal defenders. At the heart of the attack was political anti-Semitism — a movement created by the right wing which played upon the anti-Jewish feelings embedded in both organized Christianity and the history of Europe. Pamphleteers portrayed Jews in the government and Jews in general as the source of all social problems, from strikes to treason. In this atmosphere, which Herzl reported on daily, Dreyfus was convicted and stripped of his rank. At the sentencing ceremony the crowd began to shout, *"Death to the traitor! Death to the Jew!"*

Herzl was shaken by the intensity of this anti-Semitism, and became engrossed in the "Jewish problem." At the same time, an international movement organized to demand the pardon of Dreyfus. Petitions and demonstrations attracted many thousands of people who protested and fought against French anti-Semitism. Finally, Dreyfus was pardoned. But Theodore Herzl never became part of that movement. The Dreyfus trial led him to conclude that anti-Semitism was eternal and could not be eradicated. He wrote:

> In Paris, as I have said, I achieved a freer attitude towards anti-Semitism, which I began to understand historically and to pardon. Above all, I recognized the emptiness and futility of trying to "combat" anti-Semitism.[10]

Herzl argued in his book, *The Jewish State,* that the solution for Jews was to build

Theodore Herzl, founder of Zionism

a state of their own. He believed Jews were an alien nationality in Europe. The influx of large numbers of Russian and Eastern European Jews could only lead to more intense anti-Semitism. He called on middle-class Jews to join or at least to support the movement to found a Jewish state, which could attract these Jewish immigrants.

Herzl proposed either Palestine or Argentina as the site for a Jewish state, but he was not attached to any particular location. Unlike the Russian "Lovers of Zion," he felt no connection with the Palestinian "homeland." He wrote, "I shall now tell you everything about the 'promised land' except its location."[11] Herzl did not believe a state could be built on old religious claims. Neither could small bands of Jewish colonists create a state on their own. He argued that a state had to be built under the wing of one of the powerful European countries. For a European country to support the Jewish state, the state must serve European interests. This insight was Herzl's unique contribution to the Zionist movement he helped to found. Herzl's book had started to persuade middle-class Jews that Zionism could serve them. Now it remained to win over Europe's rulers.

Cecil Rhodes, architect of British colonialism in Africa

"We Must Become Imperialists"

As Herzl wrote his manifesto, the crisis-ridden European powers were in particular need of loyal servants. In the late nineteenth century, ruthless competition between capitalist industries led to the formation of giant monopolies. These new monopolies were being challenged by the millions who worked for them. Bitter, bloody strikes, food riots and even insurrections threatened the life of the capitalist system. In France in 1871, French workers had taken over Paris and established the Paris Commune. This first workers' government wanted to overthrow capitalism and establish socialism. The French Army crushed the fighting Commune in a massive attack, but the ideals of socialism were not so easily crushed.

The socialist movement grew as people endured the crisis of the 1880s. The stark poverty brought on by economic depression exposed the failure of capitalism to meet people's basic needs. Workers knew that the monopolies had gathered under their control the most massive system of production in the history of the world.

They could churn out textiles, steel, and other goods in almost endless amounts. And yet when prices dropped, the plants lay idle, producing nothing. People were laid off their jobs and had no money. Desperate and starving, they confronted the monopolies to demand bread and work. Capitalism could not survive these growing challenges without crucial changes. The monopolists needed to expand; they needed markets for their unsold goods, new places to invest their idle capital, and new sources of raw materials and cheap labor. Capitalism was reaching a new and higher stage: *imperialism*. Cecil Rhodes, a British imperial strategist whom Herzl called a "visionary," explained the reasons bluntly:

> I was in the East End of London (a working class quarter) yesterday and attended a meeting of the unemployed. I listened to the wild speeches which were just a cry for "bread, bread!" and on my way home I pondered over the scene and I became more than ever convinced of the importance of imperialism . . . . [I]n order to save the forty million inhabitants of the United Kingdom from a bloody civil war we colonial statesmen must acquire new lands to settle the surplus population, to provide new markets for the goods produced in the factories and mines. The Empire, as I have always said, is a bread and butter question. If you want to avoid civil war, you must become imperialists.[12]

Rhodes spoke as the age of imperialism was dawning. The European powers were searching for new ways to dominate the nations of the world for the benefit of the monopolies. Theodore Herzl was quick to see that the Zionist colonial project offered one way. He explained to a German statesman how Zionism served two of imperialism's main needs: "My movement can help on two fronts: through draining off the surplus Jewish proletariat [working class] and through harnessing international capital."[13]

Herzl sought the help of Cecil Rhodes. Herzl himself was a great admirer of Rhodes' activities in Africa. Rhodes had headed a colonial army to conquer southern Africa for the British. British settlers poured into Africa in the wake of Rhodes' army, conquering the Black population and forcing them to work in the mines and plantations that fed raw materials to British factories. A band of settlers marched into Zimbabwe, in the heartland of Africa, and renamed it Rhodesia, in honor of Rhodes. Herzl wrote to Rhodes, asking for his "stamp of approval on the Zionist plan." He appealed to Rhodes on the basis of common interests in colonialism:

> You are being invited to help make history. This cannot frighten you . . . .
> It is not your accustomed line; it does not involve Africa but a piece of Asia Minor, not Englishmen, but Jews.... How then do I happen to turn to you since this is an out-of-the-way matter for you? How indeed? Because it is something *colonial*.... [emphasis added][14]

To Herzl, Rhodesia and the Jewish state were similar settler-colonial projects. He hoped Rhodes would help him secure the necessary imperial backer.

In *The Jewish State*, Herzl vigorously protested the way earlier Jewish immigration to Palestine had occurred. Without the power of imperialism behind the settlers, these individual efforts — which Herzl called "infiltration" — were doomed to failure:

> An infiltration is bound to end badly. It continues until the inevitable moment when the native population feels itself to be threatened and forces the

Soldiers of Rhodes' Chartered South African Company invade Zimbabwe.

Government to stop further influx of Jews. Immigration is futile unless based on an assured supremacy.[15]

"Assured supremacy" meant having a large, well-equipped army to back up colonization.

The First Zionist Congress charged Herzl with finding an imperial backer. He began a series of trips to the European capitals. He approached the German Kaiser, the Russian Czar and the Pope. He argued that Zionism would rid European society of rebellious Jews and he stressed how a Zionist settler colony would serve the particular needs of whichever ruler he was courting.

The Turkish Sultan, whose weakened empire still formally controlled Palestine, received an offer of help from Herzl. During a visit to Constantinopole in 1903, Herzl tried to play on the popular stereotype of Jews as financial wizards. He promised the Turkish ruler, "If His Majesty the Sultan were to give us Palestine, we could in return undertake the complete management of the finances of Turkey."[16] In the chambers of the Turkish parliament, Palestinian deputies raised a storm of protest. Other Arab members backed them up. With trouble brewing all over his empire, the Sultan could not openly promise Palestine to the Zionists.

Herzl finally focused on the rising empire of Britain. Herzl understood where Great Britain's interests lay. He wrote:

England with her possessions in Asia should be most interested in Zionism, for the shortest route to India is by way of Palestine. England's great politicians were the first to recognize the need for colonial expansion. That is why Great Britain's ensign flies on all the oceans. And so I must believe that here in England the idea of Zionism, which is a colonial idea, should be easily and quickly understood in its true and most modern form.[17]

British imperialism was eager to use Zionism to expand its empire, but Britain didn't control Palestine yet. Instead, British Colonial Minister Joseph Chamberlain searched the lands controlled by Britain for a suitable location for a Zionist colony. He was looking for, in the words of the Zionist slogan, "a land without a people for a people without a land." To Chamberlain, "a land without a people" meant a land without *white* people. Chamberlain was ready to offer Zionism a colony anywhere "in the English possessions where there were no white people as of yet."[18] He finally proposed Uganda, an African country.

Herzl was enthusiastic. He argued at the Seventh Zionist Congress for the colonization of Uganda. Herzl's proposal was defeated at the Congress because Russian Zionists would hear of no other place but Palestine. When Herzl died a year later, Chaim Weizmann, a Russian Zionist, became the new leader. He planned to combine Herzl's quest for an imperial backer with the desire of most Zionist followers to acquire Palestine. Palestine had now become the only target, and the sponsor of the Zionists had to be the power which controlled Palestine.

As a new century dawned, imperial competition among the European countries erupted into World War I. Britain, France and Czarist Russia were at war with Germany. When the Ottoman Empire entered the war on the side of Germany, it became clear that the colonies under Turkish control, including Palestine, would be prizes of war. Weizmann knew that Britain wanted control of Palestine. Thus he went to England to campaign for British support for Zionism.

Footnotes

1. Uri Avnery, *Israel Without Zionism* (New York: 1971), pp. 92-93
2. Alan R. Taylor, *Prelude to Israel; An Analysis of Zionist Diplomacy, 1897-1947* (New York: 1959), p. 6.
3. Howard M. Sachar, *The Course of Modern Jewish History* (Cleveland: 1958), pp. 246-48.
4. Henry J. Tobias, *The Jewish Bund in Russia* (Stanford: 1972), p. 223.
5. Ibid., p. 253.
6. Ibid., p. 224.
7. V.I. Lenin, *Collected Works* (Moscow: 1962), 29:252-53.
8. Cited by Arie Bober, ed, *The Other Israel,* (Garden City, NY: 1971), p. 152-53.
9. *The Diaries of Theodore Herzl,* edited and translated by Marvin Lowenthal (New York: 1956), p. 390.
10. *The Diaries of Theodore Herzl* (London: 1958), p. 6, cited in *The Other Israel,* p. 168.
11. Cited by Jabbour, *Settler Colonialism in Southern Africa and the Middle East,* p. 25.
12. Cited by Lenin, *Imperialism, the Highest Stage of Capitalism* (Peking: 1973), p. 94.
13. *Diaries,* Lowenthal edition, p. 120.
14. *The Diaries of Theodore Herzl,* cited by Jabbour, p. 25.
15. Theodore Herzl, *The Jewish State* (New York: 1955), pp. 29-30, cited by Jabbour, p. 25.
16. Herzl, *The Jewish State,* cited in Arthur Hertzberg, ed., *The Zionist Idea,* (New York: 1959), p. 222.
17. Theodore Herzl, *The Complete Diaries* (New York: 1960), cited by Abdullah Schleifer, *The Fall of Jerusalem* (New York: 1972), p. 23.
18. *The Diaries of Theodore Herzl,* cited by Eli Lobel, "Palestine and the Jews," in *The Arab World and Israel* (New York: 1970), p. 115.

3: World War I: Pledges And Betrayals

On October 1, 1918, Arab and British troops liberated Damascus. After 400 years of Turkish rule, Greater Syria was independent at last.

For soldiers and civilians, the battlefields of World War I were vast scenes of death, disease and starvation. Eight million soldiers died in the blood-soaked trenches of Europe. In Greater Syria, one-eighth of the population died of starvation. But for the empires of Europe, the war was a necessary means of re-dividing the world. The decaying empires of Turkey and Austro-Hungary were the biggest prizes. Both Britain and France coveted the Turkish colonies in the Middle East.

Britain acted quickly to gain the inside track. Throughout the first year of the war, the British forged an alliance with Sharif Hussein, the ambitious Arab ruler of the Hejaz, the eastern coast of the Arabian Peninsula. Britain promised to make the Arab countries independent after the war if Hussein would call for an Arab revolt against the Turks. Sir Henry McMahon, the British Consul in Cairo, wrote several letters to Hussein, detailing the lands that would become independent. They included Palestine.[1]

27

Hussein sent his son Feisal to Damascus and Beirut to contact the secret Arab nationalist organizations. Feisal joined the largest and most important group, *al-Fatat,* early in 1916. *Al-Fatat's* members, professionals and sons of the merchant and land-owning class, wanted to wrest control of their countries from the Turks and Europeans. They wanted to establish an independent government in all of Greater Syria. Hussein and Feisal, as feudal leaders, preferred an alliance with the British as long as their personal power was secured. On May 5, 1916, Jemel Pasha, the harsh Turkish overlord of Greater Syria, rounded up and executed twenty-one key Arab nationalists, including leaders of *al-Fatat.*

The Arab Revolt

On hearing news of the executions, Feisal called for all Arabs to take up arms against the Turks. After years of repression by the Turks, the Arab people were ready to fight. That June, the Arab Revolt began, under the leadership of Hussein and Feisal. By late 1916, Arab troops had captured most of the Hejaz and laid seige to the Turkish garrison at Medina, pinning down over twelve thousand Turkish troops until the end of the war. Arab attacks on the Hejaz railway slowed Turkish communications and supplies.

Within the Turkish army, massive desertions by Arab soldiers ground military actions to a halt. Throughout Greater Syria, the official press suppressed all stories of the rebellion, but the news spread by word of mouth from village to village. Desertions increased and the spirit of rebellion grew. Enraged, Jemel Pasha placed the country under martial law and ordered wholesale arrests. Suspected members of independence organizations were beaten, confined and starved. But the secret Arab organizations were not destroyed.

By late 1916, as Arab soldiers held down the Fourth Turkish Army, British General Edmund Allenby advanced through Palestine and Syria. British planes showered the villages of Palestine with leaflets reminding the people of the British promises of independence. Palestinians came to the aid of the advancing British. Entering Jerusalem, the British received a warm welcome from the population, which had shrunk to half its pre-war size from starvation and emigration. Hundreds of people in Jerusalem jammed recruiting stations to join the Arab Army.

On October 1, 1918, Arab and British troops entered Damascus. A government had already been formed. The flag of the Arab Revolt was flying, and the people of the city celebrated their long-awaited liberation from the Turks. For the people, it was more than an end to the famine and murder of the war years. Greater Syria was independent at last. Or so it seemed.

The British had won their military victory in the area by promising support for Arab independence. But from the beginning, they never intended to honor their pledge. In 1916, as McMahon wrote his promises to Hussein, a French and a British official met secretly to negotiate the fate of Greater Syria. Sir Mark Sykes of the British War Office and Henri Picot, French Consul of Beirut, planned the dissection of the area after the war. Under their plan, known as the Sykes-Picot Agreement, France was to receive most of present-day Syria and Britain most of present-day Iraq. Both powers wanted Palestine. They compromised on a proposal for an international administration. This betrayal of British promises was kept hidden from the Arab peoples during the war.

Arab workers lay pipeline for the British. By the beginning of World War I, the British viewed Middle Eastern oil as an important prize.

The Balfour Declaration

Britain was equally prepared to betray the French. Palestine was too valuable to share with a less powerful ally. British diplomats resolved to use the Zionist movement to gain full control of Palestine. The Zionists understood their potential role in the British Empire. Chaim Weizmann, the Zionist leader, wrote in a 1914 letter to a British newspaper:

[S]hould Palestine fall within the British sphere of influence and should Britain encourage Jewish settlement.... [we could] develop the country, bring back civilization to it and *form a very effective guard for the Suez Canal.*[2] [emphasis added]

In February of 1917, Chaim Weizmann and Sir Mark Sykes sat down to work out an agreement. Weizmann guaranteed that the Zionists would accept only British control of Palestine in return for an official expression of British support for Zionist settlement in Palestine.[3] Throughout the spring and summer of 1917, British statesmen and Zionist leaders worked on the British declaration of support for Zionism. The first draft stated:

His Majesty's Government accepts the principle that Palestine should be reconstituted as the national home of the Jewish people ... and will be ready to consider any suggestions on the subject which the Zionist organization may desire to lay before them.[4]

29

The draft was reworded several times to find a version that didn't offend English Jews, many of whom opposed Zionism. The largest Jewish organization in England strongly protested against the declaration because it "must have the effect throughout the world of stamping the Jews as strangers in their native lands."[5] The final version of the declaration was a compromise. The Zionists' real goal — the Jewish state — was concealed in the diplomatic term "national home." On November 2, 1917, the declaration was released publicly in the form of a letter from Lord Balfour of the British government to Lord Rothschild, a wealthy English Jew.[6] It read:

Foreign Office,
November 2nd, 1917.

Dear Lord Rothschild,

I have much pleasure in conveying to you, on behalf of His Majesty's Government, the following declaration of sympathy with Jewish Zionist aspirations which has been submitted to, and approved by, the Cabinet.

"His Majesty's Government view with favour the establishment in Palestine of a national home for the Jewish people, and will use their best endeavours to facilitate the achievement of this object, it being clearly understood that nothing shall be done which may prejudice the civil and religious rights of existing non-Jewish communities in Palestine, or the rights and political status enjoyed by Jews in any other country"

I should be grateful if you would bring this declaration to the knowledge of the Zionist Federation.

The Balfour Declaration was meant to be kept secret from the Palestinian Arabs, the "existing non-Jewish communities" in Palestine that were 93 percent of the population and owned 95 percent of the land! On the other hand, British planes dropped copies of the Declaration over cities in Russia and Eastern Europe which had large Jewish populations. Britain hoped the Declaration would win Russian Jews to the war effort and help stem the tide of revolution against the Czar.

But five days after the publication of the Balfour Declaration, the Russian revolution swept Lenin and the Bolsheviks into power. The rule of the Czar was ended forever. The Bolsheviks knew that the workers and peasants had nothing to gain by continuing to fight in a war between imperialist powers. Russian soldiers left the trenches and returned home. The new Soviet government withdrew from the war, and announced its peaceful intentions towards the previously colonized people of the Middle East and Asia:

> Henceforth, your beliefs and customs, your national and cultural institutions are decreed free and inviolable .... We declare that the secret treaties of the dethroned Czar ... are now null and void.[7]

As the Bolsheviks had pledged, the Soviet government published all the secret agreements that Russia had made under the Czar. They released a copy of the Sykes-Picot Agreement and news of the Agreement filtered through to the Arab countries. Soon, the Palestinians also learned of the Balfour Declaration.

The first Arab reaction to the Sykes-Picot Agreement and the Balfour Declaration was disbelief. The Arabs had fulfilled their part of the bargain with Britain by fighting long and courageously against the Turks. Hussein demanded immediate clarification from Britain. In a series of telegrams, letters and meetings, the British tried to pass off the news of the Agreement as a Bolshevik lie and a plot by the Turks and the Germans to fool the Arabs. The British renewed their pledge of self-determination.

The end of the war in November of 1918 revealed the real value of this pledge. France, Britain and the United States, the late-comer into the war, were the victors. They organized the Versailles Peace Conference in January of 1919. When Feisal arrived in Europe as the Arab delegate to the conference, his worst fears were confirmed. The "imaginary" Sykes-Picot Agreement emerged as the subject of a heated debate between the British and the French. The British, stronger than ever after the war, wanted a bigger slice of the Middle East — complete control of Palestine and the Mosul oil fields in Iraq. The use of tanks, planes and ships in World War I had created a strong demand for secure sources of oil, and the British wanted the lion's share of the rich oil fields of the area. They planned to construct a pipeline from Iraq and the Arabian Peninsula to the Palestinian port of Haifa on the Mediterranean Sea.

The Mandate: A Mask for Colonialism

The principle of self-determination, heralded by both Europe and the United States throughout the war, was ignored as the winners began to divide up the spoils of war — the colonies of Germany and Turkey. They created the mandate system, a new name and a new face for colonialism. A nation receiving a mandate would control the land and resources of another people until that people had "progressed far enough along the road to self-government." The nation given the mandate had the right to decide when enough progress had been made.

At the peace conference, Feisal denounced the Sykes-Picot Agreement. He submitted a statement to the conference which read:

Palestinians protest the reading of the Balfour Declaration in Jerusalem, 1919.

> As representing my father, who, by request of Britain and France, led the Arab rebellion against the Turks, I have come to ask that the Arabic-speaking peoples of Asia ... be recognized as independent sovereign peoples....[8]

Feisal urged that an international commission visit Syria and Palestine to determine the wishes of the people. Under pressure from President Woodrow Wilson, the conference reluctantly agreed. Wilson wanted an American mandate in the area and hoped that the commission would propose just that. He immediately appointed two U.S. representatives, Henry King and Charles Crane, to the commission. Feisal left for Damascus, confident the commission would soon follow.

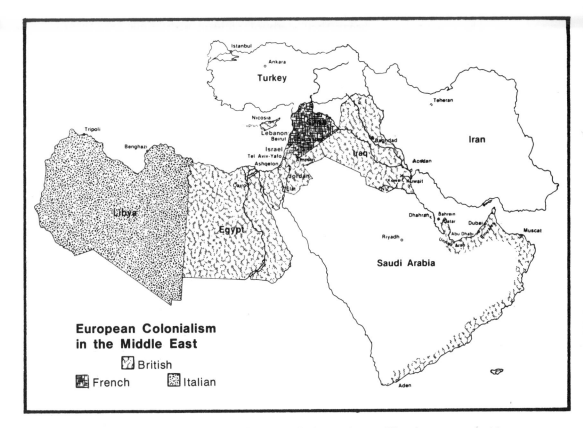

**European Colonialism
in the Middle East**

◫ British

▦ French   ▦ Italian

People in Greater Syria organized for their independence. Elections were held throughout Syria, Palestine, and Lebanon for delegates to a national congress. On July 2, 1919, the General Syrian Congress, meeting in Damascus, unanimously condemned the Sykes-Picot Agreement, the Balfour Declaration, and the plans of the Zionists. They put a pointed question to the Great Powers:

> How can the Zionists go back in history two thousand years to prove that by their short sojourn in Palestine they have now a right to claim it and return to it as a Jewish home, thus crushing the nationalism of a million Arabs?[9]

The Congress denounced the mandate system. It demanded that Greater Syria become one united and independent nation. As the resolutions became known, people demonstrated throughout Syria, Palestine and Lebanon in support of the Congress.

In the meantime, the King-Crane Commission had arrived in Jaffa. It consisted of only the two American representatives; France, Britain and Italy had backed out. The Commission spent six weeks in Syria and Palestine, interviewing delegations and reading petitions. King and Crane recommended an American mandate with two important provisions. First:

> The unity of Syria (Palestine, Syria and Lebanon) ought to be preserved in accordance with the earnest petition of the great majority of the people of Syria.

And second, they recommended "serious modification of the extreme Zionist program." The report stated:

33

The commissioners began their study of Zionism with minds predisposed in its favor .... The facts came out repeatedly in the Commissioners' conferences with Jewish representatives that the Zionists looked forward to a practically complete dispossession of the present non-Jewish inhabitants of Palestine by various forms of purchase.... No British officers, consulted by the Commissioners, believed that the Zionist program could be carried out except by force of arms .... The initial claim, often submitted by Zionist representatives, that they have a "right" to Palestine based on occupation of two thousand years ago, can barely be seriously considered.[10]

On April 5, 1920, Britain, France and the United States met at San Remo, Italy. The findings of the King-Crane Commission were ignored. The United States was not powerful enough to enforce its desire for a U.S. mandate in the Middle East. No government at the conference cared what the peoples of Greater Syria thought or wanted. France received a single mandate for Syria and Lebanon; Great Britain received two mandates, one for Iraq and one for Palestine. The mandate gave Britain a free hand to implement the Balfour Declaration.

But a formal public reading of the Balfour Declaration by a British official in Palestine in February of 1920 had already sparked large demonstrations in Palestinian cities. In April, the month of the San Remo Conference, riots broke out in Jerusalem during Easter Week and Palestinians attacked recent Jewish immigrants. As British officials prepared to govern Palestine, Palestinians had already given warning that they would not accept a British-sponsored settler colony on their land.

Footnotes

1. *The McMahon Correspondence,* cited by George Antonius, *The Arab Awakening* (New York: 1965), p. 419.
2. Letter to C.P. Scott, editor of the *Manchester Guardian,* November 1914, cited by Taylor, *Prelude to Israel,* p. 12.
3. Antonius, p. 263.
4. Leonard J. Stein, *The Balfour Declaration* (London: 1937), p. 664.
5. *London Times,* 24 May 1917, cited by Stein, p. 454.
6. Antonius, p. 266.
7. Ivar Spector, *The Soviet Union and the Moslem World, 1917-1958* (Seattle: 1959), p. 33, cited in "Soviet Policy in the Middle East," *MERIP* no. 39, (Washington, D.C.), p. 3.
8. Cited by Antonius, p. 286.
9. "Syrian Protests Against Zionism," *Literary Digest* no. 66, 3 July 1920, p. 31, cited in *The Transformation of Palestine,* p. 58.
10. Cited by Antonius, pp. 444-49.

4: Building Zion Under The British Gun

The advantages to the British Empire are obvious. The Suez Canal and air stations, the oil-pipe outlet in Haifa and its harbor, have become vital to our naval strategy in the Mediterranean. The security of the imperial complex of interests can be better assured by a large European population than by the few battalions that can be spared.

—British Lord Melchett

A 1920 editorial in a Palestinian newspaper predicted the bloody era of the British mandate. It said:

> Palestine is Arab — its Muslims are Arab — its Christians are Arab — and its Jewish citizens are Arab too. Palestine will never be quiet if it is separated from Syria and made a national home for Zionism.[1]

Arabs call 1920 *Am Al Nakba,* the Year of Catastrophe. Greater Syria was artificially divided into Syria, Lebanon and Palestine, and placed under French or British occupation. The occupying troops met strong resistance. French troops

The British High Commissioner's Garden Party in Jerusalem.

mowed down Syrians defending Damascus and imposed a harsh military dictatorship on Syria. In Iraq, armed rebellion challenged the British mandate.

The British bargained shrewdly with Feisal, who fled Syria after the French occupation. They gave him the throne of Iraq in return for his acceptance of British control. They struck a similar agreement with Feisal's brother, Abdullah. He became the king of Trans-Jordan, a country which the British carved out of eastern Palestine. The feudal chiefs who had led the Arab Revolt during World War I readily accepted a sham independence.

In Palestine, Britain had different plans. It did not offer the government to the local Arab leaders. By issuing the Balfour Declaration, the powerful British Empire had committed itself to overseeing the growth of a Zionist colony on Palestinian land. Britain appointed a leading British Zionist, Sir Herbert Samuel, High Commissioner of Palestine.

"Palestine Will Never Be Quiet"

In December 1920, the Palestine Arab Congress met in Haifa. It was the first all-Palestinian political congress. The delegates discussed the grave dangers confronting the Palestinian people. Palestine faced more than another occupier. The Zionist colony threatened the national life and the individual livelihoods of all Palestinians.

Present at the Congress were members of the powerful merchant and land-owning families of Palestine, along with some professionals. They feared that

Zionism would undermine their position as political leaders and their economic role in Palestine. They elected a twenty-four member Arab Executive that included Christian and Moslem delegates. It began a long round of petitioning the mandate government. The three demands of the Executive remained constant throughout this period.

1. An end to British support for Zionism.
2. An end to Jewish immigration.
3. Formation of a representative national government.

Members of the Executive hoped to convince Britain that they were the rightful leaders of Palestine.

The majority of Palestinians, including peasants and working people in the cities, supported the Arab Executive and their demands in the early years of the mandate period. The month before the Congress, people demonstrated on November 2, the anniversary of the Balfour Declaration. November 2 continued to be a day of mourning for Palestinians throughout the mandate. Arab shops closed their doors, newspapers appeared with black borders, and people draped black crepe paper on their houses and flew black flags. Similar events marked December 9, the day General Allenby entered Jerusalem in 1918 — with the promise of Palestinian independence. Now he had proven to be another conqueror.

Peasants, in particular, felt their survival was at stake. In 1920, Zionists paid Sursuk, an absentee landowner who lived in Beirut, £300,000 for a huge block of land, including twenty-two villages, in the fertile Esdraelon valley of northern Palestine. Six hundred eighty-eight peasant families were driven off the land. Their fields were given to new Jewish immigrants. As Zionist immigration and land purchases increased, the frustration and misery of the peasants and urban poor led to protests stronger than petitions or days of mourning.

In the spring of 1921, Palestinian anger turned into violence in the city of Jaffa. A clash between two Zionist groups at a parade spilled over into the Arab quarter. Palestinians attacked a Jewish immigration center and killed thirteen Jews. Fighting spread throughout the city.

The British appointed the Haycraft Commission to investigate the 1921 "disturbances." It pointed to the source of the bloodshed: Palestinian anger at increased Zionist immigration and at the Zionist goal of a national home in Palestine.[2] But Britain was not about to halt the flow of Jewish immigrants. The year before, in a British policy statement known as a White Paper, Britain had promised to set immigration quotas that would match Palestine's "economic capacity at the time to absorb new arrivals." The pledge was empty. The real guides for British policy were the needs of the British Empire and the capacity of the mandate government to control Palestine. The logic was simple. A Zionist colony would serve the British Empire better than an independent Arab Palestine. European Jewish settlers were more reliable allies than Arab nationalists. Therefore, Jewish immigration had to continue and a representative government could not be allowed. Lord Balfour put the point bluntly in a confidential memorandum of 1919:

[I]n Palestine we do not propose even to go through the form of consulting the

British police constantly harassed Palestinians.

wishes of the present inhabitants of the country .... The Four Powers are committed to Zionism ....[3]

A young Zionist settler from America echoed British logic. Golda Meir, who was later to become prime minister of Israel, wrote in a letter in 1921:

If we dig in here, England will come to our aid. It is not the Arabs whom the English will pick to ... colonize Palestine, it is we.[4]

Colonizing Palestine required a Jewish majority which, in turn, demanded a steady flow of immigrants. Zionism meant, as the Zionist leader Dr. Eder testified in 1921, "one National Home in Palestine, and that a Jewish one, and no equality in the partnership between Jew and Arab, but a Jewish preponderance."[5]

There were fifty-six thousand Jews and about a million Palestinians in Palestine at the end of World War I. Between 1919 and 1923, thirty-five thousand Jewish immigrants arrived. Another thirty-five thousand arrived in 1925 alone. The number of immigrants was directly related to crises in Europe. In these years, a majority came from Poland, where economic depression and virulent anti-Semitism caused many Jews to flee their homes. In 1923, the U.S. government decided that Eastern European immigrants were too "socialistic" and it slashed the immigration quotas for Eastern Europeans. Many of those who had hoped to follow their friends and relatives to the United States could not do so. They went to Palestine instead.

Socialist Dreams—Colonial Reality

It would have been hard under the best circumstances for the economy of Palestine to absorb so many new arrivals without disrupting the economic life of the Palestinians. Zionist plans for the new immigrants made it impossible. Zionists set out to build separate Jewish factories, banks, schools, a trade union, villages, and even a port city. Tel Aviv, founded in 1903, grew up near Jaffa as an all-Jewish city that tried to draw away Jaffa's shipping and trade. When the Jewish National Fund bought Palestinian land, it bought more than farms. It bought pieces of the future Jewish state. Such actions set the Jewish colony on a collision course with Palestine.

The leaders of "Labor Zionism" were the strongest supporters of Jewish separatism. They founded the exclusively Jewish trade union, the Histadrut, in 1920. It rapidly became the spearhead of anti-Palestinian activity. The Histadrut called its program "socialist." It proclaimed that the Jewish state had to be built by the toil of Jewish workers. In lofty statements, the Histadrut insisted that Jews should not exploit native Palestinians by hiring them to work in fields or factories. Histadrut leaders coined three slogans to guide the Jewish colony: "Jewish Land, Jewish Labor, Jewish Produce." Following these slogans, Zionist agencies only leased land to Jews; Jewish agricultural settlements and industries only hired Jews; and Jews boycotted fruits and vegetables from non-Jewish farms. Thus, in the name of "socialism," Palestinians were excluded from the Jewish sector of the economy.

Jewish businesses, tempted by cheap Palestinian labor, sometimes violated the "Jewish Labor" principle. They saw no reason why industrialists in the Jewish settler colony could not profit from cheap labor as European settlers in Rhodesia and South Africa did. But the Histadrut program appealed to the large number of new settlers coming from Europe who arrived in Palestine penniless and anxious to find work. Many had been active in European socialist movements. The idealistic speeches of Zionist leaders struck a sympathetic chord among these immigrants. They agreed with the Histadrut argument that jobs and higher incomes for Jewish workers rested on the exclusion of the Palestinians. Like their leaders, the new immigrants ignored the impact of the "Jews only" policy on the Palestinians. They had brought to the shores of Palestine ideas of European "superiority" and the conviction that Jews were the historic owners of Palestine. They quickly began to treat Palestinians as their enemies.

As the Jewish colony grew during the 1920s, so did the strength of Labor Zionism and the boldness of its actions. Members of the Histadrut picketed and stood guard at Jewish orchards to prevent Arab workers from getting jobs. Squads of activists stormed through marketplaces, pouring kerosene on tomatoes grown in Arab gardens or smashing eggs that Jewish housewives might purchase from Arab merchants. The Jewish National Fund gave its agents large sums of money to buy land from rich absentee landowners or to pressure small farmers who were deeply in debt to sell their land. Zionists then evicted the peasants who lived on the newly purchased land.[6]

Increasingly, the leaders of the Histadrut became leaders of the Zionist movement. Three future prime ministers of Israel — David Ben-Gurion, Golda Meir and Levi Eshkol — would come from the ranks of this "trade union." The

Histadrut, with each passing year, became more of a training ground for the administrators of the future Jewish state. It ran businesses, financed construction, directed the placement and growth of the agricultural settlements, and extended its influence over many aspects of its members' lives.

Among Jewish organizations in Palestine, only the small Palestine Communist Party pointed to the reality behind the myth of Zionist "socialism":

> The party must explain to the masses of Jewish workers that the Zionist bourgeoisie (businessmen, trade union officials, etc.) exploited their situation as victims of persecution in Eastern Europe and turned them into an instrument to oppress and dominate the masses of Arab workers.[7]

But the Communists remained a minority voice. Most Zionists proudly showed visitors from Europe and America the Zionist agricultural commune, called a kibbutz, and praised its spirit of equality and hard work. They impressed visitors with its cooperative decision-making, daycare centers, and well-irrigated fields. Hidden was the fact that each kibbutz was also a small military base of the Haganah, the Jewish Army founded in 1923. The "equality" of the kibbutz was for Jews only. A kibbutz often needed military protection because it stood on land farmed by Palestinians for generations.[8]

1929 Uprising: A Turning Point

By 1929, Zionist settlement had driven almost two thousand Palestinian families off the land. Sometimes these peasants found work tenant-farming, or they became laborers in small Arab factories. But often they remained unemployed. The growing Jewish sector was closed to them. Wage differences between Palestinian and Jew increased each year: in 1929 the average Jewish worker made nine times the wages of a Palestinian. The economy of the Zionist colony was capitalist. As that economy expanded, the traditional economy of Palestine became shakier.

The Zionist colony expanded rapidly. International donations supplied the capital to open new businesses and buy more land. Zionist fundraising got a boost with the creation of the Jewish Agency in 1928, a world-wide umbrella organization that raised money for Zionism. In addition, the British showered favors on the Zionists, granting them 90 percent of all economic assistance from the mandate government.[9] The British were deaf to Palestinian requests for such things as a bank to give low-interest loans to Palestinian farmers or a plan to build credit cooperatives to boost the Palestinian economy. Zionists were granted all the major concessions for the economic development of Palestine. They received a monopoly on the use of the Jordan river water for electricity and irrigation. Under these concessions, Zionist businesses extracted salt from the Dead Sea and constructed new ports.

Zionists in Palestine also mounted an offensive to get more political power. On August 15, 1929, Zionist settlers from outlying areas poured into Jerusalem to demonstrate at the Wailing Wall. The Wall was sacred to the Jews as part of the ancient Temple of the Second Kingdom and sacred to Moslems as part of the Dome of the Rock, one of the three holiest shrines in the Islamic religion. It was the practice of Zionists to turn the symbols of Judaism, like the Star of David, into emblems of the Zionist movement. To Palestinians, these emblems became symbols of conquest. At the Wall, the settlers raised the Zionist national flag and sang the Zionist

1929 rebellion suppressed by British soldiers.

national anthem, acts calculated to provoke Palestinian anger. During the demonstration, members of a right-wing Zionist group passed out pamphlets that advocated an armed takeover of Palestine. The next day, Palestinians held a counter-demonstration. Word spread to the countryside that the Moslem shrine was in danger. On August 23, peasants streamed into Jerusalem, and a riot broke out. Rioting spread from the city to surrounding towns. British troops were called in. When the fighting was over, 133 Jews and 116 Palestinian Arabs were dead. Most of the Palestinians were killed by British soldiers.

The British issued another report, citing the familiar causes of the violence. The Arab Executive presented the usual petitions for a representative government. But the people were beginning to lose faith in petitions. Britain stood squarely behind the Zionists and showed no indications of granting any Palestinian demands. Fearful of confrontation, the Arab Executive had condemned the 1929 events and ordered the peasants to retreat. The Executive, still at the head of the family and clan structure of Palestine, continued to try to represent the Palestinians. But it opposed any activity that might develop into a mass movement beyond its control.

After 1919 new organizations of women, students and farmers arose that allowed for political expression outside the old structures. In 1929, three hundred women participated in a Women's Congress in Palestine. They wore no veils, a radical gesture for the time. These women left the traditional confines of home and fields to demand freedom for Palestinian political prisoners, an end to arms purchases by the Zionists and independence for Palestine. The Congress founded the Arab Women's Union to continue organizing around these demands.

Angry writers and intellectuals broke the tradition of respect for prominent familes, and began to aim barbs at those who had sold land to the Zionists. The poet Ibrahim Toquan launched a sharp attack:

> They have sold the country to their enemies because of their greed for money; but it is their homes they have sold. They could have been forgiven if they had been forced to do so by hunger, but God knows that they have never felt hunger or thirst.[10]

The uprising of 1929 marked a shift in the Palestinian resistance to Zionism. Many Palestinians were becoming increasingly impatient with the Arab Executive's do-nothing policy. They realized that it would take more militant and sustained action to free their country from both Zionism and British occupation.

Footnotes

1. *Al-Nafa'is,* cited by Ghassan Kanafani, "The 1936-39 Revolt in Palestine: Background, Details and Analysis," *PFLP Bulletin* (January-February 1975), p. 7.
2. Robert John and Sami Hadawi, *The Palestine Diary,* 2 vols. (New York: 1970), 1:176.
3. Memorandum by Lord Balfour, 19 September 1919 (FO:371/4183/2117/132187), cited by William B. Quandt, *The Politics of Palestinian Nationalism* (Berkeley: 1973), p. 9.
4. Marie Syrkin, *Golda Meir* (Paris: 1966), p. 63, cited by Maxime Rodinson, *Israel: A Colonial-Settler State?* (New York: 1973), p. 106.
5. William B. Ziff, *The Rape of Palestine* (New York: 1938), p. 171, cited by John and Hadawi, 1:176.
6. Cited by Bober, ed, *The Other Israel,* p. 12.
7. Cited in "The Left in Israel," *MERIP* no. 49, p. 8.
8. Amos Perlmutter, *The Military and Politics in Israel* (New York: 1969), p. 32.
9. Nathan Weinstock, *Le Sionism-Contre Israel* (Paris: 1968), cited by Kanafani, *PFLP Bulletin* (September-October 1974), p. 7.
10. Cited by Kanafani, *PFLP Bulletin* (January-February 1975), p. 7.

5: 1936: The Palestinian Revolt

> Seize your rights,
> Al-Qassem trod that path before you.
> —Palestinian poet, 1936

After the 1929 uprising, Palestine simmered with rebellion from the quiet hamlets to the bustling cities. A popular song heard in the villages and towns urged the people to arm themselves. The refrain went, "revolt relieves all cares." The sixty Palestinian newspapers continued to criticize the British government for its callous disregard of the Palestinian people's desire for independence. The sentiments spread as a revival of poetry and song swept the country. Recent university graduates, unable to find jobs, used their energies to compose stirring manifestos against British colonialism. They began to organize and to join with peasants in small cells that trained for armed revolt against the British.

Palestinians were tired of continually petitioning the mandate government with demands the British had no intention of granting. The British claim of being "evenhanded" with Jews and Arabs became an ironic joke, as every Palestinian protest was met with evasive diplomacy or ruthless repression. In 1933, during a one-day work stoppage called by Palestinians against the mandate, British soldiers opened fire on a crowd of Jaffa demonstrators, killing twenty-seven people, including the eighty-year-old head of the Arab Executive. Demonstrations spread to Nablus, Jerusalem and Haifa — and to Syria, Iraq and Transjordan as well.

The year 1933 also brought the first massive wave of Jewish immigrants fleeing the Nazi terror in Europe. As Hitler seized power in Germany and stepped up the vicious anti-Semitic campaign that helped propel him into office, thousands of Jews entered Palestine both legally and illegally. British officials did little to stem the tide as the yearly immigration figures increased dramatically from nine thousand in 1932 to sixty-one thousand in 1935. At this rate, within ten years, Palestinians would be a minority in their own country. As the Zionist colony increased in size, it became more aggressive. The interception of a shipment of eight hundred rifles and ammunition from Europe to Zionists in Tel Aviv sparked another Palestinian general strike in October 1935.

When the worldwide depression hit Palestine in 1935, Palestinian workers and peasants were the main victims. The Zionist economy was supported by large amounts of capital brought in by the wealthier German Jews and by international contributions, including a $2.5 million loan from England. This influx of money helped protect the Zionists from the effects of the depression. They used the money to buy more Palestinian land and to open new businesses. In 1935, Jewish wages went up 10 percent, while Palestinian wages declined at the same rate. Among women working in textiles or tobacco, Jewish wages were already higher than Palestinian wages by as much as 443 percent! Jewish factory owners responded to the depression by laying off any Arab workers they still employed.

The Palestinian Arab economy suffered a devastating blow in the depression years. Arab businesses folded and Arab workers lost their jobs in construction, mining and industry. Palestinian agriculture declined sharply. By 1936, as many as twenty thousand families had been evicted from land bought by the Zionists. At least half of the peasantry could no longer sustain themselves on the land they did farm. Drifting into the cities in search of work, most joined the large ranks of unemployed workers. Workers returned to their ancestral villages only to find the peasants starving. Increasingly, the anger of workers was matched by the rebelliousness of the peasants. When the British refused to allow a thousand unemployed workers to demonstrate in Jaffa in June 1935, the Federation of Arab Workers warned: "The government will soon have to give the workers either bread or bullets."[1]

"Die as Martyrs!"

On November 12, 1935, Sheik Izz ad-Din al-Qassem went into the hills of Galilee with twenty-five followers to issue the call for armed revolt against the British. Qassem had arrived in Palestine in 1921 as a seasoned fighter against French colonialism in Syria. After 1929 he patiently built cells of young people and peasants to prepare for the day when the Palestinian people would stand up against the British — not in spontaneous demonstrations, but in an organized uprising. He spoke for the misery of the peasants and the hopes of thousands of them went with him into the hills. Qassem was killed one week later by a British patrol; but his ideas

were soon to spark a massive uprising of the people. He died uttering three words that echoed over Palestine, *"Die as martyrs!"* News of his death and final words spread quickly. Hundreds upon hundreds of peasants and workers walked for miles, following his body to its burial ground.

The Palestinian fight against Zionist settlers and the British began to take new forms. Qassemite guerrillas struck in February, surrounding a Haifa orchard that enforced the "Jewish Labor" policy, and again in April, attacking a coach on the Tulkarm Road. Their killing of two Jews was countered by a Zionist raid that killed two Palestinian farmers. Zionists marched through Tel Aviv on April 16, shouting, "We want a Jewish Army!" They began a march on nearby Jaffa. The next day, Zionist squads picketed businesses that hired Arabs. On Sunday morning, Palestinians in Jaffa gathered before British headquarters demanding permission for a parade. They were turned down. An angry crowd swept through the streets, stoning cars and buses, moving towards Tel Aviv. The two cities, the ancient Palestinian city of Jaffa and the newly rising Tel Aviv, center of the emerging Jewish state, symbolized two conflicting goals for Palestine.

On April 19, a Jaffa committee called a general strike of Palestinians against the mandate government. It spread to almost every city — Tulkarm, Nablus, Jerusalem, Jenin, Haifa. Each town committee had slightly different demands, but at the forefront, one blazed out: "Independence for Palestine!" Everyone participated — trade unions, women's associations, sports clubs, Boy Scouts and the YMCA. Christian and Moslem alike rose up to say "No!" to British rule over Palestine. By April 22, Arab shops, businesses and markets were shut. Transportation and communication had ground to a halt. The nation was on strike and hopes were high.

Zionist night squad searches an Arab village.

The people who started the strike had little experience of national politics. For national coordination, they fell back on the leadership of the old wealthy families of the Arab Executive. It reorganized on April 25 as the Arab Higher Committee, under the leadership of Haj Amin El-Husseini, the Mufti or religious leader of Jerusalem. Independence remained the rallying cry, with a halt of Jewish immigration as the condition for any Palestinian negotiation with the British. The leaders of the Higher Committee mouthed the slogans that arose from the lives of their people, but they anticipated leading only a short strike. They viewed the strike as a means to enhance their bargaining power with the British and their role in a future Palestinian government.

The majority of the people of Palestine believed that the strike might bring them independence. The Syrian people had just won a promise of self-government from the French after a fifty-day strike. As soon as the Palestinian strike began, Committees for Palestine sprung up in Damascus, Beirut, Baghdad and Cairo. Palestinians welcomed this support from Arab countries and eagerly awaited the British response.

The mandate government's answer to the strike was immediate and harsh. It announced a substantial increase in the immigration quotas for Jews for the next month and ordered the cutting of all telephone and telegraph wires from Palestine to surrounding Arab countries. The long-term strategy for dealing with the strike was simple: force and more force. The High Commissioner announced that British soldiers were free to fire on demonstrators.

In quick succession, a strike by Haifa sailors and a demonstration by hundreds of women in Gaza defied the armed troops. The British decided to destroy the leadership of the strike. They ordered the round-up of all known Communists in Palestine to prevent any actions on May 1, International Workers' Day. Yet on that day, two thousand people demonstrated in Haifa. After the British arrested sixty-one key leaders of local committees, other people took up their tasks. British Emergency Regulations, rigidly enforced against Palestinians, led to punishments like these: "Five years hard labor for possessing twelve bullets; eight months for misdirecting a detachment of British soldiers; two weeks imprisonment for possessing a stick."[2]

Punishment of individuals could not stop the tide of rebellion. Entire cities and villages defied British control. The British turned their attention to breaking the backbone of the strike, the communities of Palestinian men, women and children. They levied collective fines and imposed collective punishments on troublesome villages. If British troops heard one shot fired from a house, they made the entire village suffer.

Jaffa, where the strike had begun, was the target of especially vicious treatment. Dockworkers, sailors and students led the city in militant confrontation. Their organizing center was the ancient walled city. British soldiers feared to enter its narrow winding streets, impenetrable to tanks and cars. In June, under the pretense of "urban renewal," the British sealed off the quarter and dynamited hundreds of houses, leaving thousands of people without shelter. Another thousand homes were blown up in a nearby village.

Martial Law in Palestine

That same June the British High Commissioner reported that Palestine was in a "state of incipient revolution." There was, he reported, "little control of lawless elements outside principal towns, main roads and railways."[3] Over twenty-five hundred Palestinians had been arrested. Over a thousand had been killed.

In July, with the support of the Zionist colony, the British placed Palestine under martial law. They rushed more troops from England. Over twenty thousand troops patrolled Palestine, still failing to control a population of less than one million people. Ships arrived loaded with tanks and machine guns. The Royal Air Force began strafing the countryside. The British formed Zionist settlers into "night squads" to attack Palestinian villages. Members of the Haganah, the Zionist army that had flourished since 1929, got their first taste of war, crushing the Palestinian rebellion. In Europe, the Zionist leader Weizmann pledged that Palestine would not fall to "the forces of destruction, the forces of the desert."[4] The Zionists threw their full weight behind the British.

The unrelenting fury of the British and the Zionists made the Arab Higher Committee doubt the wisdom of continuing the strike. As the peasants became more militant and organized in response to the British, Haj Amin and the other wealthy leaders sensed a challenge to their own positions and power. The strike had lasted much longer than they had bargained for, largely because the economy of mandate Palestine was kept alive by the Zionist settlers who continued to produce and sell goods.

Many Zionist workers willingly scabbed, taking over Arab jobs in the civil service, the ports and the railroads. When Arab strikers closed the port of Jaffa, Zionists built the port at Tel Aviv and expanded the Haifa port. With Palestinian agriculture at a standstill, fruits and vegetables from Jewish fields captured the export market.

The members of the Arab Higher Committee were not interested in sacrificing their own wealth and traveling the road of all-out revolution. They were relieved when, in the summer of 1936, Britain approached King Abdullah of Transjordan and King Ghazi of Iraq with a proposal that the kings intervene in the strike. The intervention of the British "client kings" might stop the spread of the Palestinian rebellion that threatened to sweep away all in its path — the British mandate government, Zionism and perhaps the traditional Palestinian leadership itself.

Many Palestinians opposed the kings' meddling in the strike. At a large demonstration in Jerusalem in August, fifteen newspapers that reported Abdullah's proposal for peace were burned. But the members of the Higher Committee, still the sole national coordinating body, exercised all their authority and power as heads of family clans and villages, as landlords and employers, to force an end to the strike. Finally, after a series of negotiations, the kings called upon the Higher Committee to end the strike. The Higher Committee obeyed gratefully. This betrayal by the Arab kings created bitter disappointment among the people which was expressed by the poet Abu Salma:

Shame to such kings, if kings are so low
By God, their crowns are not fit to sole shoes
We are the ones who will protect our homeland and heal its wounds.[5]

Rebellion and Betrayal

The Palestinian general strike lasted six months, the longest general strike in the history of the Middle East or Europe. It was a high point of consciousness, sacrifice and unity in the history of the Palestinian people. But it rapidly became clear that none of the demands of the strike were to be met. Britain, with both the Zionists and the Arab kings on its string, refused to give Palestine independence.

Britain's new ploy, recommended by the Peel Commission of 1937, was to partition Palestine into a Zionist and a Palestinian state, with both areas dominated by Britain. Although the Zionists owned only a tiny percentage of the land, under this plan they would receive much of the most fertile land in the country. The Zionists accepted the proposal. David Ben-Gurion stated clearly that the acceptance of this plan was but a stepping stone to a larger Jewish state:

No Zionist can forgo the smallest portion of the Land of Israel. The debate has concerned which of two routes would lead quicker to the common goal.[6]

Palestinians rejected the proposal. Guerrillas assassinated the pro-Zionist Commissioner of the Galilee, who schemed to include the Arab Galilee in the Jewish state. Open warfare flared once again.

Palestinian men and women take up arms in 1936.

The British began a wholesale roundup of Palestinian leaders and deported most of the Higher Committee. This tactic only added fuel to the revolt. By the summer, guerrilla warfare spread in the hills of Palestine and rebellion engulfed the whole country. Most of the fighters were peasants. The British began arresting anyone in town wearing a *keffiyah,* the traditional peasant scarf. In support of the peasants, townspeople donned *keffiyahs* and stopped carrying IDs so the British could not check where anyone lived.

Peasants took over some towns. A British general reported in September that "the situation was such that civil administration and control of the country was, to all practical purposes, non-existent."[7] British offices in most cities were closed and British troops placed Jerusalem under a five-day seige. In a four-month period, the British dynamited five thousand houses, added a thousand more prisoners to the three thousand already in jail and executed one hundred forty-eight prisoners in Acre prison alone. Still, they could not crush the rebellion.

Confronted with the prospect of a prolonged Palestinian resistance, the British took a long, hard look at their situation in the Middle East. War with Hitler's Germany was fast approaching. Just as in World War I, Britain would need Arab help, Arab oil and secure shipping routes. This was not the time to be fighting the Arabs. Furthermore, the rebellion in Palestine was tying down *one-third* of all British troops. To avoid greater damage to its empire, Britain decided to turn once again to paper promises for the Palestinians.

The British White Paper of 1939 suddenly reversed Britain's twenty-year policy toward Palestine. It promised a ceiling on Jewish immigration — only a total of seventy-five thousand Jews would be admitted in the next ten years. It pledged some restrictions on Zionist land purchases. It included an extremely vague pledge that Palestine would become independent in ten years. But the turn-around from guns and tanks to slippery diplomacy did not convince the Palestinians. They rejected the White Paper.

The Zionists were unanimously angry at what they considered a British "betrayal." For them, the White Paper was a major turning point. Britain, their imperial sponsor for more than twenty years, had abandoned the Zionist cause in the face of more pressing needs of the British Empire. The majority of Zionists did not want an open break with Britain, but they knew they would have to find a new sponsor.

In the meantime, Zionists launched a campaign against the Palestinian community. They organized strikes, bombed Palestinian marketplaces and increased secret military training.[8] They had learned from the Palestinian rebellion that the people of Palestine would never peacefully accept conquest. A strategy that had been imbedded in Zionism from the beginning became explicit: the native people would have to be driven from Palestine. J. Weitz, head of the Jewish Agency's Colonization Department, wrote in his diary in 1940:

> There is no room for both peoples together in this country .... We shall not achieve our goal of being an independent people with the Arabs in this small country. The only solution is Palestine, at least Western Palestine [West of the Jordan River], without Arabs .... And there is no other way but to transfer the Arabs from here to the neighboring countries, to transfer all of them: *not one village, not one tribe should be left.*[9] [emphasis added]

In 1940, the Zionist movement, carefully nurtured by imperialism, faced a devastated Palestinian people. Twenty thousand Palestinians had been killed or wounded, and thousands jailed. Many of the best fighters and organizers, the most trusted leaders, were dead. The great rebellion was over, but it would not be forgotten. It would be chronicled by writers, analyzed by political leaders and passed on through stories told in the villages and towns.

As the Palestinians mourned their dead and tended to the wounded, events that would profoundly affect their future were unfolding in Europe and America. For the next several years, the actions of the Palestinians were eclipsed by the great struggle for power in the Middle East and elsewhere that was unleashed in the Second World War.

Footnotes

1. *PFLP Bulletin* (September-October 1974), pp. 6-7.
2. *PFLP Bulletin* (June 1975), p. 6.
3. High Commissioner telegram to CO, 2 June 1936 (CO 733/297/75156) cited by William Quandt, *The Politics of Palestinian Nationalism*, p. 35.
4. Cited by Matiel E.T. Mogannam, *The Arab Woman and the Palestine Problem* (London: 1937), p. 295.
5. *PFLP Bulletin* (January-February 1975), p. 7.
6. David Ben-Gurion in a speech at the 20th Zionist Congress, Zurich, Switzerland, 15 August 1937, cited by Childers, "The Wordless Wish," in *The Transformation of Palestine*, p. 178.
7. General Haining, GOC, Report to War Office, 30 November 1938, paragraph 14; St. Anthony's College, Oxford, private papers collection, cited by William B. Quandt, *The Politics of Palestinian Nationalism*, p. 38.
8. John and Hadawi, *The Palestine Diary*, 1:320-21.
9. Joseph Weitz, *Diaries and Letters to the Children* (Tel Aviv: 1965), p. 181.

6: World War II: Channelling Europe's Jews to Palestine

The heroic men and women who died on the barricades of Warsaw belonged to a section of the Jews who held their home was in the countries where they had been born, had worked, and had contributed to wealth and culture.
—**American Jewish Newsletter, 1946**

On September 1, 1939, almost two million German troops stormed out of Germany in a *Blitzkrieg,* or "lightning war," against Poland. Waves of aircraft and column after column of tanks swept over the half-million Polish defenders. Fascist Germany, under the leadership of Adolf Hitler, was on the march. Hitler's aim was to build the greatest empire the world had ever seen. Britain and France, their survival as world powers at stake, declared war on Germany. World War II had begun. France quickly fell to the Germans, leaving Britain alone to face Hitler's legions.

As German armies swept over Europe, Britain urgently prepared to defend the Middle East, its primary source of oil. Palestine became a major military garrison. British soldiers and war materials began arriving at Palestinian ports. But Britain's own troops were not enough; it needed the support of the Arab countries. Britain added to the promises of the 1939 White Paper a series of pledges to support independence throughout the Middle East.

Palestinian Arabs distrusted Britain's promises. As they reopened their shuttered shops and replanted their fallow fields, they remembered vividly the crushing of their recent rebellion. Already they had sacrificed many lives in the struggle for an independent Palestine. Now the fate of Palestine was tied to another raging worldwide conflict. World War I had taught many Palestinians that European wars were collisions of empires in which Arab peoples were used and then discarded. Would World War II be different?

As the war began, despite the promises of the White Paper, Britain made no move to form a representative government in Palestine. Instead, it tightened its grip over the country. Nonetheless, nine thousand Palestinians joined the British armies to fight against Germany. Some joined the other side. Haj Amin El-Husseini, the exiled leader of the Arab Higher Committee, made a bid to increase his power by cooperating with the Germans. Fleeing to Berlin, he made pro-Nazi radio broadcasts that emphasized British betrayal of the Arabs and promised Arab independence under the rising star of Germany. Husseini's path was followed by other Arab reactionaries. They thought it was better to curry favor with the likely winner of the imperial war than to break the grip of Europe over their countries. Haj Amin's small political party continued to operate in Palestine secretly, but his collaboration with the Nazis discredited him in the eyes of many Palestinians.

With most organizations shattered, people began to meet in small groups at their work-place or village to discuss the future of Palestine. The League of Arab Students, founded in Jerusalem during the war, proposed a program of fighting fascism, spreading progressive ideas among the people and teaching peasants to read. The League tried to unite around these goals with some Zionists it considered progressive. But the Zionists told them there could be no "common ground" with any Palestinians who opposed a Jewish state in Palestine.[1]

WW II: Turning Point for the Jewish State

The outbreak of World War II made many Zionists think their goal for Palestine might not be so distant. In 1938, David Ben-Gurion, who chaired the Jewish Agency in Palestine, predicted: "The First World War brought us the Balfour Declaration; the Second ought to bring us the Jewish State."[2] He believed that the war would create the conditions for the Zionist movement to build up a Jewish majority in Palestine. Zionists knew that without a large Jewish population, there could be no Jewish state. Even if they could wrest control of Palestine from the British, a small Jewish population with even smaller landholdings would not be able to rule over the Arab majority. During the 1930s it had seemed likely that the wave of immigrants fleeing Hitler's attacks could soon create a Jewish majority. But Britain's 1939 White Paper cut off that immigration. In 1940, in a further effort to gain Arab support, Britain announced its policy of diverting Jewish refugees who tried to come to Palestine to "an alternative place of refuge in the Colonial Empire."[3]

Zionists vowed to defeat this British policy. If it were allowed to stand and if Jews in other countries concentrated on pressuring their governments to admit Jews fleeing from Europe, the Zionist experiment would be doomed. Ben-Gurion had

Jewish refugees entering Palestine illegally

seen this as early as 1938. Describing how pre-occupation with rescuing Jews might hurt the work of building Jewish institutions in Palestine, he said:

> If Jews will have to choose between the refugees, saving Jews from concentration camps, and assisting a national museum in Palestine, mercy will have the upper hand and the whole energy of the people will be channelled into saving Jews from various countries. Zionism will be struck off the agenda .... If we allow a separation between the refugee problem and the Palestine problem, we are risking the existence of Zionism.[4]

In order to achieve their goal of a Jewish state, the Zionists focused on getting the refugees to Palestine and Palestine only. Jews who accepted Zionist help in escaping from Europe became caught in a vicious crossfire. The Zionists were bent on getting them to Palestine at any cost, and the British government was equally determined to settle them anywhere except in Palestine or Britain. The refugees

53

became pawns in the clash between the Zionists and the British, sometimes with tragic results.

In 1940 the British discovered two steamships carrying 1,171 illegal immigrants toward the coast of Palestine. In line with the White Paper policy on immigration, the mandate authorities transferred the passengers to another ship, the *S.S. Patria,* and ordered them taken to Cyprus. On the morning of November 25, most of the Jewish population of Haifa stood crowded on the docks, watching the preparations. Suddenly, an explosion rocked the *Patria,* and it sank in fifteen minutes. Two hundred fifty-two refugees and several Jewish police officers died.

Immediately, officers of the Jewish Agency announced that the refugees had sunk the *Patria* as an act of protest; they would rather die than be turned away from Palestine. This explanation dominated headlines around the world. The resulting international outcry forced Britain to allow the survivors to remain in Palestine.

A later commission of inquiry revealed a different chain of events. A commando group of the Irgun, a faction of the Zionist movement led by Menahem Begin, had been ordered by the Jewish Agency to plant a bomb on the ship to disable its engines. The commandos used too much explosive and sank the ship instead. The Jewish Agency invented the "mass suicide" story to cover up its role. The sinking of the *Patria* became a weapon in the Zionists' propaganda campaign against the British.[5]

Zionist Drive Turns to the U. S.

Stories like the *Patria* affair made good newspaper copy. They found a receptive audience in the United States where the Zionist movement was escalating its drive for support. With British support eroding, the Zionists needed a new imperial sponsor. Even before the war broke out, Ben-Gurion was convinced that the United States would play that role:

> For my part, I had no doubt that the center of gravity of our political efforts had shifted from Great Britain to America, who was making sure of being the world's leading power and where the greatest number of Jews, as well as the most influential, were to be found.[6]

When the Zionists launched their organizing campaign in the United States, they demanded free immigration of Jews to Palestine, not to the United States. They knew that American leaders, whom they wanted to win to the Zionist cause, had a consistently callous disregard for the plight of European Jews.

In the late 1930s, before the Nazis sealed their borders, thousands of German Jews had applied to immigrate to the United States. U.S. immigration quotas were set primarily to serve the demands of American corporations for cheap labor. In the depression years, American business had no need of more workers. Thus, immigration officials turned away Jewish refugees unless they had money, a good job prospect and a "certificate of good conduct" from Nazi officials. Even these did not guarantee admission.

The economic depression also intensified racism and anti-Semitism among Americans. A *Fortune* magazine poll indicated that 15 percent of all Americans

54

thought that "Germany would be better off if it drove away the Jews." The hate-filled radio broadcasts of Father Charles Coughlin blamed Jews for everything from strikes to lay-offs.[7]

In this environment, few American Jews spoke out against U.S. immigration policy. Zionism encouraged them to direct their attack at Britain. A Zionist historian, Robert Silverberg, observed:

> ... the fear of creating an anti-Semitic backlash stifled the urge to attack restrictive immigration laws. Yet something had to be done to save the sufferers in Germany. Among American Jews, Zionism became a comforting substitute for the domestic political agitation in which they did not dare indulge.[8]

The Jewish Labor Council, a group of progressive Jewish workers, was one of the few voices to challenge the "closed door" of the United States. Most Zionists were adamant about their loyalty to the United States and its policies. During the hearings on the Wagner Bill of 1939, which proposed admitting ten thousand German Jewish children to the United States, Rabbi Stephen Wise, a top Zionist leader, gave only timid testimony in its favor. He hastened to add his unconditional support for the current immigration laws:

> I have heard no sane person propose any departure or deviation from the existing laws now in force .... If there is any conflict between our duty to these children and our duty to our country, speaking for myself, as a citizen I should say, of course, that our country comes first; and if the children cannot be helped, they cannot be helped.[9]

As Zionism gained ground among American Jews in the first years of the war, it became more open about its final goal. The vague diplomatic language of the "national home" in Palestine disappeared. In May 1942 David Ben-Gurion arrived in New York to chair the Zionist Conference at the Biltmore Hotel. The six hundred delegates approved unanimously the "Biltmore Program" which demanded "the establishment of a Jewish Commonwealth in Palestine." For the first time since Herzl, the Zionist movement publicly stated its goal of a Jewish state.

Genocide in Europe: Who Can Be Saved?

In that same year, 1942, Adolph Hitler ordered what he called the "Final Solution" to the "Jewish problem": the murder of all European Jews. No longer did the Nazis harass and expel those they considered "racially unfit." The fascist storm-troopers began to round up Jews, Gypsies and Slavs and send them to concentration camps. In these grim slaughterhouses, efficient work crews exterminated millions of people in the next several years. Among them were most of Eastern Europe's Jews. The organized, political anti-Semitism that had festered inside the structure of European capitalist society since the Czar's pogroms, had reached its ultimate expression, genocide.

In the face of this vicious murder campaign, the Jews of Europe had to act. From the beginning of the war, some Jews had been active in the underground resistance against fascism. As the Nazis began the "Final Solution," building clandestine organizations became at once more difficult and more necessary. Jewish and non-Jewish resistance fighters organized underground escape routes to help Jews flee to

Jewish partisans at the barricades of Warsaw in 1944.

safety. They tried to stockpile weapons for eventual use against the Nazis. They gathered intelligence on the Nazis' plans which they tried to share with the still disbelieving Jewish communities. Even as the Nazi death machine ground on, most European Jews did not know exactly what Hitler was doing. Up to the end of the war, many Jews boarded trains to the death camps unaware of their destination.

When they did know the true situation, they did not go peacefully. In 1943, in the Warsaw ghetto of Poland, Jewish fighters rose up against the Nazis who tried to evacuate them. They fought the Nazis for six months, hiding in bombed-out buildings and the maze of sewer tunnels below the city. German commanders recorded in their notes: "Over and over again we observed that Jews, despite the dangers of being burned alive, preferred to return to the flames rather than be caught by us."[10] The Germans reported that, when surrounded, women came out with their guns blazing rather than surrender. Against impossible odds, Warsaw Jews fought to the end.

All along, they and the other underground resistance fighters of Europe hoped for direct aid from the Western Allies. It did not come. In 1944, the United States government refused to bomb the railroad tracks into Auschwitz and other concentration camps in order to save thousands of doomed people. A U.S. official said that such an operation would require "diversion of considerable air support" and would be of "doubtful efficacy."[11] The United States made no effort to supply and assist the leftist partisans in occupied Europe.

The Zionist leadership in Palestine did little more. According to Uri Avnery, a contemporary Israeli politician who was then a member of the underground Stern Gang in Palestine:

56

Throughout the war, nothing much was done by the Zionist leadership to help the Jews in conquered Europe about to be massacred .... Many people think that things should and could have been done: hundreds of Haganah and Irgun fighters could have been parachuted into Europe; the British and American governments could have been pressured into bombing the railways leading to the death camps.[12]

But rescue and defense of Europe's Jews were not the Zionist priority. In 1943, the year of the Warsaw uprising, Itzhak Greenbaum, head of the Zionist Jewish Rescue Committee, declared:

If I am asked could you give from UJA (United Jewish Appeal) money to rescue Jews? I say, "No, and again no." In my opinion, we have to resist that wave which puts Zionist activities in the second line.[13]

When Zionist leaders faced a conflict between the needs of the Jewish state and the needs of Europe's Jews, they usually decided in favor of the Jewish state. Almost a half-million Hungarian Jews paid with their lives for one such decision.

Dr. Rudolf Kastner was the vice-president of the Zionist Organization in Budapest, Hungary, during the war. He had cooperated with the Nazis through all phases of their "Jewish program," including the "Final Solution." In the early period, when the Nazis favored expelling Jews, he had been able to arrange for some Jews to leave for Palestine with Nazi cooperation. Later, when the Nazis prepared to evacuate Hungary's Jews to the concentration camp at Auschwitz, they approached Kastner. If he would help coordinate the evacuation, they would allow him to select a fixed number of Jews to emigrate to Palestine. In her book, *Eichmann in Jerusalem,* Hannah Arendt describes the bargain:

Dr. Kastner ... saved exactly 1,684 people with approximately 476,000 victims. In order not to leave the selection to "blind fate," "truly holy principles" were needed "as the guiding force of the weak human hand which puts down on paper the name of the unknown person and with this decides his life or death." And whom did these "holy principles" single out for salvation? Those "who had worked all their lives for the *zibur* [community]" — i.e., the functionaries — and the "most prominent Jews," as Kastner says in his report.[14]

Dr. Kastner and his company of "prominent Jews" were able to go to Palestine. Unaware of their final destination, thousands and thousands of Jews who might otherwise have resisted, boarded the trains for Auschwitz.

As word of Nazi genocide trickled to the United States, it galvanized American Zionists into action. Zionist pleas for U.S. support of the Jewish state found a receptive audience, especially among government and business leaders. During the war, the U.S. government's interest in the Middle East and its oil had skyrocketed. By 1942, a year after America entered the war, C.L. Sulzberger of the *New York Times* was describing the Middle East as "the most important single geographic area of the war."[15] Already U.S. leaders were intent on dislodging Britain from the region. The Zionists' anti-British campaign fit perfectly with their own plans.

Against the backdrop of Hitler's crimes in Europe, the Zionists were able to organize tremendous popular support for their cause. In the election year of 1944, more than three thousand non-Jewish organizations, from church groups to labor unions, passed pro-Zionist resolutions. Telegrams and letters poured into

Washington. Of the 534 members of Congress, 411 called for American approval of the Jewish state.

Many of the same anti-Semites who refused to open the doors of America to the Jewish refugees clamored for an open door to Palestine. Some critics of the Zionist goal questioned the ethics of making the Palestinians sacrifice their country for the sins of Europe and America. A Midwestern minister answered bluntly:

> To say it is internationally unethical to take Palestine away from the Arabs and give it to the Jews has about as much rightness to it as to say European settlers had no right to settle on what has become the great continent of America because it happened to be peopled by American Indians.[16]

President Roosevelt, responding to strong corporate interest in the Middle East and growing public support for Zionism, pledged support for a Jewish state in Palestine if he was re-elected. But less than six months after his re-election, Roosevelt met with King Ibn Saud of Saudi Arabia. Roosevelt told him that the United States would consult the Arabs before taking any action in Palestine. Clearly, the United States could not honor both pledges.

As the war drew to a close, fighting broke out in Palestine between the Zionists and the British. The Zionists intensified their campaign for American backing. The policy of the United States — now the most powerful nation in the world — had become a crucial factor in deciding the fate of Palestine.

Footnotes

1. The Esco Foundation, *Palestine,* 2:1011.
2. Michael Bar-Zohar, *Ben-Gurion: The Armed Prophet* (Englewood Cliffs, New Jersey: 1968), p. 69.
3. Christopher Sykes, *Crossroads to Israel* (London: 1968), p. 223.
4. Letter to the Zionist executive, 17 December 1938, cited in Bober, ed., *The Other Israel,* p. 171.
5. *Morning Freiheit* (New York), 27 November 1950, cited by John and Hadawi, *The Palestine Diary,* 1: 338.
6. Bar-Zohar, p. 64.
7. Robert Silverberg, *If I forget Thee O Jerusalem: American Jews and the State of Israel* (New York: 1970), p. 142.
8. Ibid., p. 141.
9. Rabbi Stephen Wise, U.S. Congress, Senate and House Subcommittees on Immigration, and on Immigration and Naturalization, respectively, *Admission of German Refugee Children,* Joint Hearings on S.J. Res. 64 and H.J. Res. 168, 76th Cong., 1st sess., 1939, pp. 155-60, cited in Walid Khalid, ed., *From Haven to Conquest: Readings in Zionism and the Palestine Problem Until 1948,* (Beirut: 1971), p. 452.
10. Sachar, *The Course of Modern Jewish History,* p. 452.
11. Henry Feingold, *The Politics of Rescue: The Roosevelt Administration and the Holocaust 1938-1945* (New Brunswick, New Jersey: 1970), p. 141.
12. Avnery, *Israel Without Zionism,* p. 106.
13. Ben Hecht, *Perfidy* (New York: 1961), p. 50, cited by Tabitha Petran, *Zionism: A Political Critique* (Washington, D.C.: 1973), p. 6.
14. Hannah Arendt, *Eichmann in Jerusalem* (New York: 1963), p. 118.
15. C.L. Sulzberger, "German Reparation in the Middle East," *Foreign Affairs* (July 1942), p. 663, cited by the Esco Foundation, *Palestine,* 1:957.
16. Cited by Wm. L. Burton, "Protestant America and the Rebirth of Israel," *Jewish Social Studies* (October 1964), p. 284.

7: Green Light from the White House

SAUDI ARABIA: "Where the oil resources constitute a stupendous source of power and one of the greatest material prizes in history."
—State Department Memo to Truman, 1945

On April 12, 1945, the death of Franklin Roosevelt propelled Harry Truman into the White House. A few days after Truman's inauguration, the new President prepared for a visit from American Zionist leader Rabbi Stephen Wise. Presidential advisers gave Truman a hasty briefing on U.S. policy toward the Middle East. They explained the promises Roosevelt had showered on Arab and Zionist alike. The contradictory promises had a single purpose: to secure allies for an American drive into the Middle East.

Truman listened intently. Like most members of Congress, he had endorsed Zionism while he was a United States Senator. As a shrewd politician and an unelected President, he appreciated the vote-getting potential of his support for the Jewish state. But as President, he had to weigh more important considerations — for example, what the oil companies wanted in the Middle East. The United States was

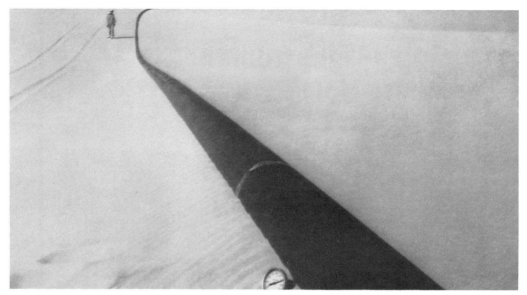
U.S. oil companies' pipelines crisscross the Middle East.

emerging from the war as the most powerful nation in the world. The old colonial empires of Britain and France were fatally weakened. The era of U.S. imperialism's supremacy had begun.

American corporations, which had boomed in the war economy, needed global markets and resources to keep growing after the war. Three of the top five American corporations were giant oil companies involved in the Middle East. Personnel from the oil companies filled top posts in the State Department and Pentagon. They wanted to see the United States control the Middle East and its oil, the most vital resource of the post-war period.

In the 1930s Britain had dominated Middle Eastern oil. American corporations then controlled less than 10 percent of the area's known oil reserves, mostly in Saudi Arabia. The discovery of vast new reserves in Saudi Arabia at the outbreak of the war increased the U.S. stake in the area. From the start, competition between the United States and Britain for Middle Eastern oil had broken into open conflict. But the United States had gained the upper hand. In the course of the war, Britain had gone deeply in debt to the United States to finance its war effort. The terms of American aid to Britain, called "lend-lease" aid, had been stiff. In essence, Britain had mortgaged its empire in order to continue fighting the war. For the United States, "aid" was a tool to open up a country's economy to U.S. penetration.

By the end of the war, U.S. oil companies controlled 42 percent of the known oil reserves in the Middle East. After the war, American policymakers created the Marshall Plan to replace lend-lease aid as a lever to control war-ravaged Britain and Europe. Massive amounts of American aid poured into Europe to rebuild European economies along lines profitable to American business. Creating a market for newly acquired oil was a central item on the U.S. agenda. When European countries asked for forty-seven thousand freight cars that ran on coal, the major energy source for Europe, the United States sent only twenty thousand coal-operated cars, and sixty-five thousand trucks that ran on oil.[1] Oil soon replaced coal as the major energy source for Europe. Europe and Japan became major markets for Middle Eastern oil.

Once U.S. oil companies had gotten control of the major oil sources and developed large markets, the U.S. government sought "stability" in the Middle East. "Stability" meant a good investment climate and constant and secure access to the area's oil, ports and waterways. That stability was immediately challenged by Arab nationalists. In July 1946, oil workers in Iran struck against the huge Western oil corporations and the Western-backed government of Iran. During the year, over half of all industrial workers in Iran went out on strike. Similar strikes stirred in the oil-rich kingdom of Iraq. Britain had to summon its troops from India to quell the disturbances.

Although the United States and Britain blamed these strikes on the "subversion of Moscow," the strikers were militant nationalists. These workers' demands were the demands of all genuine nationalists in the Middle East since the First World War: the establishment of a national government free from Western imperialism. If this Arab nationalism grew stronger in the years ahead, it might eventually strike at the heart of U.S. interests. But for the moment, the more threatening source of conflict in the Middle East continued to be Palestine.

Palestine: Which Way for the U.S.?

Throughout 1946 Truman and his advisers walked a path of careful diplomacy on the question of Palestine. Their goal was to push Britain out of the area without inflaming Arab nationalism in the process. They supported the creation of a Jewish state in Palestine because they knew that the Zionist settler colony would more willingly serve the needs of U.S. imperialism than would the Palestinian Arabs. U.S. leaders expected the Arabs eventually to accept the Zionist state.

Zionists in the United States encouraged this wishful thinking. In their post-war campaign, they continued to ignore the existence of the Palestinian people. They focused on the demand for unlimited Jewish immigration to Palestine. The Jewish victims of fascism in Europe were still the Zionists' means of mobilizing world opinion in favor of the Jewish state. At the end of the war in Europe, lengthy interviews and heart-rending pictures of the survivors of German concentration camps told, for the first time, the story of German fascism's savage attack on Europe's Jews. Millions of Jews had perished. Those who escaped languished in Displaced Persons camps. A tremendous guilt, horror and anger swept Jews and many non-Jews in the United States. They wanted to do something for the victims of fascism.

Of all the Allies, the United States was in the best position to help the refugees. The economies of Eastern Europe and the Soviet Union were devastated. In contrast, the U.S. Department of Labor announced that the United States could easily absorb four hundred thousand immigrants. But American policy continued to keep the door shut to Jewish immigrants. In the anti-communist atmosphere following the war, the admission of Jews who might have been influenced by socialist ideas threatened American businessmen. American leaders and opinion-makers demanded the opening of Palestine to Jewish immigration. Polls showed that 80 percent of American Jews and 75 percent of *all* Americans who had heard of Palestine favored establishing a Jewish state there.

Zionist rally in New York City, 1947

The Jewish Agency demanded that Britain grant one hundred thousand immigration certificates for European Jews to go to Palestine. *Bricha,* the organization responsible for illegal immigration to Palestine, sent organizers into the Displaced Persons camps. They helped thousands of potential immigrants get to Mediterranean ports for illegal departure to the shores of Palestine aboard rickety ships. Despite this intense campaign, a later report to the American Jewish Congress by a Zionist organizer, Chaplain Klausner, contended that most of the refugees had actually wanted to come to the United States. Klausner concluded, "I am convinced that the people must be forced to go to Palestine."[2]

Nonetheless, Americans responded to the dramatic attempts of the Zionists to break the British naval blockade of Palestine. The wishes of the refugees were ignored. Grief and shock at the Nazi genocide helped Zionists raise millions of dollars to send to Palestine. In 1946 and 1947 alone, American Zionists sent over $130 million to Palestine.[3] Editorials in American papers roundly condemned the British and called for the granting of the immigration certificates to the Jewish Agency. In this atmosphere, anyone who spoke out against Zionism was immediately labeled "anti-Semitic."

A recruitment poster displayed in Displaced Persons camps in Germany. In Yiddish, the poster says in part: "Men and women between the ages of 17 to 35 should report for duty to the Jewish people. All those of age to be mobilized who do not fulfill their duty will be excluded from the social and political life of the community and prohibited from holding any official office in the DP community.

In the summer of 1945, Truman wrote British Prime Minister Clement Atlee to support the admission of a hundred thousand immigrants into Palestine. Atlee replied by reminding him of America's promise to consult the Arabs in such matters, adding, "It would be very unwise to break these solemn pledges and so set aflame the whole Middle East."[4] On Atlee's urging, an Anglo-American Committee of Inquiry was set up and went to Palestine to study the question of Jewish immigration. The Arab Office in Jerusalem testified that:

> The whole Arab people is unalterably opposed to the attempt to impose Jewish immigration and settlement upon it, and ultimately to establish a Jewish State in Palestine. Its opposition is based primarily on right. The Arabs of Palestine are descendants of the indigenous inhabitants of the country ... and they claim the democratic right of a majority to make its own decision in matters of urgent national concern.[5]

In its report in March 1946, the Committee of Inquiry supported the admission of the one hundred thousand immigrants, but rejected the proposal for a Jewish state and the Zionist principle that all Jews had the right to go to Palestine.[6] Britain offered to admit the one hundred thousand if the Zionists would disarm. In June the Zionists responded by blowing up eight road and rail bridges. In July the Irgun, with the consent of the Jewish Agency, placed a high-powered bomb in the British governmental wing of the King David Hotel. Eighty people — Arab, Jewish and British — died.[7] Armed clashes flared up between British and Zionist forces, and Palestine moved towards war.

Great Britain, unable to cope with the escalating violence in Palestine or with the growing pressure from the United States, announced in 1947 that it would take the problem of Palestine to the United Nations. It was almost like announcing an

AMERICAN LABOR DEMANDS
A JEWISH PALESTINE

250 delegates representing 114 International, State, City and local unions of the American Federation of Labor and the Congress of Industrial Organizations met at a three-day Trade Union Conference for Labor Palestine in Atlantic City, May 16th through 18th. These delegates, Jews and non-Jews, represented millions of organized workers in various parts of the United States and Canada. Out of their deliberations came this call to the American people and to the entire democratic world:

THE CASE OF THE JEWISH PEOPLE IS BEFORE THE CON-SCIENCE OF THE WORLD. JUSTICE DEMANDS THAT THE DECISION BE: A JEWISH HOMELAND IN PALESTINE

WILLIAM GREEN, President of the American Federation of Labor, told the delegates:

"The 7,500,000 members of the American Federation of Labor are wholeheartedly in favor of a Jewish Homeland in Palestine. The AFL will fight by the side of the Histadrut—the General

JAMES B. CAREY, secretary-treasurer of the Congress of Industrial Organizations, told the delegates:

"The C.I.O. stands behind the Jew-

The New York Times, May 23, 1947.

American mandate for Palestine. The United States, with war looming in Palestine, threw the full weight of its support to the Zionists.

The United States had taken sides, and it dominated the United Nations. Like the countries of Europe, most UN member nations depended heavily on U.S. aid to rebuild their shattered economies in the post-war period. The nineteen Latin American countries were virtual colonies of the United States. American corporations owned much of their economies, and for half a century American Marines and gunships had put down "unrest" and installed friendly governments. On the urging of the United States, some Latin American countries had declared war on Germany in the last days of the war to qualify for admission to the United Nations. There were only four African countries among the fifty-five members of the United Nations; the rest of the countries of Africa were still colonies. In any showdown, the United States could count on a majority of the votes.

The UN Decides

The stage was set for the decision on Palestine. The United Nations Special Commission on Palestine (UNSCOP), which had no African or Arab members, recommended by a narrow margin that Palestine be divided into a Jewish and an Arab state. The partition plan granted 55 percent of Palestine to the Jews, who were 30 percent of the population and owned only 6 percent of the land. Some 407,000 Arabs, a number nearly equal to the number of Jews, were to live in the area assigned to the Jewish state. The Arab state was to include ten thousand Jews and 725,000 Arabs in the remaining 45 percent of Palestine.[8]

The United States and its allies strongly supported partition. The Soviet Union, after decades of official opposition to Zionism, had changed its position. It wanted to

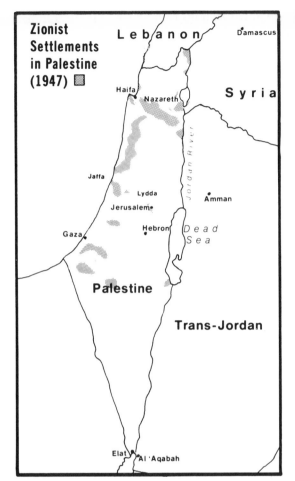

see the British Empire weakened in the Middle East and decided to vote for partition. Whether the Zionists could obtain the two-thirds of the votes necessary for victory depended on the undecided states.

On the opening day of the United Nations session on Palestine, in November 1947, the delegate from the Philippines declared:

> We hold that the issue is primarily moral. The issue is whether the United Nations should accept responsibility for the enforcement of a policy which is clearly repugnant to the valid nationalist aspirations of the people of Palestine. The Philippines Government holds that the United Nations ought not to accept such responsibility.[9]

Two days later the Philippine delegate was on a ship back to Manila, recalled from his post. A phone call from Washington to President Roxas of the Philippines had reversed the Philippine position on Palestine.[10] Ben-Gurion's decision to concentrate on the United States had paid off. In fact, columnist Drew Pearson reported, "President Truman cracked down harder on his State Department than ever before to swing the United Nations vote for the partition of Palestine."[11]

The example of the Philippine delegate was repeated. The delegate from Siam,

65

who had voted against partition in the United Nations Committee, was also recalled. A telegram signed by twenty-six Senators went to wavering countries. The president of the Firestone Rubber Company cabled Liberia, where it owned extensive rubber plantations, urging Liberia to vote for partition.

Palestine was divided on November 29 by a vote of thirty-three for, thirteen against, and ten abstentions. Only three African and Asian states voted in favor: South Africa, ruled by white European settlers, and Liberia and the Philippines, under pressure from the United States.

As the decision was announced, Arab delegates rose and walked angrily out of the Assembly. The United Nations was dead, one declared. "Not dead," said the Syrian delegate, "murdered." In the next days, Syrian demonstrators attacked the French and American embassies. Fifteen thousand Egyptians poured into the streets of Cairo, fighting the police and stoning the British consulate. Lebanese and Iraqis stormed United States offices. Many Arab people saw the hand of the United States behind the partition plan. A Palestinian leader commented: "We do not recognize Jewish and American illusions about partitioning Palestine. We are fighting an advance guard of America."[12]

Footnotes

1. Joyce and Gabriel Kolko, *The Limits of Power* (New York: 1972), p. 445.
2. Cited by Alfred Lilienthal, *What Price Israel?* (Chicago: 1953), pp. 194-96.
3. Samuel Halpern, *The Political World of American Zionism* (Detroit: 1961), p. 325.
4. Francis Williams, *A Prime Minister Remembers: The War and Post-War Memoirs of the Rt. Hon. E. Atlee* (London: 1961), pp. 181-201, cited in Khalidi, ed., *From Haven to Conquest,* p. 565.
5. *The Arab Case for Palestine: Evidence Submitted by the Arab Office, Jerusalem, to the Anglo-American Committee of Inquiry, March 1946,* cited in Walter Laqueur, ed., *The Israel-Arab Reader,* (New York: 1971), p. 94.
6. Ibid., pp. 87-89.
7. John and Hadawi, *The Palestine Diary,* 2:81-83.
8. Ibid., pp. 178-80.
9. United Nations, General Assembly Plenary Meeting, 2nd Session, November 1947, vol. 5, pp. 1313-14, cited by John and Hadawi, 2:262.
10. Alfred Lilienthal, *There Goes the Middle East* (New York: 1958), p. 6.
11. *Chicago Daily Tribune,* 9 February 1948, 8:1, cited by John and Hadawi, 2:262.
12. *New York Times,* 22 December 1947, 10:1, cited by John and Hadawi, 2:290.

8: Clearing the Land of Palestinians: The 1948 War

I noticed the tears in the eyes of our people. There was a bitter feeling in every heart. Some of the old men were willing to die fighting for our land. But they were without arms.

—Fouad Yasin, Palestinian radio announcer

On November 29, 1947, the night partition was announced in Palestine, Zionist settlers danced through the streets of Jerusalem and Tel Aviv. When some dancers burst into David Ben-Gurion's study, he hurried them away and returned to poring over military maps. The maps showed that over one-half of all Jewish settlers lived in three major cities, while the Palestinian Arabs lived in every city and in Arab villages throughout Palestine. Ben-Gurion studied each Arab village, focusing on the details of its strategic importance, its inhabitants, and its surrounding terrain.

Ben-Gurion had already ordered a secret mobilization of all soldiers in the Zionist army, the Haganah, and in the Palmach, the assault troops of the Haganah. Earlier in November, four special agents had departed for Europe with three million dollars of credits raised in the United States. Their mission was to buy rifles, machine guns, airplanes and artillery. In the outlying kibbutzim, secret arms factories, built from smuggled materials supplied by American Zionists, turned out small arms. Zionists were negotiating with Czechoslovakia for a large arms purchase.[1] Ben-Gurion was preparing a military offensive designed to seize much more of Palestine for the Zionist state than the United Nations had assigned to it. He called this offensive "Plan Dalet." It would begin as soon as enough British troops withdrew from Palestine.[2]

For Palestinian Arabs, the threat of war hung heavy in the air the night of partition. They listened to the wild celebration in the streets. They talked of how to defend their nation in the upcoming fight. No arms were arriving from Europe for the Palestinians. The weapons they possessed dated from the 1936 rebellion. In all of Jaffa, there were only eight machine guns. The British Emergency Laws, enacted during the 1936 Palestinian rebellion, still condemned to death any Palestinian found with a gun. Two small Palestinian guerrilla groups had continued to train in the hills throughout the Second World War. The only central leadership, the Arab Higher Committee, had been banished ten years ago. Recently re-formed, it no longer had the power to rally Palestinians behind it. The Palestinians faced a Zionist military that was perhaps the best led and best organized of all European settler armies.

The hopes of many Palestinians turned to the other Arab countries. The Arab League, formed at the end of the war to coordinate the activities of Arab countries, was quick to issue scores of statements expressing solidarity with the Palestinians. But it failed to train Palestinians or to provide them with arms. Arab leaders depended on Britain and the United States to maintain their power. Several, like Prime Minister Nuri es-Said of Iraq, were more employees of Western oil companies than independent leaders. They did not want to challenge imperialism by giving full support to the Palestinians.

There were those among the Arab peoples, however, who had an understanding of Western imperialism born from decades of resistance. Through demonstrations and in organizations, they pressured their governments to do more than pay lip service to the Palestinian cause. Some Arab organizers suggested a powerful weapon: an oil boycott against the United States and Britain. In 1947, Syria had refused to sign an agreement with the United States to complete an oil pipeline. Workers in Lebanon and Transjordan stopped work on the line in enthusiastic support. But King Ibn Saud of Saudi Arabia sabotaged the work stoppage to protect the royalties that flowed directly into his palace from the profits of United States oil corporations. Palestinians understood from betrayals like this that they could expect only token help from the Arab governments.

In December 1947, the British announced that they would withdraw from Palestine by May 15, 1948. Palestinians in Jerusalem and Jaffa called a general strike against the partition. Fighting broke out in Jerusalem's streets almost immediately. The Zionists were prepared to seize every opportunity to escalate the fighting. A lightning war was their only hope to defeat the Palestinians, who outnumbered the Zionists and lived in all parts of the partitioned country. A lengthy battle could only favor the Palestinians. Violent incidents mushroomed into all-out war.

Palestinians fought in small guerrilla bands, in village militias, or in the ranks of the Arab Liberation Army, a poorly armed force of a thousand Palestinians and

68

Zionist soldiers invade a town.

three thousand volunteers from other Arab countries. The people of Palestine supported the fighters as best they could. Women organized groups called "daisy chains" to smuggle arms into the hills, to dig trenches and to organize medical supplies. Casualties were high. By February the Palestinians were outmatched with twenty-five thousand Arabs fighting fifty thousand Zionist troops.[3]

Plan Dalet

Throughout the winter of 1948 Haganah and Irgun soldiers carried out night raids on Arab villages. The Haganah defined the purpose of these raids as "not to punish but to warn." Soldiers attacked quiet villages that had not been involved in the fighting to demonstrate "the Haganah's long arm."[4] Haganah troops entered a village and silently placed dynamite around the stone houses, drenching the wooden

69

doors and window frames with gasoline. Then, stepping back, they opened fire with their guns. The sleeping inhabitants died in the explosion and fire that destroyed their homes.[5]

Such "warnings" caused some villagers to flee their homes, but often only to another part of Palestine, not far enough away for the Zionists. The Zionist goal was to "clear the land" of its Arab inhabitants, but Palestinian leaders urged the people to stay and fight. In March Ben-Gurion put Plan Dalet — an all-out attack throughout the whole of Palestine — into effect.[6] At the heart of his strategy was the systematic expulsion of the Palestinian Arab population. As long as most Palestinians stayed in Palestine, the Zionists could not win a decisive victory.

The attack began with the use of psychological terror. On March 28, the Zionist Free Radio broadcast this warning in Arabic:

> Do you know it is a sacred duty to inoculate yourselves against cholera, typhus and similar diseases, as it is expected that such diseases will break out heavily in April and May among Arabs in the cities?[7]

Such broadcasts were not directed at Palestinian soldiers. Their purpose was to create fear in villagers, farmers and families in the cities and encourage them to flee. At Deir Yassin, a small Arab village near Jerusalem, psychological terror turned into a full-fledged massacre.

Deir Yassin was a quiet village. Its inhabitants had cooperated with the Jewish Agency and kept Arab troops out of their town.[8] On April 9, Irgun soldiers entered the village and told the residents they had fifteen minutes to abandon their homes. Then the bands of soldiers attacked. In a few hours, the Irgun had murdered two hundred fifty-four people — men, women and children — in cold blood.[9] Over the protests of the Jewish Agency, Jacques de Reynier of the International Red Cross visited Deir Yassin a few days later. He met the soldiers of the Irgun in the process of "cleaning up." This is what he reported:

> I found some bodies cold. Here the "cleaning up" had been done with machine guns, then hand-grenades. It had been finished off with knives, anyone could see that .... As the [Irgun] gang had not dared to attack me directly, I could continue. I gave orders for the bodies in this house to be loaded on the truck, and went into the next house, and so on. Everywhere, it was the same horrible sight. I found only two more people alive ....[10]

The Irgun took the few survivors to Jerusalem and paraded them through the streets as crowds spit upon them. Although the Jewish Agency piously condemned the massacre at Deir Yassin, the Irgun was admitted to the Joint Command of the military with the Haganah the same day.[11] The actions of the Irgun served the Zionist plan well. The destruction of Deir Yassin, which was skillfully publicized by the Zionists, sparked an exodus of Palestinian families who feared a similar fate. During the joint Irgun-Haganah attack on the Palestinian quarter of Haifa, the news of the massacre which had occurred twelve days before convinced many to flee.

On April 21, 1948, the British commander of Haifa advised the Zionists that he was withdrawing his troops. He did not tell Palestinian leaders. At sundown the Zionists began their attack on Haifa Arabs with *Davidka* mortars, which hurled sixty pounds of explosives about three hundred yards into the crowded Arab quarter. Barrel bombs, which were casks filled with gasoline and dynamite, rolled down the narrow alleys and crashed, creating an inferno of flames and explosions. Haganah

Palestinians flee Jaffa.

loudspeakers broadcast "horror recordings" that filled the air with the shrieks and anguished moans of Arab women, interrupted by a booming sorrowful voice that called out in Arabic, "Flee for your lives! The Jews are using poison gas and atomic weapons!" As Palestinians fled their city, the Irgun commander reported that they cried, "Deir Yassin! Deir Yassin!"[12]

Within a week the same "psychological blitz," as the Zionists called it, emptied the port city of Jaffa, a city designated as part of the Arab state. Only three thousand of the eighty thousand Arabs of Jaffa remained. Jon Kimche, a Zionist historian, reported that the soldiers "commenced to loot in wholesale fashion .... Everything that was movable was carried from Jaffa [and] what could not be taken away was smashed."[13] From the fertile fields of Galilee to the fortress city of Acre, the Zionist campaign drove the Palestinians from their homes, their villages, their lands. The several hundred thousand who remained lived under Zionist occupation.

During that fateful April of 1948, eight out of the thirteen major Zionist military attacks on Palestinians occurred in the territory granted to the Arab state by the United Nations.[14] By May 15, as the British ended their long rule over Palestine, three hundred thousand Palestinians were exiles, living hand-to-mouth in the Jordan Valley, Lebanon and Syria. The Jewish Agency cynically announced that the exodus of Arabs from Palestine was due to "flight psychosis."[15]

71

Ben-Gurion proclaims the State of Israel.

"Proclaim the State, No Matter What"

On Passover, April 24, Ben-Gurion had announced at a victory feast in Jerusalem: "We stand on the eve of a Jewish State." He had already set the date in his mind. As the British ended their rule on May 15, 1948, the Zionists would begin theirs. Ben-Gurion planned to cut off the lingering debate in the UN about the partition plan by confronting the world with the actual existence of the new state. Chaim Weizmann, the elder statesman of Zionism, telegraphed his advice: "Proclaim the state, no matter what else ensues."[16]

Zionist leaders approached President Truman and worked out the details of U.S. recognition. At 6:00 P.M. on May 15, David Ben-Gurion proclaimed the existence of Israel. Eleven minutes later, President Truman cabled American recognition of the Jewish state.

A messenger rushed into the United Nations to inform the members of the turn of events; even the U.S. ambassador had not been informed. Arab delegates charged that the United Nations had again served as a backdrop for the maneuvers of the United States. The Soviet Union, still hoping that the creation of the new state might mean an end to imperialist control of Palestine, added its recognition a few days later.

People in the Arab countries knew better. The news of Deir Yassin and other violent incidents had created an intense concern and anger over the fate of the Palestinians. As Committees for Palestine called meetings and demonstrations throughout the Arab countries, Arab leaders knew they had to respond. The Arab League hastily called for its member countries to send regular army troops into Palestine. They were ordered to secure only the sections of Palestine given to the Arabs under the partition plan. But these regular armies were ill-equipped and lacked any central command to coordinate their efforts. King Abdullah of Transjordan, the official commander-in-chief, was busy negotiating with British and Zionist leaders for a slice of Palestine.[17] Abdullah wanted to attach to his own kingdom any Palestinian territory not occupied by the Israelis. He promised that his troops, the Arab Legion, the only real fighting force among the Arab armies, would avoid fighting with Jewish settlements.[18] Under Abdullah's self-serving leadership the armies of the Arab League had little effect. A few individual units — most notably those of young Egyptians — fought fiercely, but often with no support from their generals. Yet Western historians record this as the moment when the young state of Israel fought off the "overwhelming hordes" of five Arab countries!

In reality, the Israeli offensive against the Palestinians intensified. British Major Edgar O'Ballance described the new phase:

> [T]he Arab inhabitants were ejected and forced to flee into Arab territory, as at Ramleh, Lydda and other places. Wherever the Israeli troops advanced into Arab country, the Arab population was bulldozed out in front of them.[19]

On July 11, 1948, Moshe Dayan led a jeep commando column into the town of Lydda. Rifles, Sten guns and submachine guns blasted at everything that moved. Within minutes, the streets were silent, strewn with corpses of men, women and children.[20] The next day, the Israelis seized the adjoining town of Ramleh. Loudspeakers announced that all Arabs had forty-eight hours to leave. Israeli soldiers stripped each person of all belongings — even food — at the bridges leaving the town. As Israeli troops sacked the town, a hundred thousand Palestinians began a painful march into exile.[21] For three days, without food and water, the refugees walked in the sweltering sun towards the Transjordanian hills. Many old people and children died of thirst.

"An Insuperable Problem"

When the fighting persisted and it became clear that the partition plan had broken down, the United Nations sent a mediator, Count Folke Bernadotte, to try to arrange a cease-fire and to secure the rights of the Palestinians. Numerous cease-fires which he arranged broke down as the Israelis continued their drives into Arab territory.[22] Bernadotte urged Israel to allow the Palestinians to return to their homes. Israeli Foreign Minister Moshe Shertok replied: "On the economic side, the reintegration of the returning Arabs into normal life ... would present an insuperable problem."[23]

In reality, the "problem" was that the new state depended on the homes, land and shops left behind by the exiled Palestinians. New Jewish settlers were already arriving, moving into Arab houses and reopening Arab businesses. The wealth of the exiled Palestinians — 80 percent of the land, 50 percent of the citrus groves, 90

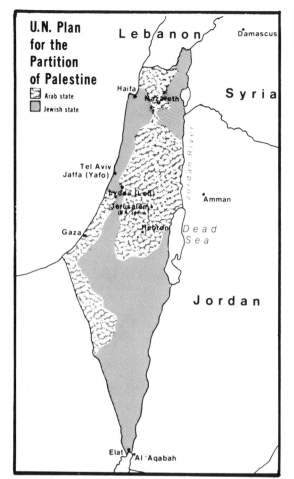

U.N. Plan
for the
Partition
of Palestine

Arab state
Jewish state

Lebanon
Damascus
Haifa
Nazareth
Syria
Tel Aviv
Jaffa (Yafo)
Lydda (Lod)
Jerusalem
Gaza
Hebron
Amman
Dead Sea
Jordan River
Jordan
Elat
Al 'Aqabah

Israel
(1949-1967)

Lebanon
Damascus
Haifa
Nazareth
Syria
Nablus
WEST BANK
Tel Aviv
Jaffa (Yafo)
Lydda
Jerusalem
Gaza
GAZA STRIP
Hebron
Amman
Dead Sea
Jordan River
Israel
Jordan
Elat
Al 'Aqabah

percent of the olive groves, and ten thousand shops — was needed to build the new state of Israel.[24]

Bernadotte continued to press for Palestinians' right to return. His reports documented the forced flight of the Palestinians and their desire to return once peace was established. Finally on September 17, members of the Stern Gang assassinated Bernadotte. Waves of shock rippled through the United Nations and Western capitals at the news of his murder. New pressure mounted on Israel to accept a cease-fire. On January 7, 1949, a prolonged cease-fire went into effect. The new state of Israel encompassed 80 percent of Palestine! The key to victory had been the forcible eviction of the Palestinian Arab population. Chaim Weizmann observed that the exodus of the Palestinians was a "miraculous simplification of our tasks."[25]

The Western world celebrated the birth of the new state. In America, Senators, members of Congress and the President applauded the "miracle of Israel." A rush of books and articles, like the best-seller *Exodus,* told the story of Israel as the victory of a valiant and intelligent people, the Israelis, over hordes of dark-skinned, dishonest and backward Arabs. The story had the drama of the popular Hollywood

Westerns that dominated the American screen. It also had the same point: the attack on native people and the conquest of their land, whether Palestinian or Indian, was not only legitimate, but courageous and inspiring. It was a useful lesson to teach as American leaders launched the Cold War. It helped mobilize the American people behind the U.S. drive to seize the resources of other countries. An atmosphere of fear and hatred of "backward and uncivilized" people, from the Koreans to the Arabs, gripped the country. Israel represented a victory that both recaptured America's pioneer days and gave Israel's American supporters an emotional stake in U.S. domination of the Middle East.

The truth about the Palestinian Arabs lay buried in this avalanche of propaganda. In 1959 an American Jew, Nathan Chofshi, who had settled in Palestine in 1908, wrote to the American *Jewish Newsletter,* protesting an article by Rabbi Mordecai Kaplan. Kaplan had argued that Arab leaders told the Palestinians to leave. Chofshi wrote:

> If Rabbi Kaplan really wanted to know what happened, we old Jewish settlers in Palestine who witnessed the flight could tell him how and in what manner we, Jews, forced the Arabs to leave cities and villages which they did not want to leave of their own free will. Some of them were driven out by force of arms; others were made to leave by deceit, lying and false promises.[26]

Over seven hundred fifty thousand Palestinians had been driven out of Palestine to create the state of Israel.[27] King Abdullah annexed the Palestinian West Bank to Transjordan, renaming his enlarged kingdom simply Jordan. King Farouk of Egypt took over the administration of the Gaza Strip. Palestine disappeared from Western maps.

The people of Palestine did not forget. The memories of the terror of the spring of 1948 mingled with the memory of other springs in Palestine, when the land was theirs and grew under their care. Ghassan Kanafani, an exiled Palestinian writer, described the flight of his family from Jaffa in a story called *The Land of Sad Oranges.* He recalled

> ... the long queue of lorries, leaving the land of oranges far behind and spreading out over the winding roads of Lebanon. Then I began to weep, howling with tears. As for [my] mother, she eyed the oranges silently and all the orange trees [my] father had left behind to the Jews were reflected in his eyes; all the wholesome orange trees he had acquired one by one were visible in his face and glistened through the tears he could not check, even in front of the officer. When we arrived in Sidon that afternoon, we had become homeless.[28]

Footnotes

1. Tabitha Petran, *Zionism, A Political Critique,* p. 10, using sources from Walid Khalidi, "Plan Dalat, The Zionist Master Plan for the Conquest of Palestine," *Middle East Forum* (November 1961).
2. Nathaniel Lorch, *The Edge of the Sword* (New York: 1961), p. 87, cited by Childers, "The Wordless Wish," in *The Transformation of Palestine,* p. 180.
3. Compiled from various sources, including Fred J. Khouri, *The Arab-Israeli Dilemma* (New York: 1969), cited by Dana Adams Schmidt, *Armageddon in the Middle East* (New York: 1974), p. 123.
4. Jon Kimche and David Kimche, *Both Sides of the Hill* (London: 1960), cited by Childers, p. 182.
5. Ibid.

6. David Ben-Gurion, *Rebirth and Destiny of Israel,* translated and edited by Mordechai Nurock (New York: 1954), p. 39, cited by Childers, p. 183.
7. *BBC Monitoring Records,* British Museum, cited by Childers, p. 183.
8. Sykes, *Crossroads to Israel,* p. 416.
9. Numerous sources cited by Childers, p. 185.
10. Jacques de Reynier, "A Jerusalem un Drapeau Flottait sur la Ligne de Feu," in Khalidi, *From Haven to Conquest,* p. 764.
11. George Eden Kirk, *A Short History of the Middle East* (London: 1948), cited by Sykes, p. 418.
12. From numerous pro-Zionist sources cited by Childers, pp. 188-89.
13. Jon Kimche, *Seven Fallen Pillars* (London: 1950), p. 233, cited by Childers, p. 191.
14. Petran, p. 11, citing Khalidi, "Plan Dalet, the Zionist Master Plan for the Conquest of Palestine."
15. *New York Times,* 4 May 1948, 1:6,8, cited by Robert John and Sami Hadawi, *The Palestine Diary,* 2:342.
16. Sykes, p. 432.
17. Jon Kimche and David Kimche, *A Clash of Destinies: The Arab-Jewish War and the Founding of the State of Israel* (New York: 1970), p. 60, cited by John and Hadawi, 2:295.
18. Aref el-Aref, *The Tragedy 1947-1952* 2 vols. (Sidon, Lebanon: 1956), 1:65-67, cited by John and Hadawi, 2:295-96.
19. Edgar O'Ballance, *The Arab-Israeli War, 1948* (London: 1956), pp. 171-72, cited by Childers, p. 194.
20. Kenneth Bilby, *New Star in the Near East* (New York: 1950), p. 43, cited by Childers, p. 194.
21. Kimche, *Both Sides of the Hill,* p. 228, cited by Childers, p. 194; *London Economist,* 21 August 1948, cited by Childers, p. 194.
22. Sykes, pp. 435-36.
23. United Nations Security Council, *Official Records,* Suppl. 108 (S/949), August 1948, pp. 106-9, cited by Childers, p. 195.
24. Don Peretz, *Israel and the Palestine Arabs* (Washington, D.C.: 1958), cited by Childers, p. 195.
25. James G. McDonald, *My Mission to Israel 1948-1951* (New York: 1951), cited by Childers, p. 196.
26. "The Bitter Truth about the Refugees," *Jewish Newsletter* (New York), 9 February 1959, cited by Childers, p. 184.
27. Janet Abu-Lughod, "The Demographic Transformation of Palestine," in *The Transformation of Palestine,* pp. 147-61.
28. Anni Kanafani, *Ghassan Kanafani* (Beirut: 1973), p. 10.

9: The Exile: From Bitterness To Strength

Teach the night to forget to bring
Dreams showing me my village
And teach the wind to forget to carry to me
The aroma of apricots in my fields!
And teach the sky, too, to forget to rain.

Only then, I may forget my country.
　　　　　　　—Rashed Hussein

The winter of 1949, the first winter of exile for more than seven hundred fifty thousand Palestinians, was cold and hard. Snow glistened on the mountains of Lebanon and the Galilee as thousands of families trudged along the roads seeking shelter. Families huddled in caves, abandoned huts, or makeshift tents which tore, were patched, and tore again as the cold rains pounded the ancient material. In October of 1948 the U.S. ambassador to Egypt reported that "thousands of refugees would die of cold if help was not sent soon."[1] As the United Nations debated the status of the refugees and Americans sent donations to Israel, forty people died of cold each night in the Ramallah area of Jordan.[2] Food was scarce. The *New York Times* of February 27, 1949 stated:

> American eyewitnesses in Jordan told of swarms of children with matchstick arms and legs and protruding bellies produced by progressive starvation and of babies dying because there was no milk.

Many of the starving were only miles away from their own vegetable gardens and orchards in occupied Palestine — the new state of Israel. Months before, in July of 1948, David Ben-Gurion had stated the Zionist policy toward the refugees: "We shall do everything possible to ensure that they never return."[3]

The American press placed no blame on Israel for the exiles. When they mentioned the "refugee problem," the newspapers told their readers that the solution was simple: Arab countries could easily absorb all the refugees. This solution, of course, was unacceptable to the exiles. They were tied to Palestine not just by livelihood, but by thousands of threads that link a people to their country. Also, the Arab countries who received the streams of refugees — four hundred sixty thousand in Jordan, two hundred thousand in the Gaza Strip, one hundred thousand in Lebanon and eighty-five thousand in Syria — were poor. Western colonialism had taken its toll. Arab cities were already swollen with people looking for work. Egypt, for example, exported cotton to the West, but lacked enough food to feed its own people. Lebanon spent 20 percent of its annual budget on food and shelter for the Palestinians,[4] but it was not enough. Religious organizations and individuals added their aid, but still the needs of three-quarters of a million displaced people were staggering. Some Palestinians had money, connections or saleable skills to ease the pain of exile. But most arrived with nothing.

At the end of 1949 the United Nations finally acted. It set up the United Nations Relief and Works Administration (UNRWA) to take over sixty refugee camps from voluntary agencies. It managed to keep people alive, but only barely. Refugees who qualified for aid received roughly thirty-seven dollars a year. ID cards branded each person as a permanent refugee. Since there was little possibility of refugees getting jobs, UNRWA made an institution of hunger and humiliation.

The Disinherited

Three hundred thousand Palestinians were crowded into refugee camps located on desolate land. There was no sanitation and only basic health care in the camps. For the first several months of exile, nightly radio broadcasts named those who had died in the war. In this way families learned the fate of relatives. Some were close by in exile; others were in distant camps or in occupied Palestine. As men who had stayed behind in Palestine to fight found their families again, the joy of reunion turned quickly to despair. There was nothing to do, no way to ease the hunger of the children, to keep them warm and dry, to find a book to teach them to read. Many people had been farmers; now there was no land. Traders, craftspeople and professionals lived in the camps with no outlet for their skills.

Days passed by as people waited in endless lines — lines for water, lines for food, lines for medicine. The simplest household task took hours. Some jobs, like cleaning, were impossible, as every rain turned the "floor" of a tent into mud. Women gave

TENT NO. 50 (SONG OF A REFUGEE)

Tent No. 50, on the left, is my new world,
Shared with me by my memories:
Memories as verdant as the eyes of spring,
Memories like the eyes of a woman weeping,
And memories the color of milk and love!

Tent No. 50, on the left, that is my present,
But it is too cramped to contain a future!
And - "Forget!" they say, but how can I?

    Teach the night to forget to bring
    Dreams showing me my village
    And teach the wind to forget to carry to me
    The aroma of apricots in my fields!
    And teach the sky, too, to forget to rain.

Only then, I may forget my country.

                  By Rashed Hussein

"We studied like ones possessed."

birth with only the help of neighbors. A baby born in the cold and rainy winter survived with donations of clothes and extra food rations from neighbors. Oil lamps ineffectively heated the tents with a misty steam. The traditions of celebration at the birth of a child were haunted by the question: What can the future hold?

For Palestinians in the Arab cities, the future was not much brighter. Thousands crowded into the slums of Beirut, Amman and Damascus. In a 1953 visit, a British journalist described the scene in a mosque, an Islamic house of worship, where refugees had lived for three years:

> At first I could see nothing. The little light there was was yellow and sticky like fog. Then I got used to it. High above, the whitewash of the domed roof was stained with patches of brown damp; water ran down the walls. The floor space was stone-paved and black from use. It was partitioned — if that is not the wrong word for such flimsiness. Ropes were slung from wall to wall. Odd poles stuck in the floor, supported them. And from them hung drab strips of sacking, patched, torn and brown with age. These strips were the walls of the partitions, and each pen — that is the right word — was a home and in the mosque were twenty-three families.[5]

Preparing to Return

The journalist accurately reported the misery faced by Palestinian refugees each day. But he missed the seeds of a new life that were growing out of the poverty and humiliation. Fawaz Turki, a Palestinian who grew up in a refugee camp in Lebanon, wrote:

Those people outside the camp (not to mention the Western "tourists" with

their blessed sympathy, their cameras, their sociological degrees, and their methodological and statistical charts) seeing our tattered rags hanging on us like white flags of surrender ... did not know what we had. A feeling inside us. Growing. A hope.[6]

At night in the camps, Palestinians gathered inside a tent to play the *oud,* a Palestinian stringed instrument, or dance the *dabke,* a village folkdance of Palestine. Women hoarded small bits of thread to embroider traditional designs on a daughter's wedding dress. People from the same village in Palestine found each other and passed around cherished snapshots, discussing the fate of their olive trees or planning a spring planting on their return to Palestine. Women wondered aloud if the Israeli immigrants living in their house would cut down the jasmine or remember to mend the wall by the garden in the spring.

Just as often, people clustered around poets who recited the stories of Ramleh and Lydda or sang of the 1936 rebellion. Children learned from the poets about Palestinian history and resistance. They made up games of evading the Israeli border patrols and returning to Palestine to bring back a treasured heirloom or a favorite possession of their mothers.

Parents strongly urged their children to study as a way of escaping the deadliness of camp life. In makeshift classrooms, teachers encountered their most eager students. One Palestinian described her generation as studying "like one possessed." Worn newspapers and leaflets with news of resistance to Israel were passed from tent to tent. Palestinians were preparing for one thing only — to return home. *Life* magazine reported in 1951:

> The refugees don't want to be compensated for their lost lands and homes. They don't want to be sent off anywhere. They want to go home to what they consider properly theirs.
>
> "I want to go to my home," said Said Kewash, a lean-faced man who comes from Mayroon, near the Lebanese border. "I will never change this idea no matter what they offer me. There is no place in the world, not even Truman's White House that I would take for my home."
>
> Maud Saleem agrees. He says he has the key to his home in his pocket and he has told his son that if he dies, the key is to be buried with him.[7]

The United Nations, in November of 1948, affirmed the right of the refugees to return to Palestine, resolving:

> ... refugees wishing to return to their homes and live in peace with their neighbors would be allowed to do so as soon as practicable, and that compensation would be paid for the property of those choosing not to return.[8]

As Said Kewash and Maud Saleem stated, the refugees were not interested in "compensation." Real compensation, which Professor Samuel Penrose of the American University of Beirut calculated in 1953 at *$12 billion,* was never under discussion.[9] The return of refugees received even less attention. The United States, the main ally of Israel, vetoed every United Nations resolution that might allow a trickle of refugees to re-enter their homeland. Refugees in the camps confirmed that the expulsion of Palestinians by Israeli soldiers continued.

On May 5, 1951 General Bennike, head of the United Nations Treaty Supervision Organization, reported that Israeli troops had expelled seven thousand Arabs from el-Auja, a demilitarized zone near Egypt, and added the territory to Israel.[10] Nothing was done. As reports of Israeli violations of the cease-fire filled the UN offices, Palestinians affirmed that return to Palestine was the only issue. Israel's only offer involving return of Palestinians was to accept one hundred thousand refugees from the Gaza Strip, if the Strip were added to the state of Israel.[11]

Palestinians rejected this solution and any other that did not promise the return of their land. In 1950, twenty-five thousand refugees went on a hunger strike against UNRWA, stating they would rather starve than settle outside Palestine. When UNRWA built concrete houses to replace the tent settlements, Palestinians in the camps began destroying the new buildings until they were assured that better houses did not mean they were giving up their claim to return to Palestine.[12]

Young Palestinians saw the role that the Western powers had played in creating Israel from the start. In Beirut, Amman and Damascus, they joined other demonstrators in marches to the American Embassy and United States Information Agency to protest the growing role of the United States in the Middle East. At the demonstrations they spoke of the history of the conflict between Zionism and the Palestinian nation. On important anniversaries like November 2, the date of the Balfour Declaration, or May 15, the date of the creation of Israel, Palestinians led

Children learned the history of Palestine from the old.

student strikes and marches through the Arab cities. Even elementary school pupils participated.

Palestinians protested not only against Israel and the United States. In 1951 the Committee for Resisting Peace with Israel began distributing in the camps and cities leaflets that exposed the deals that Arab leaders, especially King Abdullah of Jordan, were making with the Israelis. Demonstrations broke out in Jordan. That year a Palestinian tailor from Jerusalem shot and killed Abdullah as he was leaving a mosque.

Abdullah and his successor, King Hussein, ordered Jordanian police to help Israel guard its new borders against the return of the Palestinians. It was at these borders that protest became face-to-face confrontations with the new "owners" of Palestine. The jagged line of barbed wire outlining Israel's border had been erected in 1948, wherever Israeli troops had advanced. Often it divided villages down the middle, separated cattle from their grazing land and tore farmers from their fields. Over one hundred thirty thousand farmers in eighty villages along the Israeli-Jordanian border were cut off from their fields. They could not even qualify for UN aid; they had "only" lost their source of income, not both their homes and source of income, as UNRWA required.[13]

That first spring of exile the Israeli government allowed Palestinian farmers to cross the border to plant their fields. In the fall Israel decided they could not return to cultivate their crops. As people came to pick their oranges or harvest their wheat, they were met by the border patrol. Sir John Glubb reported in the quarterly journal *Foreign Affairs:* "A great number of them were shot dead, without question or answer, by the first Israeli patrol they met. Others were maltreated or tortured."[14] The Israelis claimed that the farmers were "infiltrators." In reality, most were trying to reweave their lives after the horrors of war. The Palestinian writer Turki explained:

> A great many of these simple folk, to whom politics, war and frontiers were alien concepts, had the naive notion that once the hostilities had ceased they could return home to resume their lives, to meet the members of their families they had left behind, to sleep in their warm houses, and to be in their orange groves — for soon it would be the orange-picking season.[15]

Israeli guns shattered these innocent assumptions forever. Merchants crossing Beersheeba from the Gaza Strip, their pack animals loaded with rice and sugar, found their centuries-old caravan routes blocked by Israeli troops. Israeli bullets killed others as they looked for work or searched for relatives. Soon many people had fathers and sons, mothers and daughters who had been killed on the Gaza caravan, at the Jordanian border, or in their own olive groves. Many Palestinians no longer crossed the border unarmed. The longing to return home, among students, farmers, and camp-dwellers, gave way to a determined search for the path back to Palestine.

Footnotes

1. *New York Times,* 17 October 1948, cited in *The ABC of the Palestine Problem,* 2 vols., Arab Women's Information Committee (Beirut: 1969 and 1974), 2:9.
2. Ibid.
3. Michael Bar-Zohar, *Ben-Gurion* (French Edition), cited by Maxime Rodinson, *Israel and the Arabs* (Middlesex: 1970), p. 66.
4. "Peace and Refugees in the Middle East," *Middle East Journal* (July 1949), p. 252.
5. Owen Tweedy, "The Arab Refugees," *International Affairs* (July 1952), p. 339.
6. Fawaz Turki, *The Disinherited* (New York: 1972), p. 46.
7. James Bell, "Forgotten Arab Refugees," *Life,* 17 September 1951, pp. 91, 92ff.
8. United Nations General Assembly Resolution 194 (3/1), para. 11, 11 December 1948, cited by Rodinson, p. 66.
9. Samuel Penrose, *The Palestine Problem: Retrospect and Prospect* (New York: 1954), p. 18, cited in *The ABC of the Palestine Problem,* 2:11.
10. Fayez Sayegh, *The Record of Israel at the United Nations* (New York: 1957), p. 46, cited in *The ABC of the Palestine Problem,* 2:9.
11. Rodinson, p. 66.
12. Leila Kadi, ed., *Basic Political Documents of the Armed Palestinian Resistance Movement* (Beirut: 1969), p. 15.
13. Janet Abu-Lughod, p. 161, and Gerard Chaliand, *The Palestinian Resistance* (Middlesex: 1972), p. 36.
14. Cited by Turki, p. 38.
15. Turki, p. 38.

10: Building the Jewish State

An Arab peasant asked an official at the Israel Lands Administration, "What are you offering me? Is my land worth only two hundred pounds per dunam?" The official replied, "This is not your land, it is ours, and we are paying you watchman's wages, for that is all you are. You have 'watched' our land for two thousand years and now we are paying your fee. But the land has always been ours."

Inside the new state of Israel, the work of wiping out the memory of Palestine began as soon as the war ended. Printing presses churned out maps which marked the boundaries of Israel and displayed its new name. Writers hastily corrected manuscripts, scratching out the name of Palestine. Editors revised history textbooks for the schools. Road signs in Hebrew directed travelers to ancient Palestinian cities with new names. Jaffa, the lively port city, was forced to merge with Tel Aviv and become Tel Aviv-Yaffo. Lydda, emptied of its Arab citizens since July of 1948, became Lod. Many Arab villages, turned over to Jewish settlements, disappeared from the map entirely.

Zionist leaders planned to erase the Arab character of Palestine. They wanted to make Israel, in the words of the Zionist slogan, "as Jewish as England is English." As long as three hundred thousand Palestinians remained in Israel and on their land, that could not happen. Israel had already closed its borders to the refugees who wanted to return. It passed the Law of Absentee Property to seize the land they had left behind — 60 percent of the land of Palestine suitable for farming.[1] Now Israeli leaders turned their attention to the Palestinians living inside the new state's borders.

Ironically, Israel's leaders launched their campaign against the Palestinians and their land by applying the old British Defense Laws. The British had passed these laws in 1945 to repress Zionist attacks on the mandate government. That year a conference of Zionist lawyers had demanded their repeal. One of the lawyers, Yaacov Shapiro, said then:

> The system established in Palestine since the issue of the Defense Laws is unparalleled in any civilized country; there were no such laws even in Nazi Germany . . . . No government has the right to pass such laws.[2]

Three years later, as the Attorney General of Israel, Shapiro ordered the vigorous enforcement of these laws against the Palestinians.

The Military Government

Israel used the Defense Laws to set up a Military Government in the areas where most of the Palestinians lived — the Galilee, the little Triangle and the Negev. Ben-Gurion explained why: "The Military Government came into existence to protect the right of Jewish settlement in all parts of the state."[3] Its purpose was to confiscate land and to suppress any Palestinian resistance.

In the first ten years of Israel's existence, Palestinians *inside* the country lost more than a quarter of a million acres of land.[4] Israel seized some of this land under the Law of Absentee Property. This law defined an "absentee" as any Arab absent from the areas under Jewish control after the date of the United Nations partition, November 29, 1947. Thus a family from Nazareth that went on its annual Christmas pilgrimage to Jerusalem, which was under Arab control, was "absentee" even if the family returned the very next day. The people of Acre, who fled to another quarter of the city during the May 1948 Haganah attack, lost their homes and shops under this law.[5]

The Military Government also seized land by expelling Arabs from their villages for "security reasons." Then after a period of time, the Minister of Agriculture could claim the land for the state because it was technically "uncultivated." In the case of the village of Ikrit, in the Galilee, the Military Government went even further.

During the 1948 war, the Israeli Army had occupied Ikrit. Its farmers, who were mostly Catholics, offered no resistance. When the soldiers ordered everyone to leave their homes for two weeks until "military operations in the area were concluded," the villagers went to a nearby town. A military governor took over the area and repeatedly denied the villagers' appeals to return to Ikrit. The people of Ikrit petitioned the Israeli Supreme Court, which made a rare decision in their favor in

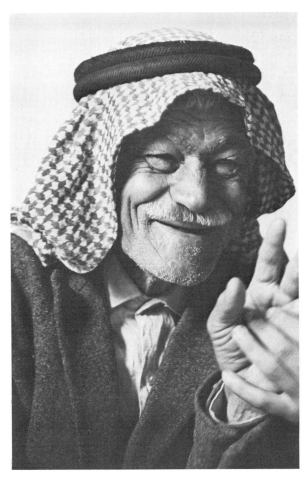

July 1951. But the Military Government still refused to allow them to return. On Christmas day, a month before the court was to hear a new appeal from the villagers, Israeli soldiers entered Ikrit and systematically blew up every house. Ikrit's land was then given to Jewish immigrants.[6] These new settlers "made the desert bloom," in the words of Israeli press releases, by reclaiming land once green and fruitful under Arab hands.

Between 1948 and 1950, three hundred fifty of three hundred seventy new Jewish settlements were built on land taken from Palestinians.[7] The Israeli government tried to "compensate" many Arabs for their land with small payments. But the Palestinians did not want the money. Many simply set up camp near the occupiers' settlements. Israel Hertz, a Zionist writer, reported:

> [These refugees] mostly live in humble houses of tin, sacking or wood, that they have erected on the outskirts of their villages . . . . The great majority of these refugees — nearly all of them — ask to be allowed to return to their villages, refusing to sell their rights to their land, in spite of unfavorable material conditions.[8]

Even when Palestinians managed to hold on to their land, the settlers, police and the Military Government harassed them constantly. In his book, *To Be An Arab in*

From: IDENTITY CARD

Record!
I am an Arab
and my Identity Card
is number fifty thousand
I have eight children
and the ninth is coming in midsummer
Will you be angry?

Record!
I am an Arab
You have stolen the orchards
of my ancestors
and the land
which I cultivated
Along with my children
And you left us with those rocks
So will the State take them
as it has been said?

                                    By Mahmoud Darweesh

Israel, the political journalist Fouzi el-Asmar described what happened to him as a child when he was picking figs one morning in his family's orchard. An armed settler ordered him to stop. When he refused, the settler took him to the police station, where a police officer interrogated him:

"Aren't you ashamed to steal, you little thief?"
"I didn't steal. It's our orchard — my father's. I went there to pick figs."
"There is no such things as 'ours.' The land belongs to the Jews. Do you understand?"
"No."
"You dog. You are answering arrogantly!"
He took me and put me in an inner room and locked the door behind me. I burst into tears. I did not know what the policeman was talking about . . . . An hour later the policeman came again and took me to the room where he had previously questioned me. This time he asked me, "So whose land is this?" And I answered, "Ours. But I did not know my father had sold it to Jews." To this I received a crushing answer in a mocking tone. "I told you that the orchard is not yours. Your father did not sell it to the Jews. It belongs to the Jews."[9]

Such harassment was not confined to children. The Military Government and police made daily life almost unbearable for many Palestinians. Until the Military Government was finally ended in 1966, no Palestinian could enter or leave his military district without a special permit. The Military Governor of each area had absolute power to punish violators, including the authority to levy huge fines.[10] Often he exiled Arabs to distant villages and forced them to return to their old village to report at the police station each day. In the Galilee, the authorities frequently expelled breadwinners from Israel, in the hope that their families would be forced to follow them into exile.[11]

Despite these attempts to expel the Palestinians, most remained and claimed their rights as citizens. Yet even their right to Israeli citizenship was threatened. The Israeli Knesset (Parliament) passed the "Law of Return" in 1950. It guaranteed immediate Israeli citizenship to any Jew who came to Israel from any country in the world. Palestinians living in Israel had to pass through a series of obstacles to become citizens. They had to prove that they had stayed in Palestine throughout the war and they had to show "some knowledge of Hebrew." During the Knesset debate on the Nationality Law that set these terms, Moses Sharret, Israel's Foreign Minister, criticized his colleagues for being too easy on the "foreigners," referring to the Palestinian Arabs.[12]

In the face of all these assaults, many Palestinians risked fines, jail and expulsion to fight for their rights. In 1951 the people of Nazareth organized a general strike to protest confiscation of their land. Their action sparked large solidarity demonstrations in other major towns in the Galilee. The Military Government did not tolerate such open defiance. It tried to find and expel the leaders of any demonstration or organization that Israel considered "hostile to the state." Yet by 1954 Palestinians had organized the Popular Arab Front, which demanded equality for all peoples in Israel and an end to the Military Government. The Front enjoyed strong support until it, too, was destroyed by the Military Government.

"Ingathering the Exiles"

This continuing Palestinian resistance led Zionists to insist on the need for an even larger Jewish majority in the new state. More immigrants would be needed to protect Israel from the Palestinians in exile and from those inside Israel. As Ben-Gurion said, "We can have no real security without immigration."[13] To attract Jewish settlers, the new government and the Zionist agencies gave all the support they could to immigrants, including jobs, housing and land.

Zionists had hoped that the "ingathering of the exiles" — the "return" to Israel of the Jews of the world — would bring millions of eager pioneers to build a "Greater Israel" whose final borders were still not defined. Instead, Israel's open invitation to Jews throughout the world was accepted by a far smaller number than expected. Most of those who came were poor and desperate. Among these were three hundred thousand Eastern European Jews and seventy thousand survivors of Nazi concentration camps who left war-ravaged Europe to go to Israel in its first three years of existence. Most American and European Jews simply expressed their commitment to the Jewish state by making annual donations, not by moving to Israel.

Yemeni immigrants wait in the shadow of the plane that will carry them to Israel.

When the "ingathering" of Western Jews did not happen in large enough numbers, the Israelis turned their attention to the communities of dark-skinned so-called "Oriental" Jews who lived in the surrounding Arab countries. The appeal of a better living standard made many willing to emigrate. Others left their homes because the creation of the Jewish state and the resulting Arab anger and suspicion had poisoned relationships among Jews, Christians and Moslems in the Arab countries. Jews were often suspected of being disloyal citizens and sympathetic to Israel. As a result of violent outbursts against Jews in Libya, Syria, Egypt and Lebanon, many fled to Israel.[14]

The Zionists took advantage of these tensions in order to swell the number of immigrants from Arab countries. One target of the Zionists was the Jewish community of Baghdad, the capital of Iraq. This community of Jews had existed for more than twenty-five hundred years. Its people lived peacefully and prosperously among the Moslems of Baghdad. At first, the Jews of Baghdad had no interest in going to Israel. However, a series of bombings aimed at Jewish stores, synagogues and cafes stampeded a hundred thousand Iraqi Jews in a panicked flight to Israel. Many years later, an Israeli magazine, *Ha'olam Hazeh,* published the confession of an Israeli agent, Yehuda Tager. Israelis had been responsible for the bombings in Baghdad, to "encourage immigration."[15] At community gatherings the new Iraqi immigrants to Israel often sang this song:

> What did you do, Ben-Gurion?
> You smuggled all of us!
> Because of the past we gave up our citizenship and came to Israel
> If only we had come riding donkeys and hadn't arrived yet!
> Alas, what a black hour it was
> To hell with the plane that brought us here.[16]

Other planes chartered by the Israeli government flew forty-five thousand Jews from Yemen to Israel in a program called "Operation Magic Carpet." The Yemenites were told that the flight fulfilled an ancient Messianic prophecy; they were being lifted to a heavenly land on "giant silver wings."[17] Hundreds of miles away from their traditional life, most Yemeni Jews ended up as unskilled workers in Israel, subject to ridicule and discrimination from European Jews.

These streams of penniless immigrants were vital for building the Jewish state, but they strained the Israeli economy to the breaking point. By 1951, seven hundred sixty thousand — half from Europe and half from the Arab countries and Asia — had entered Israel. The state spent an average of $2,250 on each immigrant, which it could barely afford. Many of the new arrivals were dissatisfied with the conditions they found in Israel. In 1950 immigrants demonstrated against the government, demanding better housing and an end to food rationing. Some Oriental Jews — such as the Jews from India — petitioned to return home, where they said they had not experienced the discrimination they faced in Israel.[18] There were many complaints about the preferred treatment given to European Jews and to members of Ben-Gurion's Mapai Party.

Watchdog for the West

The Israeli state could not meet the demands of the dissatisfied immigrants. A growing economic crisis seriously threatened Ben-Gurion's government. The wealth which Palestinian refugees left behind had helped sustain Israel through its first years of life, but Israel's needs were staggering. Its small industries needed constant injections of new money to grow. By 1950 Israel imported ten times as much as it exported. The Arab League's boycott of trade with Israel added to the new state's problems. A bloated military budget devoured half of the government's annual spending. Funds to cover the massive deficit had to come from somewhere.

Such a large sum of money could only come from outside Israel. Fund-raising from Jews in other countries had always kept the Jewish colony in Palestine afloat. However, this kind of fund-raising, although significant, could not keep the Jewish state solvent. In 1949 the U.S. government decided to make donations to Israel tax-exempt, to encourage private contributions. That same year the Export-Import Bank, controlled by the United States, loaned Israel $100 million. But this was not enough either. In 1951 Ben-Gurion shocked Jews in Israel and around the world by turning to West Germany for aid. The year before, the West German government had offered to pay Israel "reparations" for Nazi war crimes. Ben-Gurion ignored a storm of protest from Israelis who felt taking money would be a blatant whitewash of Nazi crimes. The Israeli government decided to accept $862 million as reparations payments over a period of twelve years. The money solved Israel's immediate crisis.

However, Ben-Gurion knew that in the long run only the Western powers, and especially the United States, could give Israel the massive aid it needed. They would do this, Ben-Gurion reasoned, because Israel was the West's most reliable ally in the Middle East. The publisher of the leading Israeli daily newspaper, *Ha'aretz,* expressed similar views in an article in 1951:

The West is none too happy about its relations with the [Arab] states in the

Middle East. The feudal regimes there have to make such concessions to the nationalist movements, which sometimes have a pronounced socialist-leftist coloring, that they become more and more reluctant to supply Britain and the United States with their natural resources and military bases .... Therefore, strengthening Israel helps the Western powers to maintain equilibrium and stability in the Middle East. Israel is to become the watchdog. There is no fear that Israel will undertake any aggressive policy toward the Arab states when this would explicitly contradict the wishes of the U.S. and Britain. But if for any reason the Western powers should sometimes prefer to close their eyes, Israel could be relied on to punish one or several neighboring states whose discourtesy toward the West went beyond the bounds of the permissible.[19]

United States policy-makers, however, were not preoccupied with Israel or the Middle East in the early 1950s. American troops were fighting in Korea as the U.S. government tried desperately to "contain" the expansion of socialism and of the Soviet Union's influence around the world. In the Middle East, the United States was attempting, with mixed success, to make allies of right-wing leaders of the Arab states and to support them against the nationalist movements in their own countries. American leaders were not yet ready to pin all their hopes on Israel. But events in the Arab countries would soon make the idea of the Israeli "watchdog" a popular one in Western capitals.

Footnotes

1. Don Peretz, "The Arab Refugee Dilemma," *Foreign Affairs* (October 1954), pp. 137-38, cited by Turki, *The Disinherited,* p. 23.
2. Cited by Sabri Jiryis, *The Arabs in Israel,* 1949-1966 (Beirut: 1969), pp. 4-5.
3. *Knesset Debates,* vol. 36, p. 1217, 20 February 1963, cited by Jiryis, p. 46.
4. Jiryis, p. 56.
5. Don Peretz, *Israel and the Palestine Arabs,* p. 152.
6. Jiryis, pp. 69-70.
7. Don Peretz, *The Middle East Today* (New York: 1963), p. 297, cited by Petran, *Zionism,* p.13.
8. *Ner,* April 1960, cited by Jiryis, pp. 86-87.
9. Fouzi el-Asmar, *To Be An Arab in Israel* (London: 1975), cited in *MERIP* no. 40, p. 25.
10. Jiryis, pp. 15-21.
11. Jiryis, "The Land Question in Israel," *MERIP* no. 47, p. 7.
12. *Knesset Debates,* vol. 6, p. 2134, 10 October 1950, cited by Jiryis, *The Arabs in Israel,* p. 179.
13. Ben-Gurion, *Israel: Years of Challenge* (New York: 1963), p. 60.
14. The whole question of the conditions of Jews in Arab countries, their relation to Zionism and the creation of Israel and the conditions under which they came to Israel is a matter of some dispute and much distortion. The classic work on the question from a Zionist perspective is Joseph B. Schectman, *On Wings of Eagles: The Plight, Exodus and Homecoming of Oriental Jewry* (New York: 1961), especially pp. 93, 138, 151, 158-163, 178 and 190. Also referred to was the book, *The Israelis: Founders and Sons,* by Amos Elon (New York: 1972), pp. 30-3. Another source which contains much documentation and presents an Arab perspective on the question is Ali Ibrahim Abdo and Khairieh Kasmieh, *Jews of Arab Countries* (Beirut: 1971).
15. *Ha'olam Hazeh,* 29 May 1966, cited in *Middle East International,* (January 1973), pp. 18-20.
16. *Middle East International,* p. 34.
17. Schechtman, p. 55.
18. Alfred M. Lilienthal, *The Other Side of the Coin* (New York; 1965), p. 225.
19. *Ha'aretz,* 30 September 1951, cited in *The Other Israel,* ed. Bober, p. 17.

11: Birth of the Fedayeen

Let me tell you why these people fight. It's because of their condition. I believe that if you would stay in a camp for one week, you would feel that you had to fight your father, not to speak of fighting Israel.

—Inam Yasin, Priest from Nazareth

When a tree is uprooted, the ground around the tree cracks open. Like the uprooting of a tree, the exile of the Palestinian people and the implanting of Israel on Arab land shook the surrounding Arab countries. In 1952 an officers' coup in Egypt overthrew the corrupt rule of King Farouk. Within two years, Gamal Abdel Nasser emerged as the dynamic nationalist leader of Egypt. He promised to end the misery of the peasants by breaking up large landholdings and giving land to those who tilled it. He also pledged to expel the British from Egyptian soil and to fight the Zionist occupation of Palestine.

In Syria the Ba'ath Party, under the slogan "Unity, Freedom and Socialism," took power in 1954. It united with the Communist Party of Syria, the largest communist organization in the Middle East, to form a new government. From Cairo and

Gamal Nasser was acclaimed in Cairo after he announced the nationalization of the Suez Canal.

Damascus to the smallest village along the Nile, Egyptians and Syrians debated the future direction of their countries. Newspapers and wall posters attacked the United States and Britain, as well as the Zionists and rich Arab landowners who served colonialism.

The Western powers were alarmed. Loss of their economic control over Egypt and Syria loomed dangerously on the horizon. The new governments' embrace of "socialism" could mean an opening to Soviet influence in the Middle East. The United States and Britain did not want that. When Nasser surprised the United States by asking for American aid and arms, U.S. officials told him he would first have to join a military alliance to "contain" communist influence in the Middle East. Nasser refused. He insisted that Egypt wanted a *neutralist* foreign policy — no military alliance with either the socialist or the capitalist camp.

The American Secretary of State John Foster Dulles refused to concede that there was such a position as neutralism. To him, countries had to be either for the United States or for the Soviet Union, for capitalism or for socialism. For Dulles and the oil companies he had represented as a corporate lawyer, the Middle East was a giant pool of oil to be guarded for U.S. corporations. Their major concern was that some countries and leaders who weren't firm enough allies of the United States might eventually turn toward socialism and claim their oil for themselves. Dulles thought that Nasser's neutralism was the beginning of an alliance with the Soviet Union and a threat to U.S. power in the area.

Israel, too, was concerned about Nasser and the upsurge of Arab nationalism. Six years after the 1948 war, none of the Arab countries — including those like Jordan and Saudi Arabia which were ruled by conservative regimes — had yet recognized Israel. The Arab boycott of Israel was hurting its economy badly. Unless there was a breakthrough soon, Israel's economic problems would get worse. Already, immigration had practically fallen to zero. Some way had to be found to gain Arab recognition and trade.

Ben-Gurion believed that Arabs — and particularly the new wave of Arab nationalists — understood only force. Ben-Gurion believed that the time was at hand for Israel to play the role of watchdog. When Nasser stepped out of line, Israel would punish him. If, in attacking Egypt, Israel could expand its territory, so much the better. As Ben-Gurion put it, "To maintain the status quo will not do. We have set up a dynamic state bent on expansion."[1]

War in Suez

In early February 1955, the Egyptian government tried and hanged three Israeli intelligence agents in Cairo for acts of terrorism. On February 28, Israeli troops attacked a camp in the Gaza Strip and killed thirty-six Egyptian soldiers. The United Nations condemned the raid, pointing out that there had been no Egyptian border crossing or other military act providing even a pretext for the raid. Furious, Nasser asked the United States for arms to defend Egypt against further attacks. The United States responded with one condition: first Egypt had to join the Baghdad Pact, the anti-Soviet military alliance the United States had set up with client states in the area.

Nasser defied both the United States and Israel. For years, Palestinians living in the Gaza had been asking for military training and arms from the Egyptian government. After Israel's raid, Nasser approved their request. During 1955 small bands of Palestinians began crossing the border to attack Israeli patrols and border settlements. They called themselves fedayeen — "people of sacrifice."

Egypt also moved to defend itself against further attack. Nasser negotiated with Czechoslovakia to get the arms Egypt needed. Secretary of State Dulles flew to Cairo to convince Nasser he was falling into "communist hands" by buying arms from the Czechs. Nasser ignored Dulles's pleas. In July of 1956, the United States withdrew its promise of aid to help build the Aswan Dam. The dam was vital to Egypt's development; it would provide irrigation for the 75 percent of Egypt which was desert. Britain and France applauded this American show of power.

But Nasser would not be intimidated. On July 26, 1956, he nationalized the Suez

Canal, a part of Egypt formerly controlled by Britain. Over one hundred twenty-five thousand Egyptians had died building the canal for the British Empire. Now the income from ships using the canal would benefit the Egyptian people by financing the dam that would irrigate the desert.

Telegrams and letters flew between the leaders of Europe and the United States. Britain and France urged immediate military intervention. Britain wanted to regain a foothold in its former colony. France wanted Nasser defeated because it was convinced that he was masterminding the revolution in Algeria, France's North African colony. However, President Dwight Eisenhower preferred the more subtle strategy of economic pressure.

Britain and France did not wait for the United States. Israel was eager to ally itself with the West and to expand into Egypt. In October 1956, under a secret agreement with Britain and France, Israel invaded the Egyptian Sinai and the Gaza Strip. Israeli troops drove as far as the Suez Canal with the help of British and French air and naval cover. Heady with success, Ben-Gurion declared, "We have created the third Kingdom of Israel!"[2] His boast was premature.

The Soviet Union feared a return of Western influence in Egypt and was anxious to heighten Soviet prestige in the Middle East. Moscow threatened to use its own military force to stop the invasion. The United States, angry at the independent actions of Britain and France, added its voice to the condemnations. With American and Soviet support, the United Nations General Assembly stopped the invasion deep inside Egyptian territory. Israel continued to occupy the territory for five months before it reluctantly withdrew. When it left, UN troops were stationed in Gaza and at the Straits of Tiran.

Israel's Suez expedition had bared its aggressive and expansionist face to many peoples of the world, especially in Africa, Asia and Latin America. But the Palestinian people experienced the harsh consequences directly. On the eve of the invasion, the Israeli Army had imposed a curfew on the border town of Kfar Kassem, a Palestinian village *inside* Israel. The order was announced at 4:30 in the afternoon. Between five and six o'clock that evening, as villagers returned from work unaware of the order, Israeli soldiers murdered thirty-seven Palestinians. The oldest killed was sixty-six; the youngest, a boy of eight. For the death of thirty-seven Palestinians, the commander of the Kfar Kassem operation was fined *one Israeli cent.*[3]

In the Gaza Strip, the Israeli occupation had been especially brutal. As the soldiers moved into Gaza, they found a list of fedayeen in an Egyptian administration center. Systematically, they rounded up and executed two hundred fifty young Palestinians. Eighty died in a mass execution in a schoolyard.[4]

The Summer of Mourning

Still, during the five long months of Israeli occupation, small groups of Palestinians risked their lives to harass the Israeli soldiers. Although Nasser stopped military training of Palestinians in Gaza after the UN troops came in 1956, the seeds of resistance that sprouted in Gaza took root among Palestinians in many Arab countries. Israel had set back the Gaza fedayeen, but the beginnings of an organized

movement arose in their place — the national liberation movement of the Palestinian people.

Throughout the fifties exiled Palestinians, from Beirut to small towns in Kuwait, had brought the cause of Palestine to political movements sweeping the Arab countries. In 1953 George Habash, a Palestinian doctor from Lydda, helped to found the Arab Nationalist Movement (ANM) in Jordan. It operated secretly in Jordan, its members subject to death or imprisonment if caught by the king's police. Aboveground in other Arab countries, it agitated for Arab unity against Western imperialism and Zionism. The ANM learned much from its fight against Israel and the West. As one woman said:

> All in all, Dulles and Ike, Eden and MacMillan, Ben-Gurion and Moshe Dayan were not a totally unmitigating evil; they gave us a rude awakening ....
> They forced us to re-examine the foundations of our society.[5]

When ANM members took a hard look at Arab society, they quickly understood the betrayal of the Arab kings in the 1948 war. The traditional leaders — kings, sheiks, landowners, businessmen, clergy — all had their own narrow interests at heart and willingly served imperialism. They claimed to represent their people. Yet Saudi Arabian oil workers made twelve cents a day; Jordanian peasants lived from hand to mouth; and Lebanese tenant farmers were thrown off their land and crowded into Beirut, where no work was to be found. Arab leaders spoke emotionally of the plight of the Palestinians, yet threw them into jail in Jordan and refused them passports and work in Lebanon. Thus Palestinians were soon at the forefront of every movement that spoke out for transforming Arab society.

Nasser's defiance over the Suez Canal led many Palestinians to hope that radical changes in the Arab world and liberation for Palestine might happen very soon. Nasser quickly became a near-legendary hero. His pictures were tacked to the walls of the refugee tents and Palestinians grouped around battered radios to hear his speeches that defied the West to conquer Egypt. In 1958, Egypt and Syria merged to form the United Arab Republic. Arab nationalists, who hoped to see one unified Arab nation in the Middle East, were elated. The two countries that most militantly opposed Zionism and the West had united. Palestinians in the schools, camps, oilfields and inside political organizations pushed for a new offensive to recover their homeland.

This rising tide of Arab nationalism did not go unchallenged. As British and French presence in the Middle East waned after the Suez invasion, the United States emerged as the major imperial power. It was determined to stop radical Arab nationalism. U.S. military bases ringed the Middle East; the Sixth Fleet patrolled the Mediterranean. In 1957 the United States had announced the "Eisenhower Doctrine," a new and more forceful statement of an old policy. The United States was prepared to "contain communism" in the Middle East by any means, including "the employment of the armed forces of the United States." "Communism" was the Americans' general term for any political force hostile to U.S. business interests. The efforts of Egypt and Syria to institute land reform and break the grip of foreign businesses over their economies fell into that category.

Soon after Syria and Egypt formed the United Arab Republic, the faithful servant of the United States and Britain, Nuri es-Said of Iraq, decided to invade Syria and detach it from Egypt. The Iraqi troops, who were influenced by nationalism themselves, refused their orders. Instead, they turned around and marched on Baghdad to overthrow the government of Nuri es-Said. As crowds rejoiced in the Baghdad streets, the Republic of Iraq was proclaimed on July 14, 1958.

The right-wing governments of Lebanon and Jordan also came under attack from Arab nationalists in those countries. In Lebanon a small-scale civil war erupted in May 1958, when pro-Western President Camille Chamoun tried to run for an unprecedented second term as president. Fighting broke out between his supporters and nationalist opponents. In the Lebanese town of Sour, members of the Arab Nationalist Movement, many of them Palestinians, took over the town government and organized its citizens to defend themselves. The people stormed the prison and police station to free those who had been arrested as "political agitators" by the Lebanese Army. A young Palestinian woman recalled, "That summer I do not remember sleeping a whole night without interruption, for I was a soldier at thirteen and I had sentinel duty."[6]

On July 16, 1958, two days after the Iraqi people overthrew their government, American Marines landed in Beirut to protect Chamoun's government. Three days later British paratroopers flew to Jordan to shore up King Hussein's regime, which was also under attack from Jordanian nationalists. With Western help, the governments of Jordan and Lebanon remained in power. Western guns had not been able to sever the union of Egypt and Syria. But by the end of 1958, with a major

U.S. Marines position machine guns on a Beirut Street in 1958.

show of force, the United States and Britain had contained the revolutionary thrust of Arab nationalism. For many Arab nationalists, the elation of a year earlier gave way to pessimism about the Arab revolution's future. One Palestinian described the summer of 1958 as a "summer of mourning." But other Palestinians did not despair. They continued to look for the path that would lead to the liberation of Palestine.

The Fedayeen Are Born

Scattered throughout the Arab world, the Palestinians faced the problem of how a small dispersed nation could organize itself to fight for the return to its homeland. For many, the Gaza fedayeen had been an inspiration. The fedayeen had fought Israel while the Arab governments merely talked about it. In 1958 twelve young Palestinians met secretly on a beach in Kuwait to discuss building an independent, armed Palestinian resistance movement — one that would not depend on any Arab government. These Palestinians had been active in student organizations and some had fought in the 1948 war while in their teens. They believed that Palestinians could not rely on the Arab leaders to liberate Palestine, no matter what they might promise. Palestinians had to take their destiny in their own hands. The twelve fighters founded an organization called Fatah, which means "victory" in Arabic. Read backwards, its letters are the initials of the words "Palestine National Liberation Movement."

Fatah's magazine, *Falasteenuna,* was passed secretly from hand to hand in the

Arab cities and refugee camps. It called for Palestinians to leave other Arab organizations and work to build an independent Palestinian movement. It urged Palestinians to prepare to fight to recover their homeland. The guns of imperialism had crushed the 1936 rebellion, and the Zionist army had forced Palestinians from their homes. Now U.S. military might backed up Israel's occupation of Palestine. Fatah argued that, as in 1936, Palestinians had to take up arms against imperialism and its allies.

At first only a small number of Palestinians joined Fatah. Many still believed that Nasser would unify the Arab peoples and liberate Palestine. However, Nasser's limits were becoming more evident. In 1961, Syria withdrew from the union with Egypt, and accused Nasser of trying to dominate its economy. The collapse of this attempt at Arab unity lowered Nasser's prestige and heightened the appeal of Fatah's call among Palestinians. By 1963 Nasser was pre-occupied with Egypt's massive economic problems and said that he had "no plans" to liberate Palestine. The constant promises broadcast over Egyptian radio suddenly rang hollow. Fawaz Turki, the Palestinian writer, described the conflict in his family:

At home there were tense scenes where I would argue mercilessly with my father, ridiculing his naive grasp of Middle Eastern politics, or in desperation, rip Nasser's picture off the wall and spit on it. I did not give the unhappy man the chance to hold on to that symbol of hope he saw in the picture of the smiling face on the wall. In those days of emotional crisis, the last years of his on earth, he had nothing except hope. And he hoped. And a million people hoped.[7]

In this same period Palestinians in the Arab Nationalist Movement, long disillusioned with Nasser's promises, broke decisively with him. Like Fatah, ANM formed its own guerrilla organization and recruited among students, workers and refugees in the camps. Its members studied together and the vague "socialism" of the early days of the ANM became a more sharply defined Marxism. ANM activists read the works of Marx, Lenin, Ho Chi Minh and Che Guevara, even though in countries like Jordan the penalty for possessing a Marxist book was imprisonment.

Dispersed in all the Arab countries, groups of Palestinians formed cells that began training for the day they would fight Israel. These groups came into existence as other countries in Asia, Africa and Latin America stirred with revolution. Palestinians studied the experiences of the Algerians, who had waged a seven-year battle against French colonialism. They also took lessons and inspiration from the Vietnamese and Cuban peoples' example. They shared the conviction that a people determined to be free from foreign domination *could* defeat even the most powerful enemies.

The old Palestinian leadership that had misled their people during the 1936 rebellion had been defeated in the 1948 war. Now new leaders arose who had no bank accounts or land-holdings to protect. They were prepared to lead the Palestinians in a *people's war* — a war that mobilized the resources of all the people and taught, trained and armed all who wanted to fight. In a people's war there would be no compromise with imperialism. The April 15, 1963 issue of *Falasteenuna* affirmed:

> The Palestinian alone is determined to refuse all colonialist plans .... He is firmly convinced that armed struggle is the one and only means for the return [to Palestine]....He refuses to allow [the Arab governments] to represent him in their lethargy, diplomacy and defeatism. As soon as he is able to tear away the fetters with which they had bound him he shall return to being what he was — a fedayeen.

The idea of the fedayeen, willing to give their lives in people's war, threatened not only Israel, but the established Arab leaders as well. These leaders had always used the Palestinian cause for their own ends, competing with each other in verbal claims of support for the Palestinians. None of them wanted to see an independent Palestinian movement. The Arab leaders called a summit conference in 1964 to try to regain their slipping control of the Palestinians. At Nasser's request, they created a Palestinian organization — the Palestine Liberation Organization (PLO) — to control the guerrilla groups.[8] To be head of the PLO, the Arab leaders chose Ahmed Shukeiry, an ambitious and conservative Palestinian lawyer who had served Saudi Arabia as Minister for Palestinian Affairs. Fatah attended the first conference of the PLO in May 1964, but maintained its organizational independence. Other guerrilla groups refused even to attend the conference. Unity between Palestinians would come "within Palestine," not in "offices," Fatah declared.

On January 1, 1965, a Fatah unit launched its first armed attack against Israel. Fatah issued its first communique under the name of its military arm, *al-Assifa,* "the storm." Like a storm, this first raid stirred the Middle East. Other guerrilla groups soon began their own operations against Israel. With these actions Palestinians had taken the first steps in a people's war against the state of Israel.

Footnotes

1. Ben-Gurion, *Destiny and Rebirth of Israel,* p. 419, cited by Petran, *Zionism,* p. 13.
2. Rodinson, *Israel and the Arabs,* p. 76.
3. Jiryis, *The Arabs in Israel,* pp. 96-113.
4. Abdullah Schleifer, *The Fall of Jerusalem,* p. 62.
5. Leila Khaled, *My People Shall Live* (Toronto: 1975), p. 40.
6. Ibid., p. 47.
7. Turki, *The Disinherited,* p. 60.
8. Schleifer, pp. 69-71 and Khaled, p. 83.

12: The Road to War

The United States and Israel employ almost identical language in speaking of reprisal actions. The formula employed is that the cost must be made so high that those involved will no longer be willing to pay it.

—Moshe Dayan after trip to Vietnam
as guest of U.S. Marines

The first Palestinian guerrillas who crossed the border into Israel lived up to the name fedayeen — "people of sacrifice." Most never expected to leave Israel alive. The well-equipped Israeli Defense Forces shot suspected guerrillas on sight. If the fedayeen made it back to Jordan, they often met death or prison at the hands of Hussein's border patrols.

At first, the fedayeen did not pose a major military threat to Israel. But they did shake a central political pillar of the Zionist state: the carefully nurtured myth that Palestine had been a "land without a people" until the Jews "returned" to it. Golda Meir summed up this view of history in an interview with the London *Times:*

There were no such things as Palestinians. It was not as though there were a

Palestinian people and we came and threw them out and took their country away from them. They did not exist.[1]

With each communique of the guerrillas, the story of the "non-existent" Palestinians came alive and Israel lost a battle with history. Zionist leaders knew that, as the Palestinian movement grew, Israel would lose more than symbolic battles. Israel had to stop the fedayeen.

Throughout 1965, the Arab governments helped Israel police its borders. The governments of Jordan and Lebanon, where the largest numbers of Palestinians lived in exile, feared the guerrillas. They knew that a successful people's war in the Middle East could sweep away imperialism and *all* its allies — the Zionist state and right-wing Arab governments. Jordan and Lebanon tried to shield Israel and themselves from the Palestinian revolution. In addition, the moderate government that ruled Syria in the mid-1960s did not allow the guerrillas freedom of movement across Syria's border. On the Egyptian front, UN troops sealed the border with Israel. This meant that the fedayeen had no reliable base in the Arab countries for their operations against Israel.

But in early 1966 a left-wing military government took power in Syria. It immediately announced that it would no longer act as a "guardian for Israel's interests." It opened its borders to the guerrillas and began to publish the communiques which the guerrilla groups put out after each operation. The number of raids increased dramatically. Their political impact grew as Syria and the Palestinians told the Arab people of the deeds of the fedayeen. The close historical ties of the Syrian and Palestinian peoples led to a special joy among Syrians at the beginnings of the armed Palestinian movement.

The new Syrian government also refused to be a guardian for the interests of the American oil companies in the Middle East. Syria declared that Arab oil was the rightful property of the Arab people. The Syrians criticized the right-wing Arab governments that served imperialism at the expense of the Arab people. The new government began a long battle with ARAMCO — the Arabian American Oil Company, dominated by the U.S. oil giants — over control of the pipeline that cut through Syria and brought oil from the Gulf states to Mediterranean ports.

Arab Nationalism on the Rise

The U.S. government and the American oil companies were alarmed. Tied down in Vietnam by a people's war, the United States could not easily fight revolution in the Middle East. Yet the American oil companies had an enormous stake in the area, and they wanted it protected. Middle Eastern oil made up 70 percent of the oil reserves of the non-socialist world. Sixty percent of the oil fueling the U.S. military machine in Vietnam came from the Middle East. Sales of Middle East oil brought in profits of *$2 billion a year* for U.S. corporations.

The major American military force in the area was the Sixth Fleet, which cruised the Mediterranean coast. One exuberant sailor said the mission of this imposing armada was to "steam around the millpond and scare the Arabs."[2] This naval show of strength did not stop the Syrians, Palestinians and other Arab nationalists from fighting. As the Palestinian guerrillas continued their attacks on Israel, further

The U.S. Sixth Fleet patrolling the Mediterranean

south, in the Arabian peninsula, war raged in the countries of Yemen, South Yemen and Oman.

In 1962 Arab nationalists in Yemen, a small country which bordered on oil-rich Saudi Arabia, declared a republic. The United States and Britain supported Saudi Arabian troops which fought against the new government. Nasser sent Egyptian troops to help defend the republic against Saudi attack. In the mid-1960s the National Liberation Front of South Yemen began fighting for independence from Britain. In 1966 the British announced plans to withdraw from Aden, the major port city in South Yemen. Guerrilla warfare also began in the adjoining province of Dhofar, Oman. The revolts in Yemen, South Yemen and Oman were a serious threat to Saudi Arabia and the U.S. oil companies there.

A high-level U.S. policy study of the Middle East in this period concluded that revolutionary Arab nationalism, which the study called "Nasserization," might well spread to Lebanon, Jordan and the Arabian peninsula. Thus it posed "a security crisis of major and possibly catastrophic proportions."[3] With almost a million troops in Vietnam, the United States could not send its own troops to shore up its weakened allies. Yet something had to be done.

In 1966 the United States began arming Israel with new planes and missiles. While Israeli Foreign Minister Abba Eban was concluding a deal for Skyhawk missiles in the United States, James Feron of the *New York Times* reported on the developing U.S. strategy for the Middle East:

The United States has come to the conclusion that it must rely on a local power — the deterrent of a friendly power — as a first line to stave off America's direct involvement. Israel feels she fits this definition.[4]

105

The Vietnamese inspire revolutionary movements around the world.

Crisis in Israel

Israel was finally to play the role of watchdog for the United States. To the hard-line Zionist leaders, the chance had come none to soon. The Palestinian raids were no longer simply a nuisance. The guerrillas were ambushing border patrols, blowing up bridges, and harassing the para-military border settlements. They were beginning to attack larger military and economic targets as well.

The upsurge in fedayeen raids came at a time of growing economic problems in Israel. The number of new immigrants was falling off rapidly. In 1966 just as many people left Israel for other countries as came to the Jewish state. A popular joke in Israel that year described a sign hanging in Israel's Lod Airport. The sign read: "Will the last person leaving kindly turn out the lights?" Zionist leaders did not find the joke terribly funny. They knew the stark reality behind this new exodus. The vital aid from the West that sustained Israel was drying up. German reparations payments ended in 1965 and even sales of Israeli bonds — a source of $3.5 billion since 1948 — had begun to slip. The result was rising taxes and prices and high unemployment — all of which were driving more and more people from the country. As long as the Arab boycott of Israel continued to stop normal trade between Israel and its neighbors, the Israeli economy could not solve these problems.

Thus when the U.S. government most needed a watchdog to guard its interests in the Middle East, the leaders of Zionism were more than anxious to do the job and to reap the benefits. The enemies of the oil companies and the U.S. government were also the enemies of the state of Israel: Syria, the Palestinians, Nasser and revolutionary Arab nationalists throughout the area. Israel would punish them for their acts against the United States and the Jewish state. Zionist leaders knew that the U.S. government would show its appreciation.

In March 1966, General Moshe Dayan toured Vietnam as a guest of the U.S.

106

military. After witnessing an American attack on the Cambodian border, he noted the similar strategies of U.S. and Israeli generals:

> The United States and Israel employ almost identical language in speaking of reprisal actions. The formula employed is that the cost involved in aiding the enemy ... must be made so high that those involved will no longer be able to pay it.[5]

That summer the new Syrian government began to pay the price for its support of the Palestinians and its defiance of the United States. As the fedayeen stepped up their attacks, Israeli troops began regular "reprisal raids" across the Syrian border. After a flurry of guerrilla operations in early July, the Israeli Air Force bombed targets in Syria. The United States increased arms shipments to Israel. Syria continued to support the Palestinians.

In September the Israeli Army Chief of Staff, General Yitzhak Rabin, formalized Israeli policy:

> The Syrians are the spiritual fathers of the Al-Fatah group .... The military engagements which Israel has to conduct in Syria in reprisal for the sabotage raids she suffers are therefore directed against the Syrian regime .... Our aim is to make the Syrian government change its mind, and to eliminate the cause of the raids.[6]

A week later, Israel's Prime Minister Levi Eshkol made it clear that Syria would be held responsible for *all* Palestinian raids, no matter what country they came from.

The Syrians took Israel's threats seriously. They began urgent talks with Nasser. In November Syria and Egypt signed a mutual defense pact. The Egyptians hastened to add that the pact did not mean "that the Egyptian Army would immediately intervene against any Israeli attack on Syrian positions."[7]

The Israeli government and media ignored these disclaimers. They used the new pact to spread alarm among the Israeli people. It was not the defensive move of a nervous Syria and a reluctant Egypt, but a new act of aggression by the "bloodthirsty Arabs." Despite the cries of alarm, many Zionists were glad to see Nasser drawn into the conflict. They thought that if events were to lead to war, there was no sense in defeating only the Syrians. Nasser, the hero of the Arab world and leader of the most influential country, should be defeated as well. A sound trouncing of Syria and Egypt might finally force them to recognize Israel.

A few days after the signing of the Egyptian-Syrian pact, a mine exploded near the Jordanian border. It killed three Israeli soldiers and wounded six. The Israeli Prime Minister did not want to test the pact immediately by attacking Syria. Instead, he ordered a reprisal raid against the nearby Jordanian village of Sammou. Eighty Israeli tanks, covered by Mirage aircraft, moved across the border and leveled the village. The school, the hospital and one hundred twenty-five houses were reduced to rubble. The Israelis killed eighteen Jordanians and wounded one hundred thirty-five.[8]

The West Bank of Jordan, the home of many Palestinians living under the rule of King Hussein, exploded with violent demonstrations from Nablus to Jerusalem. Demonstrators demanded arms to protect themselves from Israel. They accused Hussein of weakness toward Israel and betrayal of the Palestinian people through harassment of the guerrillas. Hussein's regime was almost overthrown. His Arab

Legion was able to restore order only by firing on the demonstrators and filling the jails with his opponents. Hundreds of Palestinians were killed or wounded.

To deflect the intense Palestinian anger from himself, Hussein accused Nasser of failing to act in the face of Israeli reprisals against another Arab country, and he ridiculed him for hiding behind the UN troops on Egypt's border. Hussein's verbal blasts did not divert Palestinian anger. But they did put more pressure on Nasser to take some action against Israel.

Nasser Enters the Conflict

In January 1967, the fedayeen began a new round of raids, stronger and more effective than those of the previous year. The Syrians and Israelis clashed regularly in the demilitarized zone on their common border. Some Zionist leaders demanded a reprisal raid against Syria. Shimon Peres, an ally of Ben-Gurion, said in an interview that the Syrians were the only antagonists "never to have felt any real blow from the Israelis." He added, "Perhaps the time has now come to teach the Syrians a good lesson."[9]

In April the Israelis defied the Syrians by cultivating land inside the demilitarized zone. Syrian gunners fired on an Israeli armored tractor and there were artillery exchanges across the border. Then Israel launched a major tank and air attack on Syrian border villages. Israeli planes shot down six Syrian MIGs and penetrated as far as the suburbs of the capital, Damascus. Again, Nasser did not respond and was ridiculed by Hussein and other Arab critics.

Israel's General Rabin said that he hoped the Syrians would understand "the lesson which has been administered to them." Personally, however, he thought it was "inadequate."[10] In mid-May, he went a step further, saying, "[S]o long as the ardent revolutionaries in Damascus have not been overthrown, no government in the Middle East can feel safe."[11] According to the Associated Press, a high-ranking Israeli army officer had threatened that Israeli troops might occupy Damascus to put an end to the acts of the fedayeen.

Rumors that Israel or the United States or both might attack Syria grew. The increased maneuvers of the Sixth Fleet off the Syrian coast did nothing to dispel Arab fears. There was intense pressure on Nasser to do something to protect Syria. The right-wing kings, Hussein of Jordan and Feisal of Saudi Arabia, rejoiced at Nasser's dilemma. They heaped abuse on him, calling him a dishonorable coward, afraid of Israel's shadow.[12]

Nasser did not want to fight Israel. One-third of the Egyptian Army was still tied down in Yemen. This was not the time to wage war with Israel. Yet he had to act. On May 15, amidst great fanfare, he sent Egyptian troops toward the Sinai Desert and the Israeli border. He hoped such a move would discourage Israel from attacking Syria, since the attack might lead to a war on two fronts.

No one took Nasser's action seriously. Although the Israeli leaders publicly denounced it as one more act of aggression, they knew that it was a symbolic gesture. The Syrians and Nasser's other critics were quick to condemn his "mini-mobilization" as minor saber-rattling. Hussein's Jordan Radio continued to accuse Nasser of hiding behind the UN troops.

The next day Nasser publicly asked the United Nations to restation its observers

Egyptian demonstrator supports Nasser's actions.

on the border with Israel — another symbolic move. He was told he could not request any UN troop movement; he could only ask for the removal of all UN troops. It was an either/or choice, and Nasser was trapped. Unwilling to back down from his original request, he demanded the withdrawal of all UN troops from Egypt. Egyptian troops took up positions along the Israeli border. They also occupied Sharm-el-Sheikh, which overlooks the narrow Straits of Tiran, the only sea outlet for the Israeli port of Eilat. On May 23 Nasser closed the Straits of Tiran to Israeli shipping.

The Straits had been open to Israeli ships since the 1956 Suez war. Ben-Gurion had said of that war, "For us the main purpose of the Sinai campaign was to safeguard our southern sea route."[13] The Israelis had withdrawn from Sharm-el-Sheikh very reluctantly and only with a guarantee that UN troops would keep the Straits open. By closing the Straits, Nasser was erasing the last humiliating reminder of Israel's drive into Egypt. His critics could not call this act cowardice.

No one did. The Israelis cried that the closure of the Straits meant "economic strangulation" for Israel. Israel demanded that the Straits be reopened. Although only 5 percent of Israel's foreign trade passed through the Straits, Israeli leaders now had their chance to call Nasser's bluff.

Despite Israel's verbal blasts, Nasser thought he could get away with his bold action. The Arab states applauded it. Everyone else seemed to be calling for restraint: the United Nations, the United States, and the Soviet Union. The United States assured Nasser through the Soviet Union that it was urging Israel to resolve the crisis peacefully. Nasser trusted the American assurance. For several days he proudly believed that he had spared Syria from an almost certain Israeli attack. He answered Israel's campaign of threats and warnings with a public show of bluster and toughness. Meanwhile, unknown to his audience, Nasser was trying to defuse the crisis through secret negotiations.

The Arab people greeted Nasser's public actions with heady rhetoric. Elated people· filled the streets of Arab capitals, convinced that the long-awaited hour of victory over Israel was near. They thought Nasser had taken the first step toward war. The actual weakness of the Arab armies was ignored in what one Arab observer called a "mobilization of imagination." People gathered around radios, rejoicing as Nasser said, "If Israel wants to attack us, our answer is 'You are welcome!' "[14]

Many Arab radio broadcasts and newspapers described the coming demise of Israel in vivid detail. Ahmed Shukeiry, the PLO leader, broadcast over Cairo Radio the cry, "Drive the Jews into the sea!" Israel picked up the most menacing Arab statements and broadcast them to the listening West. Western media ignored Israel's own racist attacks and slurs on the Arab people. Zionist organizations in the United States played on the theme and created a vivid picture for Western audiences: a sea of barbarian Arabs threatened to engulf a small and valiant nation!

Pentagon computers told a vastly different story about the balance of forces. They predicted that no matter who struck first, in whatever combination of Arab forces, Israel's military superiority assured its victory. Nonetheless, on May 25 the Pentagon sent battalions of Marines to the Sixth Fleet in case they might be needed. A member of the Israeli Chiefs-of-Staff stated, "The Egyptians concentrated eighty thousand soldiers while we mobilized against them hundreds of thousands of men."[15] Three days *before* Nasser announced the closure of the Straits of Tiran, Israel had already ordered a full mobilization of its troops. On May 30 Moshe Dayan, an ally of Ben-Gurion, took over as Minister of Defense. By June 2, the date of the attack was set. Israel was about to give Syria and Egypt the "lesson" it had promised. It only awaited U.S. approval. On June 4, as Nasser continued negotiations with an American envoy, President Lyndon Johnson telegraphed Dayan and gave Israel the final go-ahead from the United States.[16]

Footnotes

1. *London Times*, 15 June 1969.
2. *New York Times,* 19 June 1967, cited by Rita Freed, *War in the Mid East* (New York: 1972), p. 52.
3. Eugene Rostow, "The Middle Eastern Crisis in the Perspective of World Affairs," *International Affairs* (April 1971), p. 280, cited in *MERIP* no. 21, p. 10.
4. *New York Times*, 11 June 1966, cited by Schleifer, *The Fall of Jerusalem*, p. 95.
5. Newsreel Films, "We the Palestinian People," 1973.
6. Cited by Rodinson, *Israel and the Arabs*, pp. 180-181.
7. *Al-Ahram*, 18 November 1966, cited by Rodinson, p. 181.
8. Rodinson, p. 181.
9. Rodinson, pp. 183-184.
10. Ibid., p. 184.
11. Tabitha Petran, *Syria* (New York: 1972), p. 198.
12. The general source for material regarding events and analysis leading up to the outbreak of war is Schleifer, pp. 100-130 unless otherwise noted. Schleifer's chronology is based on Michael Bar-Zohar, *Embassies in Crisis; Diplomats and Demagogues Behind the Six-Day War* (New Jersey: 1970).
13. Terence Prittie, *Israel: Miracle in the Desert* (New York: 1967), p. 71.
14. *Le Monde*, 30 May 1967, p. 3, cited by Rodinson, p. 200.
15. *Ha'aretz*, 19 March 1972, cited in *The Other Israel*, ed. Bober, p. 85.
16. *Ma'ariv*, 3 May 1968, cited in *The Other Israel*, p. 84.

13: June 1967: Seizing New Arab Land

An occupation is an occupation. You never get used to it. To be sure, some walls have been torn down and Jerusalem is 'united' but the human walls are much higher than ever.

—Basil Sahar, Palestinian school teacher

On Monday morning, June 5, 1967, Moshe Dayan ordered the attack. Flying low to evade Egyptian radar, Israeli planes headed for Egypt's airfields. The Israelis destroyed the entire Egyptian air force while it was still on the ground. The planes, sitting wing to wing, had not even been camouflaged. Nasser had expected a peace settlement in a few days. Yet for twenty-four hours after the attack, the Voice of America broadcast unceasingly that Egypt had invaded Israel. It was a version of the war many Americans never questioned.

Without air cover Egyptian troops in the Sinai desert were vulnerable targets. Thousands of Egyptian soldiers were killed or wounded. Using the shield of Mirage jets, Israeli tank brigades pushed through the desert with lightning speed, despite some fierce fighting in the Gaza Strip by Palestinians attached to the Egyptian

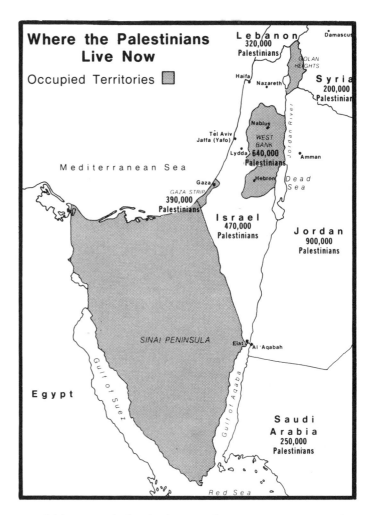

Where the Palestinians Live Now

Occupied Territories ▨

Lebanon 320,000 Palestinians

Damascus

GOLAN HEIGHTS

Haifa

Nazareth

Syria 200,000 Palestinian

Nablus

Tel Aviv
Jaffa (Yafo)

WEST BANK 640,000 Palestinians

Jordan River

Lydda

Amman

Mediterranean Sea

Gaza

Hebron

Dead Sea

GAZA STRIP 390,000 Palestinians

Israel 470,000 Palestinians

Jordan 900,000 Palestinians

SINAI PENINSULA

Elat

Al 'Aqabah

Egypt

Gulf of Suez

Gulf of Aqaba

Saudi Arabia 250,000 Palestinians

Red Sea

Army. As Israel's advance quickly proved, the Arab countries were not prepared for war.[1] The Syrian defenses crumbled rapidly. In Jordan, the Palestinians living on the West Bank had never received the arms that they demanded of King Hussein after the Sammou raid. Resistance to the Israeli invasion was individual and ill-armed. In Jerusalem there was house-to-house fighting — resistance which the Israeli Defense Ministry called "the toughest fighting of the war."[2] The people of Jerusalem were forced to defend themselves, as the Jordanian Army remained stationed on the outskirts of the city.[3]

Even as the Egyptian Army was being defeated, tens of thousands of people throughout the Arab countries rallied to the fight against Israel. Students left final exams to enlist in the army for training or to go directly to the front to help in any way they could. In the schools and marketplaces, people collected food and supplies for the soldiers. Volunteers joined the Red Crescent medical aid teams and set up blood banks. Many people prepared for a long battle, confident of an Arab victory. They were stunned when, after only six days, the war ended in a humiliating defeat. The smashing Israeli victory suddenly revealed both the hidden weaknesses of the Arab governments and the expansionist nature of the Jewish state.

112

On the first day of the war, Moshe Dayan had grandly proclaimed: "We have no aim of territorial conquest."[4] Yet even after the cease-fire, Israeli troops pushed through Syria until they captured the Golan Heights. Determined fighting by Fatah units delayed their drive, but Fatah's small arms could not stop the onslaught of Israeli planes, tanks and mortars. The Israelis expelled thirty-five thousand people from the Golan and sacked the provincial capital of Kuneitra.[5] By the end of the war, Israel had captured Syria's Golan Heights, the Egyptian Sinai and Gaza, and Jordan's West Bank. In six days, Israeli territory had *tripled* in size. A million more Palestinians — those in the West Bank and Gaza — were now under Israeli occupation. As in the 1956 Suez War, none of the battles were fought inside Israel itself.

"De-population"

Israel's triumph took thirty-five thousand Arab lives and six hundred Israeli lives. Many of the Arabs who died were civilians. In the West Bank and the Golan Heights, Israeli planes bombed villages and dropped napalm. Napalm rained on areas around Arab Jerusalem, Bethlehem, and the East Bank of the Jordan.[6] Sami Oweida told the story of his family to a British professor. During the war his family left Jericho and tried to cross the King Hussein Bridge to the East Bank of the Jordan and relative safety. According to Oweida's account:

> I saw a plane come down like a hawk directly at us. We threw ourselves on the ground and found ourselves in the midst of fire.... I tried to do something, but in vain. Fire was all around. I carried my burning child outside the fire. The burning people became naked. Fire stuck to my hands and face. I rolled over. The fire rolled with me. I saw another plane coming directly at us. I thought it was the end. I saw the pilot lean over and look at us.
>
> My daughter Labiba (four years old) died that night. Two children of my cousin also died. My daughter Adla (seventeen years old) died four days later.[7]

The Oweida family was part of a stream of two hundred thousand refugees from the West Bank. Some left to escape the bombings and napalm. Others were forced out by Israeli bulldozers. Within a few days after the war, Israeli soldiers leveled seven villages near the Jordan River. A miller from Beit Nuba, one of the seven villages, explained to A. C. Forrest, a Canadian clergyman:

> The Israelis first shelled the village. Then they moved in and ordered us all out and told us to walk towards Ramallah. Eight persons were killed. Some old people who were ill couldn't leave. They were buried alive. The Israelis said the area was a military zone. They demolished my mill and carted it away, but they bulldozed everything else under.[8]

Twenty thousand villagers became refugees. The Israelis had cleared their new border of Palestinians and readied it for possible Jewish settlement.

Israel called this policy of expulsion "de-population." In the city of Tulkarm in the West Bank, Israeli soldiers forced fifteen thousand Palestinians into trucks and dumped them at the Jordanian border. The Israelis pointed their guns at the people and told them: "Go to Hussein."[9] Many of these refugees were fleeing the Israelis a second time, having fled from cities inside Israel to the West Bank in 1948. Israeli soldiers carefully planted eucalyptus trees in the red soil of the demolished West Bank villages. Eucalyptus grows quickly. The next year tourists saw flourishing young groves on the graves of Palestinian villages.

In the Syrian Golan, Israeli soldiers expelled another ninety-five thousand people. These refugees joined those who had fled to Damascus during the actual fighting. The Syrian capital was swollen with people who had no shelter, food or jobs. Within weeks Israel put out a call to Jews all over the world, asking them to come and settle in the Golan. Soon a dozen military settlements dotted the Syrian land.[10]

Almost as soon as the firing stopped, the refugees demanded to return to their homes. Over one hundred fifty thousand West Bank Palestinians applied immediately to the Israeli government for permission to return home. Israel reluctantly approved only eighteen thousand applications.

Significantly, not one application was accepted from residents of Jerusalem.[11] The treasured city was finally in Israeli hands. Ben-Gurion arrived at the Wailing Wall in triumph to celebrate the "return" of the city to its "rightful owners." He frowned when he noticed a sign in Arabic, and an aide immediately tore it down. A flood of petitions and telegrams from religious groups around the world pleaded with the Israelis not to annex Jerusalem to Israel. They proposed an "international administration" for the city. But on June 21, Israel officially annexed Jerusalem.

Realizing that Israel was blocking their return in every possible way, many refugees from the West Bank tried to cross the Jordan River and return home without official papers. A young Israeli soldier published an account of the fate of Palestinians who tried to do this:

> Every night Arabs cross the Jordan from east to west. We blocked the passages ... and were ordered to shoot to kill without warning. Indeed, we fired shots every night on men, women and children. In the mornings, we searched the area and, by explicit order from the officer on the spot, shot the living, including those who hid or were wounded.[12]

The Israeli government banned the newspaper that published this story and arrested its distributors as sellers of "obscene literature."

Israel Reaps Rewards of Conquest

The Israeli press and the pro-Zionist media in Europe and the United States ignored the fate of the refugees and the brutal reality of Israeli occupation. They celebrated the "heroic" Israeli victory over the aggressive Arabs who had vowed to destroy the Jewish state. American publishers churned out popular books like *Six Days in June* and *Strike Zion!* that faithfully reflected the Israeli and American version of the war. A study of American reporting during the war showed that Arabs were most frequently described as dark, shifty-eyed and cowardly; the Israelis, however, were more often pictured as hard-working, handsome and brave.[13] These books, countless articles and TV and radio stories built a strong base of support for Israel's new role as the American watchdog in the Middle East.

Against this backdrop of slick propaganda, almost no one spoke out for the victims of Israel's expansion. One journalist noted:

Israeli soldiers mark the shops of Palestinians striking to protest the annexation of Jerusalem.

Writers who try to present the Arab view are vociferously condemned privately and in public; every possible kind of pressure is exerted to try to silence the unwelcome opinion, and as a last resort, charges of anti-Semitism have been leveled. It makes writers wary. . . .[14]

Few writers braved the fire. Most commentators joined in painting a picture of Nasser as a villain equal to Hitler. Nasser and the Arabs wanted to crush Israel, but the Israelis had turned the tables on the oppressor. A small David had conquered the bloodthirsty Goliath.

It was a story that captured not only the imaginations but the pocketbooks of Americans, especially American Jews. New York and other cities were the scenes of large fundraising dinners. Zionist organizers raised thousands of dollars by collecting donations on streetcorners and ringing doorbells. On the campuses, students stood in line to donate blood for Israel. When the war ended, they signed up to work

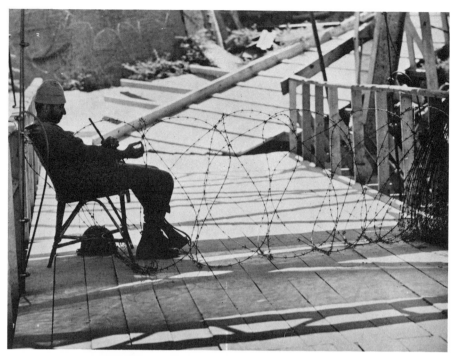

The Israelis were confident that they had defeated the Palestinian guerrillas.

on a kibbutz for the summer. In the six days of the war, the United Jewish Appeal sold $220 million worth of Israeli Bonds. Gottlieb Hammer, vice-chairman of the United Jewish Appeal, observed, "When the blood flows, the money flows."[15] Contributions for Israel from Americans in 1967 totaled $600 million.

Israel's biggest bonus from the June War was not individual support, valuable though that was. The greatest gain was the recognition in Washington that Israel had dealt Arab nationalism a stunning blow and should be rewarded. A State Department memo concluded:

> Israel has probably done more for the U.S. in the Middle East in relation to money and effort invested than any of our so-called allies and friends elsewhere around the world since the end of the Second World War. In the Far East, we can get almost nobody to help us in Viet Nam. Here, the Israelis won the war singlehandedly, have taken us off the hook, and have served our interests as well as theirs.[16]

Unlike the Thieu regime in Vietnam, Israel had not required U.S. troops to fight the U.S. government's enemies. The United States finally acknowledged Israel as regional "policeman" for American corporate interests in the Middle East. The United States sent Israel a flood of sophisticated weapons, including Phantom jets, which greatly strengthened Israel's impressive military machine. In the four years after the war, Israel would receive $1.5 billion worth of arms from the United States — ten times the amount sent in the previous twenty years. The U.S. Agency for International Development (AID) added another $75 million worth of free military aid. In subsequent years *10 percent* of all foreign aid from the United States went to Israel.

116

This aid helped solve the problems that had plagued Israel's economy before the war. As Israeli troops took up their positions on the country's new frontiers, U.S. and Israeli leaders hoped that the military defeat of the Arab nationalists had ended the fedayeen attacks on Israel's borders. The Israelis also thought Nasser would decide that it was futile for Egypt to continue fighting Israel and the United States.

In fact the war had exposed the fatal weaknesses of Nasser's leadership. Nasser's "socialism" had not been genuine socialism. The people of Egypt did not collectively run the factories and farms, fill the ranks of popular militias and a people's army, or play a major role in the political decisions of the nation. Under Nasser's rule, a class of military officers and government bureaucrats had gained power at the expense of Egypt's peasants and workers. Nasser had caved in to the Israeli offensive because he could not risk the only other real option — mobilizing the Egyptian people in a protracted war against Israel.

Nasser's political party had relentlessly driven from political power those who spoke out for such an alternative — communists, socialists and trade union leaders. Rather than arm and mobilize the people, Nasser and his circle had relied on a professional army and guarantees of support from the Soviet Union. When Israel struck, the professional army collapsed. The Soviet Union, anxious to avoid a head-on collision with the United States, did not use its own military threats to pressure for Israeli withdrawal as it had done in the 1956 Suez War. After the June War, Israel still occupied Egyptian territory.

The War Is Not Over

On June 9 Nasser went on the radio and offered his resignation to the Egyptian people. He turned over the reins of power to Zakaria Moheidden, a man eager to end the fight with Israel and the United States and to open Egypt to American investment. American and Israeli leaders had achieved what they wanted: Nasser, "the hero of the Arabs," was defeated. But within hours after Nasser's resignation, millions of Egyptians poured into the streets. They chanted, "No imperialism, no Zakaria, no leader but Nasser!" To Egyptians, Nasser was still the symbol of the fight against foreign domination. Given a choice between him and Moheidden, they stood beside Nasser.

Although Nasser resumed power, he changed none of the basic conditions that led to Egypt's defeat in the June War. Instead, he turned once again to the Soviet Union to rebuild his professional army. Eighty percent of Egypt's military capabilities had been destroyed by Israel. Egypt would get new weapons, but not the political and social changes it needed to resist the power of Israel and the United States.

Instead, Egypt relied on worldwide condemnation of Israel to force the return of occupied Arab land. In the United Nations the Soviet Union sponsored, and the United States supported, Security Council Resolution 242, demanding that Israel return the occupied areas. But the resolution did not strike at the heart of the conflict. It recognized the legitimacy of the Zionist state and referred to the Palestinians as a "refugee problem," not a people having rights to their own country. Even so, Israel refused to comply with the resolution, and the United States did not pressure it to do so. After June 1967, Israel was condemned by most countries of the world.

Its only firm allies outside the United States were South Africa and Rhodesia, settler colonies like itself.

Although Israel had defeated the Arab armies and continued to occupy Arab land with the support of U.S. imperialism, the resistance of the Arab peoples to U.S. domination was still alive. In Beirut, Amman and Damascus, thousands stormed the U.S. embassies in waves of powerful demonstrations. *Fortune* magazine, written for American business, reported:

> Not since the Boxer Rebellion [in China] has there been as rapid ... a revulsion against a foreign power as against the U.S. in the Middle East.[17]

In Saudi Arabia, where any protest is against the law, oil workers went on strike at ARAMCO, the giant U.S. oil conglomerate. The Saudi government arrested and deported eight hundred Palestinians for "anti-American activities." In Libya oil workers walked off their jobs at American installations. The king jailed the leaders of the strike and sent in the police to force people back to work. To angered Arab workers and students, the June War had shown that the United States was without a doubt the committed imperial sponsor of Israel.

Within the old city of Jerusalem, in the newly swollen refugee camps, in cities of the West Bank and Gaza, Palestinians renewed their determination to defeat Zionism and imperialism. Zionist leaders thought that the war would crush the Arab nationalist governments and end the Palestinian cry of "people's war." Instead, they found the cry raised within their new borders, as more and more Palestinians began to embrace the goals of the armed Palestinian Resistance. Amos Kenan, a well-known Israeli writer, witnessed an Israeli army unit destroying a Palestinian village during the June War. In a letter to the Israeli parliament, he wrote:

> The chickens and doves were burned in the rubble. The fields were turned into wasteland in front of our eyes. The children who went crying on the road will be fedayeen in nineteen years.... Thus we have lost the victory.[18]

Footnotes

1. Edgar O'Ballance, *The Third Arab-Israeli War* (Hamden, Conn.: 1972), p. 65.
2. Schleifer, *The Fall of Jerusalem,* p. 180.
3. Ibid., p. 166.
4. Ibid., p. 161.
5. A.C. Forrest, *The Unholy Land* (Old Greenwich, Conn.: 1972), p. 92.
6. Ibid., p. 17 and Schleifer, p. 181.
7. Forrest, p. 17.
8. Ibid., pp. 14-15.
9. Schleifer, p. 209.
10. Forrest, pp. 93-96.
11. Schleifer, pp. 218-219.
12. *Nimas* (an underground Israeli newspaper), cited by Schleifer, p. 221.
13. Michael W. Suleiman, "American Mass Media and the June Conflict," in Ibrahim Abu-Lughod, ed., *The Arab Israeli Confrontation of June 1967: An Arab Perspective,* (Evanston, Ill.: 1970), pp. 141-42.
14. Forrest, p. 45.
15. L. Mosher, *National Observer,* 18 May 1970, cited by Freed, *War in the Mid East,* p. 41.
16. *U.S. News and World Report,* 19 June 1967, p. 42, cited by Petran, *Zionism,* p. 16.
17. *Fortune magazine* (September 1967), cited by Freed, p. 91.
18. *Israel Imperial News* (an underground Israeli newspaper), cited by Schleifer, p. 210.

14: Palestine Lives

Each land has its own rebirth
Each dawn has a date with revolution.
—Mahmoud Darweesh

In the summer nights following the June War, Israeli tanks and jeeps prowled the streets of the occupied West Bank and Gaza Strip. Israeli soldiers frequently stopped Palestinians for rough questioning. Any hint of defiance could lead to further questioning behind the closed doors of the nearest prison. The first Israelis to move into the occupied territories were the prison officials, the military administrators, and the Shin Beth — the Israeli secret intelligence service. Their job was to seek out any possible Palestinian resistance and eliminate it.

Yet, except for these Israeli authorities, most people in the West Bank town of Nablus knew that Yasser Arafat, a Fatah leader, sat at a certain local cafe each day, talking with townspeople. Like many Palestinians that summer, Arafat discussed the meaning of the shattering defeat of the June War. He and other members of the armed resistance were recruiting Palestinians to fight Israeli occupation. The only

119

Israelis round up "trouble-makers" in Gaza.

answer to Israeli aggression was, in Fatah's words, "a popular war of liberation" — a war that would last not for six days, but until Palestine was liberated.

The Israelis did not allow the guerrillas to organize so openly for long. By mid-summer the net of repression was closing in on fedayeen in the West Bank and Gaza. Captured Jordanian files gave the Israelis the names of suspected guerrilla sympathizers, and mass arrests began. In August, Fatah began attacking Israeli soldiers in the West Bank. In December, the Popular Front for the Liberation of Palestine (PFLP) — a Marxist organization formed from several guerrilla groups with roots in the Arab Nationalist Movement — also began raids. At first the guerrillas' losses were high. Israeli newspapers boasted of the numbers of fedayeen killed or captured. Fatah explained the movement's way of looking at these actions:

> We did not understand the struggle in terms of profit or loss. We blow up one bridge and the Zionists will blow up ten of our bridges.... We must plant it firmly in our minds that the strategy is that of a guerrilla warfare which should be developed into a popular war of liberation.... This is mainly what frightens Israel, Zionism, and other counter-revolutionary forces. Why? Because calculations will not be made on the basis of a tank for a tank and a combat plane for a combat plane. The calculations are based on the will of a struggling people who want to fight...[1]

120

Israel planned to break the Palestinians' will to fight by harsh repression of all political activity. By early 1968 the Israeli crackdown had driven most identifiable guerrillas out of the occupied territories and into Jordan and Lebanon. Those who stayed had to work as part of an underground movement. The Israelis not only outlawed political activity, but also attacked Palestinian economic and social institutions. They shut down Arab banks, schools and hospitals in the West Bank and Gaza, replacing them with Israeli institutions. The Israelis used threats when necessary to convince West Bank "notables" who had loyally served Hussein as village officials to switch their allegiance to Israel. Others transferred their loyalties without prompting.

Israel planned to keep the rest of the population in line by a combination of force and the creation of a colonial mentality among the people. Schoolteachers in the West Bank and Gaza were forced to teach Palestinian children courses that glorified the history of Israel and belittled Arab culture. Teachers who protested were fired. One who was exiled to Jordan in 1967 said, "I can't teach that Palestine was always Jewish and we are parasites."[2]

The crowded refugee camps of Gaza were largely isolated from outside reporters and contacts. There the Israeli drive to create a passive population took its most brutal form. Heavily-armed Israeli patrols descended on the camps and cities and rounded up people indiscriminately. In one such roundup in late 1967, Israeli soldiers forced two thousand men to lie half-submerged in a lake for twenty-four hours during a storm. Other "troublemakers" were exiled to concentration camps in the Sinai Desert.[3] Still, Israeli soldiers rarely dared to leave their jeeps as they patrolled Gaza. Wires stretched across the road at windshield level often caused their jeeps to screech to a halt. In 1968, two hundred women defied a law forbidding demonstrations and marched on Gaza prison, demanding the release of two thousand Palestinian prisoners.

In Gaza and the West Bank and in the refugee camps in Jordan and Lebanon Palestinians began taking action for themselves toward the positive goal of liberating Palestine. Slowly they broke out of the defeatism that had gripped many Palestinians — a defeatism that the Arab governments had fostered in them. They began to fight against the "vengeance mentality" toward Israel which some still held on to — what Fatah called the "venom and bitterness of an oppressed people who see no way to freedom." The guerrilla organizations led the fight for these changes.

In Fatah's first communique after the June War, the guerrillas emphatically rejected the leadership of PLO figurehead, Ahmed Shukeiry. During the war, Shukeiry had broadcast tirades on Cairo Radio that vowed to "drive the Jews into the sea." Fatah condemned this racism toward Jews:

> [Palestinian] operations ... are in no way aimed at the Jewish people. Nor do they intend to "drive them into the sea'".... [O]n the day the flag of Palestine is hoisted over their freed, democratic peaceful land, a new era will begin in which the Palestinian Jews will again live in harmony, side by side, with the original owners of the land, the Palestinian Arabs.[4]

In December 1967, Fatah, the Popular Front, the General Union of Palestinian Students and other groups joined in a condemnation of Shukeiry. He was removed from the leadership of the PLO for his "misleading statements" and his backward leadership.[5] In Shukeiry's place, the fedayeen emerged as the real leaders of the Palestinian struggle.

Karameh Means Dignity

Three months later the guerrillas demonstrated the new strength of the Palestinian movement to the Arab people and Israel. In the small Jordanian town of Karameh the fedayeen waged a battle that galvanized the support of the Palestinian people for its fighters. Karameh, which means "dignity" in Arabic, had been patiently built by Palestinian refugees from a tented refugee camp in 1952 into a prosperous town that supplied vegetables and poultry to the whole region. Twenty-five thousand more refugees swelled Karameh in the months after the June War. The people of Karameh supported the fedayeen and many joined their ranks. The town became a base for guerrilla raids into the West Bank. In the first two months of 1968, the Israelis attacked Karameh from the air, shelling the town six times. Knowing the Israelis would eventually attack the town, the guerrillas moved much of the population to the mountains and prepared for battle.

Four Israeli armored columns attacked Karameh on March 21, 1968. They expected the guerrillas and their supporters to scatter. Instead, Fatah leaders decided that the guerrillas would make a stand. Inside Karameh, two hundred guerrillas, all volunteers, fought for twelve long hours, holding off the more numerous and far better equipped Israelis. Taher Saadi, a fighter who survived the battle at Karameh, told a French reporter why the Palestinians stayed in the embattled town:

> At Karameh, the Israelis had tanks and planes; they were trying to crush the fedayeen.... Many of our men who had run out of ammunition hurled themselves under the tanks, carrying explosives. The first martyr to do that was Rarbi; he threw himself under a tank. I knew him well. We stuck it out that day, so as to wipe out the memory of June 1967.[6]

Overnight the fedayeen became heroes in the Arab press. The next day photos of burned-out Israeli tanks appeared in newspapers throughout the Arab countries. Palestinians had done what the Arab leaders could not do — stand up to the military might of Israel. Arab leaders rushed in to stake out part of the victory for themselves. Even King Hussein, dressed in battle fatigues, went to Karameh and had his picture taken beside a captured Israeli tank. He declared, "We are all fedayeen."

For exiled Palestinians in Jordan and Lebanon, the victory at Karameh was more than a media image. It was a seed dropped on fertile soil. As Palestinian farmers defied Israeli shelling and moved back to the ruined town of Karameh to plant new crops, thousands of young volunteers clogged the guerrilla recruiting stations in Jordan. In the lines were Palestinians who had given up jobs as postal clerks, farmers, engineers or secretaries to offer their lives to liberate Palestine. At first many had to be turned away because there were not enough arms to hand the eager fighters.

Many of these recruits came from the refugee camps in Jordan and Lebanon where hundreds of thousands of Palestinians still lived. Among those who had come to the camps after the June War there was a special energy to be tapped. In 1968 and 1969 activists from all the guerrilla groups moved into the camps to help organize them and to explain the lessons of people's war. They recruited new members, organized militias and discussed politics with the eager and the skeptical.

The guerrilla groups set up schools in the camps to teach the children to be proud

Women march against an Israeli military parade through the occupied territories, Jerusalem, 1968.

of, and learn from, Palestinian history. One Fatah leader, a former teacher in the UN-sponsored schools, explained with a quiet passion to an American interviewer that, "The UNRWA schools are trying to destroy this generation of our children." His stories of out-of-date textbooks or no books at all, irrelevant studies and over-crowded classrooms reminded the American of ghetto schools in the United States. The Fatah leader said, "Of course, the same people plan it, the same people are responsible for it. The U.S. government runs UNRWA."[7]

The guerrilla schools gave military training as well as explaining the history and geography of Palestine, and teaching fundamental skills like reading and writing. In camps in Jordan and Lebanon, young boys and girls learned to crawl through barbed wire fences and jump hurdles, chanting together, "To Palestine!" A Palestinian mother commented:

> I am proud to see that our children are able to do that. I am only sorry that it is necessary that they should do it.... As one of our songs says, "I am fighting so that the future generations will reap the wheat."[8]

To Liberate Women Is to Liberate Society

The military training of young girls in the guerrilla schools was an example of one of the most profound changes brought about by the Palestinian revolution: the new role of Palestinian women. All the guerrilla groups recognized that Palestinian women were one of the deepest resources for revolution, and they affirmed that the liberation of women was fundamental to the liberation of Palestine.

Women working in a resistance center

Palestinian women won this recognition by fighting for it. In the 1936 revolt, the war of 1948, and the guerrilla war of the 1960s, Palestinian women took up arms. Isam Abedilhadi, president of the General Union of Palestinian Women (founded in 1965), described the role of women in resisting Israeli occupation:

> Concerning the women after 1967, they were the first to lead demonstrations asking for withdrawal, rejecting occupation, asking for something. They were the first prisoners. They were the first to ask for strikes. Won't we all be put in jail or be deported? Well, it's all right. . . . I was in prison and there were more than five hundred women in all the prisons, inside the occupied territories, and twenty-five of them were deported.[9]

Even as women fought and demonstrated, a daily struggle was going on in Palestinian homes between men and women of the Resistance and the traditional heritage of old Palestine, with it strict ideas of how to protect women's honor. Women had to argue with their families to be allowed to go alone to political meetings, to take military training or to stand guard duty. Islamic culture taught that women couldn't work outside the home and retain their honor. Yet women wanted and needed to work to support their families and the revolution. Slowly, the traditional notion of women's honor, which rested on obedience and chastity, began to crumble. A new concept of honor, forged in the crucible of revolution, began to emerge. It valued the contribution of women to the movement, and to other women's growth and development.

Women's centers in the refugee camps helped women overcome the stumbling blocks to their participation in the revolution. In Jordan, where only 15 percent of the women could read, grandmothers patiently stumbled through their first book with the help of a young guerrilla. These centers also trained women in sewing and marketed their products. "When a woman has money that she herself has earned," said a woman in a sewing center in Irbid, "she can speak more loudly in her own home."[10]

Not only Palestinian women, but all Palestinian workers and peasants in Jordan were finding their voice and speaking out against the injustices of Jordanian society. Unions had always been illegal in Jordan, and workers who tried to organize them were quickly imprisoned. When the Palestinian Resistance began organizing in Jordanian workplaces, the number of strikes increased dramatically. When police came to break up the strikes, they were often met by armed guerrillas. Employers were forced to recognize the unions their workers wanted. The guerrillas also supported Palestinian sharecroppers in disputes with their Jordanian landlords over the size of annual rents. Slowly more Jordanians began to support the Palestinian liberation movement.

Confronting the Arab Regimes

Before King Hussein's eyes, the seeds of a new society were sprouting and threatening his rule. Jordanian officials watched as goods stamped "For the Palestinian Nation" arrived at Amman. Aid from Vietnam, China, Algeria and other liberation movements around the world flowed into Jordan. In Amman guerrillas maintained their own military checkpoints, newspapers and offices. King Hussein knew that the Palestinian movement would like to see him overthrown. After all, the British had artificially carved Jordan from historic Palestine after World War I, and his grandfather had annexed the West Bank in 1948. Most of Jordan's population were Palestinians who had never strongly supported Hussein. His regime depended on American economic and military aid for survival, as his grandfather's had on British support. The U.S. government paid half of Jordan's annual budget and the CIA made personal payments to him starting in 1957. Hussein used much of this money to pay large salaries to his army, made up of impoverished bedouins whom he had turned into loyal troops.

Hussein could not tolerate the growth of this Palestinian nation within his kingdom. He decided to act quickly to protect his throne. On November 4, 1968, Hussein's soldiers opened fire on Palestinian offices in Amman and on three refugee camps. They killed several campdwellers, but the fedayeen repulsed the attack. Hussein's troops had to retreat and await a better time to strike. After Hussein's November raid, Fatah warned its Arab enemies that the Resistance was "not prepared to commit suicide with Arab bullets."[11]

President Nasser of Egypt refused to condemn the November attack, claiming he did not want to violate "Jordanian sovereignty." The refusal of even the most progressive Arab states to criticize Hussein opened a serious debate between the guerrilla organizations on the role of the Arab governments in the Palestinian struggle. The debate highlighted the central dilemma of the Palestinian movement: as a people driven off their land, they had no secure base in which to train and organize. Access to the camps in the East Bank of the Jordan and southern Lebanon was vital for the growth of the Resistance and the fight against Israel. What price should the guerrillas pay to maintain their freedom of movement in the Arab countries? How should the fedayeen relate to radical movements in the Arab countries? The major organizations in the Resistance debated these questions throughout 1969.

125

Youth training in a Palestinian camp

Fatah was convinced that the revolution could not publicly challenge the internal structure of the Arab states without losing its base of operations. Its suggested policy was "no meddling in the internal affairs of Arab countries." Zionism was the first enemy; change in the Arab countries would come after Palestine was liberated.

The Popular Front believed equally as firmly that the liberation of Palestine went hand in hand with radical changes in the Arab governments. In this view, the overthrow of Hussein and the establishment in Jordan of a democratic state was a pressing task. The Democratic Front for the Liberation of Palestine (DFLP), which broke from the Popular Front in 1969, argued that the Resistance should not even accept aid from regimes like Egypt. Both the Popular Front and the Democratic Front believed that the only reliable allies of the Palestinians were the small revolutionary movements in the Arab countries.

Differences in military strategies also developed between the Popular Front and Fatah. Fatah confined its operations to Israel and the occupied territories. The Popular Front, although also operating in the occupied territories (especially Gaza), took the cause of the Palestinian people to the world arena. Its most spectacular actions were hijackings of U.S. and Israeli planes in 1968 and 1969. Leila Khaled, a Popular Front commando who participated in hijackings, explained the strategy:

> We do not embark haphazardly on adventurous and romantic projects to fulfill "individual needs".... We act collectively in a planned manner ... to dramatize our own plight and to express our resolute determination to alter

the "new realities" that Mr. Moshe Dayan's armies have created.... [We act] with a view to disseminating revolutionary propaganda ... making our cause international ... before an unresponsive Zionist-inspired and Zionist-informed Western public opinion. As a comrade has said, "We act heroically to prove that the enemy is not invincible."[12]

And Israel was not invincible. The fedayeen raids grew more frequent and more effective throughout 1968. Targets included the Haifa pipeline, a potash factory near the Dead Sea, para-military settlments, and factories in Tel Aviv. By 1969 about three hundred guerrilla actions were occurring inside Israel and the occupied territories each month. By 1969 two thousand Israeli casualties had resulted from raids since the June War. Israel responded with a heavy counterattack.

In December 1968 Israel answered a hijacking by blowing up thirteen passenger planes in Beirut, Lebanon. In 1969 it began a steady campaign of saturation bombing in southern Lebanon. Saturation bombing hits everything indiscriminately — fields, sheep, and farmers, as well as guerrilla bases. The Israelis hoped the bombings would pressure the Lebanese government to move against the guerrillas. The right-wing government did order the army to attack the refugee camps. But strong resistance by the Palestinians and strikes and demonstrations by their Lebanese supporters forced the Lebanese government to back down. After Egyptian mediation, the Palestinians and the Lebanese government signed the Cairo Accords, which guaranteed the Palestinians' freedom of movement inside Lebanon and control of the refugee camps in exchange for non-interference in Lebanon's internal affairs. This was a major defeat for Israel's plans.

The Zionists suffered another political defeat in 1969 when Fatah and the other guerrilla organizations took control of the Palestine Liberation Organization. From the beginnings of the Palestinian armed resistance, King Hussein of Jordan and the Israeli authorities in the West Bank and Gaza had repeatedly tried to deny the Palestinians the right to their own representative organization. Since its creation in 1964, the PLO had been largely under the control of the Arab governments. But at the Fifth Congress of the Palestine National Council — the highest authority of the PLO — several hundred representatives came from trade unions, women's and student organizations and, for the first time, most of the guerrilla organizations. They chose a new leadership for the PLO Executive Committee, the body which carries out the programs and goals of the Council. This new leadership reflected the success of the armed resistance movement in winning the support of the Palestinian nation. Fatah won the majority of the seats, and Yasser Arafat was elected chairman of the Executive. Independents and nearly all the major guerrilla groups also won representation. The PLO had finally emerged as the voice of the Palestinian people.

A Democratic Secular State

Beginning that year, Fatah and other groups began discussions within the PLO to have the charter of the organization state firmly that the enemy of the Palestinians was the Zionist state, not the Jewish people. The final goal of the movement should be a "democratic, secular state in all of Palestine." Fatah described the future state as one "in which there will be no racism, no Zionism and no religious persecution."

It would serve equally Moslems, Christians and Jews, including all those currently living in Israel. The new state would reflect the history of Palestine in which the people of the three religions had lived peacefully together for hundreds of years.

The call for the democratic secular state stood in stark contrast to the Zionist state of Israel. Israeli propagandists dismissed Fatah's call and ridiculed it as a public relations ploy. They reminded Israelis of Haj Amin and his collaboration with the Nazis and Ahmed Shukeiry's 1967 radio broadcasts, in an effort to "prove" Palestinian anti-Semitism. They insisted that anti-Zionists were anti-Semites. But the Israeli government's portrayal of Palestinians as implacable enemies of the Jewish people failed to touch all Jews in Israel. The behavior of Israel in the occupied territories had produced a steady stream of protest from conscientious Israelis. In 1968, a group of Israeli teachers proclaimed:

> A people which oppresses another finishes by losing its liberty and that of its citizens. Jewish citizens! Remember how courageous non-Jews stood at our sides in moments of distress. Misfortune has now descended on our brother Arab people. Do you think it just to wash your hands and keep quiet?[13]

Palestinian organizations began making contact with progressive Jews inside Israel to begin trying to build alliances.

Within two short years the fedayeen and the PLO had matured into a force that seriously threatened Israel and the right-wing Arab governments. From the victory at Karameh to the successful defense of the camps in Jordan and Lebanon, the Palestinian movement had shown that it would fight hard to protect its people and its independence. U.S. leaders listened to the concerned reports of American diplomats in Jordan and Lebanon, who noted the growing strength of the fedayeen. Together with similar reports from State Department and Pentagon officials from Vietnam to Chile, they formed a picture of the U.S. empire under siege. Determined not to let the Palestinian liberation movement threaten their most vital resource, Middle East oil, they began planning their own offensive to defeat the Palestinian revolution.

Footnotes

1. Kadi, *Basic Documents of the Armed Palestinian Resistance Movement,* pp. 88-89.
2. Frank H. Epp, *The Palestinians, Portrait of a People in Conflict* (Scottsdale, Pennsylvania: 1976), p. 77.
3. Amity Ben-Yona, "What Does Israel Do To Its Palestinians? A letter from Israel to Jews of the American Left," *Arab American University Graduate Bulletin* no. 2. For further references also see Arlette Tessier, *Gaza* (Beirut: 1971), pp. 33-36.
4. *Palestine: Crisis and Liberation* (Havana: 1969), pp. 147-49.
5. Rashid Hamid, "What is the PLO," in Hatem I. Hussaini and Fathalla El-Boghdady, eds., *The Palestinians, Selected Essays,* (Washington, D.C.: 1976), p. 14.
6. Chaliand, *The Palestinian Resistance,* p. 74.
7. Sheila Ryan and George Cavalletto, "Palestine on the Brink of People's War," unpublished manuscript, 1970.
8. Epp, p. 164
9. Ibid., pp. 161-62.
10. Ryan and Cavalletto.
11. Kadi, p. 27.
12. Khaled, *My People Shall Live,* pp. 128-29.
13. John Cooley, *Green March, Black September* (London: 1973), p. 230.

15: Black September

**Now all day long the loudspeakers are asking the refugee camps to surrender . . . .
How can a refugee camp surrender and to whom? Is there a surrender greater than
the life of the camps?**

—Diary of a Resistance Fighter, September, 1970

The United States Assistant Secretary of State, Joseph Sisco, took off from
Washington on a "peace mission" to the Middle East in April 1970. In Amman, Jordan, tens of thousands of demonstrators, mostly Palestinians, marched through the
streets to protest Sisco's visit. They burned down the U.S. Information Agency and
damaged the U.S. Embassy. The Palestinians knew that an American "peace" meant
a drive for more U.S. control at their expense. Sisco canceled his stop in Jordan. But
he and other U.S. diplomats would soon return. They had watched the steady
growth of the Palestinian Resistance and of Soviet influence in the whole region
since 1967. Now they intended to stop both.

Significant Soviet influence in the Middle East had begun when the Soviet Union
supplied aid to Nasser to build the Aswan Dam in 1956. Since then the Soviets had

been trying to develop strong ties with regimes who were taking the "non-capitalist road" of development. The Soviet Union had signed trade and technical assistance agreements with Egypt and Syria in the late 1950s, and had armed them during the 1960s. It had supported the People's Democratic Republic of Yemen when it formed in 1967. After the June War, it helped rebuild the shattered armies and air forces of Syria and Egypt. It helped Iraq explore for and market oil after the radical Iraqi government nationalized U.S. oil companies. The number of Soviet advisers in the area and the size of the Soviet fleet in the Mediterranean grew rapidly after 1967.

The Soviet Union wanted to erode U.S. economic and military strength in the area. Soviet leaders believed that American forces and allies so near Soviet borders posed a grave threat to Soviet security. The Soviets wanted the Americans to leave and encouraged allies of the United States to adopt a neutral or pro-Soviet foreign policy. This led the Soviet Union to support, with some caution, nationalist governments and movements which confronted U.S. imperialism militarily and economically — as long as these confrontations did not seriously disrupt the stability of the area or bring the Soviets into direct conflict with the United States.

In the view of U.S. policy-makers in 1970, the Soviet Union's support of Egypt's "war of attrition" against Israel might well lead to a U.S.-Soviet confrontation. Egypt began the limited war in 1969, by shelling Israeli positions along the Suez

130

Canal. The war escalated rapidly after the United States delivered fifty sophisticated Phantom jets to Israel. Israeli pilots flew these jets deep into Egypt and struck civilian targets. In April of 1970, as Sisco proclaimed the "peaceful" intentions of the United States, a Phantom jet dropped bombs on an Egyptian school, killing forty-six children. Nasser requested and got anti-aircraft missiles from the Soviet Union to counter the Phantoms.

The Rogers Plan

To prevent a further escalation, U.S. officials tried to put into effect a plan that they had been working on since 1969. It proposed a general settlement for the Arab-Israeli conflict. The Rogers Plan (as it was called, after Secretary of State William Rogers) was based on UN Resolution 242. It offered Arab leaders the return of some of their territory lost in the June War, in exchange for their recognition of Israel and the establishment of secure borders. The Rogers Plan, like the UN resolution, denied the rights of Palestinians to their homeland. It treated them simply as a "refugee problem." Acceptance of the Rogers Plan by Arab governments would undermine the Palestinian movement and remove the Arab states from the fight against Israel.

A main aim of the American plan was to pull Egypt away from the Soviet Union and into the U.S. orbit of influence. Henry Kissinger explained in a background briefing in June 1970:

> We are trying to get a [Middle East] settlement in such a way that the moderate regimes are strengthened, and not the radical regimes. We are trying to expel the Soviet military presence. . . .[1]

Sisco's April mission to the Middle East was to test the reaction of Arab leaders to the American proposal.

King Hussein was the most responsive. He wanted to endorse the Rogers Plan, but he knew that such a betrayal of the Palestinians could cost him his throne. With each month, more Palestinians in Jordan were drawn to the program of the fedayeen. Already Irbid, Jerash and other cities in northern Jordan were controlled by Palestinian guerrillas. From his palace Hussein could see armed guerrillas patrolling the streets of Amman. Before he could accept the Rogers Plan he had to try once more, as he had tried the previous November, to subdue the fedayeen. On June 6 his Bedouin troops attacked the Palestinian guerrilla base at Zerka and shelled the nearby refugee camps. Once again the resistance of the popular militias and the guerrilla movement forced Hussein to back down and withdraw his troops.

When Hussein failed to defeat the Palestinians in Jordan, the United States stepped up its drive to persuade Nasser to accept the Rogers Plan. If Nasser — the historic "friend" of the Palestinians — accepted the plan, then Hussein could do so more easily. By the summer of 1970 the "war of attrition" between Egypt and Israel had gone far beyond the limited war Nasser's army was capable of waging. Already the Egyptian people were pressing for a settlement that returned Egypt's land or total mobilization against Israel. The United States offered him a way out of the dilemma with the Rogers Plan. Nasser endorsed it on July 24, 1970. A few days later Israel accepted the plan, realizing that it would end the "war of attrition" with Egypt and allow Hussein to attack the Palestinians in Jordan.

Women fighters in Jordan, September, 1970.

Many Palestinians were stunned. Despite Nasser's many past achievements, this act was too familiar. It reminded Palestinians of the self-serving betrayals of the Arab kings in 1936 and 1948. Nasser tried to muzzle Palestinian criticism by closing down the Cairo radio station that broadcast the "Voice of Palestine" and by expelling several hundred Palestinian students from Cairo University. In Amman, ten thousand people silently marched against the Rogers Plan. In the West Bank, demonstrators' placards branded Nasser a "traitor."

In Amman, Jordan, heavy tanks, artillery and napalm began arriving daily, directly from the United States. Jordanian troops patrolled the border to capture Palestinian guerrillas returning from the West Bank. Palestinian organizations felt themselves trapped inside a circle that grew smaller every day. They were not ready to fight Hussein. Although they had developed ties with many people in Jordan, their base of support was not well-organized. Two years of rapid growth had its shortcomings. Many guerrillas were inexperienced and poorly armed. Yet, Palestinian leaders knew the attack would come soon.

Fatah stepped up its pressure on Nasser to come to the aid of the Palestinians. Both the Popular Front and the Democratic Front thought negotiating with Nasser was a dead end. In August the Democratic Front called for setting up a democratic government in Jordan to replace Hussein. But the call came only days before the crisis broke. On August 29, 1970, Hussein officially accepted the Rogers Plan.

Hussein's army had been steadily attacking Palestinian bases in southern Jordan during the previous two weeks. On August 30, 1970, members of the Popular Front boarded jumbo jets of Swissair, TWA and BOAC and commanded the pilots to fly to Jordan. They hoped to pressure Hussein to end his attacks on the camps and

132

guerrillas in Jordan. When Hussein ignored their demands, they removed the hostages and blew up the jets. On September 13, Hussein ordered all Resistance fighters to turn in their arms. The Resistance responded by issuing a call for a general strike to demand the participation of Palestinians in the government. All guerrilla organizations met in Amman and hastily set up a unified command.

Hussein Attacks

In the pale dawn of September 15, the storm broke over the city. At 5:00 A.M. Jordanian tanks and armored cars began shelling any suspected guerrilla positions in the refugee camps. The army imposed a curfew on Amman, shooting on sight anyone caught on the streets. The guerrillas quickly prepared to fight. In a battlefield diary, a young guerrilla, code-named "Bassem", recorded Hussein's first attack on the Resistance offices, all in the same section of Amman:[2]

> Suddenly we all got together. All the barriers between organizations disappeared. We met together in a trench, behind a wall, on the sites of the ruins of offices. All of us from different groups were working together without hesitation.

They fought for four hours, holding their own. Bassem recorded:

> Then something unexpected happened. The cannons of the tanks shelled the houses in a totally unnecessary way. Savagely, without even differentiating between homes and commando offices. It was really frightening. We were paralyzed, seeing the houses collapsing and suddenly seeing in the unexpected rubble many of the small private things of people, the warm small things of people, torn, sometimes bloody.

As the tanks rolled down the streets, some fighters began to retreat. But then:

> Abu Ammar [Yasser Arafat] came down to Hussein Street. He asked the fighters who were retreating to stop running away and to plant mines and build barricades of cars, gas cans, any kind of metal. He brought his own car himself, and with some other men, pushed it into the middle of the street. Immediately high morale filled the area and men started to come back.

Leaders of the other guerrilla groups joined the fighters in the streets as the battle intensified. The Palestinians fought stubbornly with light weapons against Hussein's heavy artillery. In the camps around Amman the situation was desperate. Napalm rained from the skies and fires raged uncontrollably through the crowded camps. The desperate fighters hoped for some word of support from other Arab countries. None came. When radio reports confirmed the official silence of the Arab governments, Bassem said it was "as if a hand had caught [our] necks in the darkness." Only Syria sent a tank column across the border, but it was driven back. Bassem's last entry from the embattled Hussein camp read:

> I am afraid that here at least everything is coming to an end. I can see only that people prefer to die resisting. Death is in every square inch of the Hussein refugee camp. Also thirst and hunger .... Now our men fight starvation in the first line as they face the tanks.

After eleven days of fighting the guerrillas still held most of their military positions in the north of Jordan and in the camps. But five thousand people had been killed and twenty thousand wounded — most of them civilians. Food and supplies were running low. On September 25, the Central Committee of the Resistance sent Yasser Arafat to Cairo to negotiate a cease-fire.

As people ventured into the streets of Amman, they found among the bodies and ruins of buildings thousands of ammunition cartons stamped "Made in the U.S.A." The markings revealed the hand behind the Black September attack. At a top-level meeting in Washington during the heaviest fighting in Jordan, the Israeli and Jordanian ambassadors had met with Henry Kissinger and the heads of the Defense Department, the CIA and the Joint Chiefs of Staff. They planned an Israeli attack on the Palestinians, code-named "Operation Brass Strike," in case Hussein's army failed to do the job or Syria intervened. In the Mediterranean the U.S. Sixth Fleet steamed towards the coast nearest Jordan and U.S. troops boarded giant cargo planes at U.S. bases in Turkey.[3] After the cease-fire, U.S. planes rushed more supplies and weapons to Hussein. The U.S. government gave Hussein $35 million in emergency aid over the next three months.

While the United States was rearming Hussein, the Palestinian guerrilla organizations were meeting in the mountains of Jordan to probe the lessons of Black September. Ghassan Kanafani of the Popular Front wrote:

> Shocks like September crystallize the strength of the revolution, because they have forced it into the mountains. There are now commandos living ... in caves, with limited water and food and little ammunition. In this situation, we can't expect that the thousands who went around Amman in khakis carrying their Klashnikovs will lead this kind of life.[4]

Both the Popular Front and the Democratic Front firmly believed that Black September was the "heavy price" the Resistance paid for trusting in the Arab regimes. They argued that it was not just Hussein, but all the Arab leaders who had remained silent, who bore responsibility for the thousands killed and wounded. The Palestinians' only lasting allies would be the progressive forces in the Arab countries.

Fatah, by far the largest of all the organizations and the one with the broadest range of views among its members, was torn with internal disagreement over this question. Everyone agreed that Hussein's actions had branded him an enemy of the revolution, and that the other Arab leaders had failed to act. A few Fatah leaders agreed with the Popular and Democratic Fronts. Some thought the Resistance could rely on Egypt and Syria for support in the next lean years. Others did not think Egypt and Syria could be relied on, but argued that the Resistance could not alienate them and lose its freedom of movement in those countries.

All groups agreed that the Resistance in its two short years in Jordan had failed to fully mobilize the people behind a program to support the Palestinians and democratize Jordan. At the March 1971 Palestine National Council meeting, one hundred ten Jordanian nationals joined the Palestinian delegates. The Council resolved that the Jordanian and Palestinian people had to unite closely to fight against Hussein. Despite unresolved struggles over strategy, the Council overwhelmingly affirmed for the first time that the goal of the revolution was a democratic secular state in all of Palestine.

As the Palestine National Council was finishing its session, Hussein intensified

his drive to get every guerrilla off of Jordanian land. He pressed the attack throughout 1971. In July he ordered his Prime Minister, Wasfi Tal, to move against the last strongholds of the guerrillas. The Jordanian army moved into the forests of Ajloun, the base for eighteen hundred guerrillas. After four days of fierce fighting and heavy napalming, the Jordanians had captured or killed all but fifty guerrillas. On the orders of Prime Minister Tal, Jordanian soldiers killed the captured Fatah military leader, Abu Ali Iyad. They dragged his body behind a tank through nearby villages. They wanted to make a clear point to any potential supporters: "The Resistance is dead!"

The Resistance Will Not Die

Four months later Wasfi Tal was standing on the steps of a Cairo hotel when bullets rang out, killing him instantly. The group responsible for his death called it- self "Black September" and said that Tal's assassination was in memory of the young fedayeen leader, Abu Ali Iyad. "Black September" went on to answer the latest wave of terror aimed at the Palestinian people with a highly disciplined secret war that focused on Israel and Jordan.

Cut off from the old bases in Jordan and facing stepped-up Israeli border patrols, the Palestinian fighters from all groups tried many paths to develop a political and military strategy that could defeat Zionism and its allies. The raids into Israel and the occupied territories were increasingly difficult and dangerous. Yet there were strong differences within the Palestinian movement about the wisdom of relying on external operations like hijackings as a strategy for building the movement. Groups like "Black September" were not formally part of the PLO, and there was much debate about the effect of their actions on the Palestinian cause. But few Palestinians questioned the absolute right of the Palestinian people to use every available means in their fight for freedom.

In Israel, Europe and the United States, the actions of "Black September" inspired a flood of indignant speeches, editorials and articles. The same media that had applauded or matter of factly reported Hussein's massacre of thousands of Palestinians in Jordan were suddenly outraged at the actions of Palestinian "terrorists." Editors and commentators described armed attacks on illegal Israeli para-military settlements in the occupied territories as "terrorism." When the Israelis retaliated, their attacks were called "reprisals." Just as they had done with the wars in Vietnam, Algeria, or the Portuguese colonies in Africa, Western politicians and media shouted "terrorism" to obscure the justice of people's fight for national liberation.

So it was when "Black September" took eleven Israeli athletes hostage at the 1972 Olympics in Munich. "Black September" commandos demanded the release of two hundred Palestinian political prisoners held in Israeli jails. Israel refused to negotiate. Under Israeli pressure the German authorities moved on the planes carrying the hostages and opened fire. All the guerrillas and hostages died. Western officials and the media heaped abuse on the Palestinians and carefully refrained from criticizing Israel's role in the deaths. In September of 1972 the Israeli Air Force mounted a "reprisal raid" against southern Lebanon in retaliation for the "Black September" action at Munich. The raid killed three hundred people.

The September raid was not the first. In February and June Israeli planes had struck deep into the south of Lebanon for saturation bombing of the area that the Israelis called "Fatahland" — where many Palestinian guerrilla base camps were located. These raids were part of Israel's general offensive against the Palestinians in the wake of Black September. Israeli leaders hoped now to finish off the Resistance once and for all.

The previous year Moshe Dayan had begun to prepare the way for new Jewish settlements in the Gaza Strip. He ordered a massive "security round-up" of Palestinians he believed to be potential trouble-makers. He placed the entire Strip under a curfew and conducted house-to-house searches of some camps. Israeli troops blew up houses to widen the roads for better surveillance. They punished any resistance swiftly and strongly. After a year of operations, they considered Gaza "pacified." Yet in September of 1972, rioting broke out in the Gaza camp of Shatti. Using sticks and homemade weapons, young Palestinians fought hit-and-run battles with the occupation troops. Despite massive arrests, curfews, beatings and shootings, sporadic rioting continued all during the fall.

The Palestinian leaders recognized the importance of this resistance in Gaza and similar unrest in the West Bank. National Council meetings of the PLO in both 1972 and 1973 called for the formation of a *national front* in the occupied territories to connect the struggle there with that of the Palestinians in exile. Contacts between groups in the West Bank and Gaza took place in the beginning of 1973. Meeting in greatest secrecy, trade unions, women's and students' organizations, and political parties, including Jordanian communists, hammered out the organization of the

From: DEFIANCE

You may fasten my chains
Deprive me of my books and tobacco
You may fill my mouth with earth
Poetry will feed my heart, like blood
It is salt to the bread
And liquid to the eye
I will write it with nails,
    eye sockets and daggers
I will recite it in my prison cell—
    in the bathroom—
        in the stable—
            Under the whip—
                Under the chains—
                    In spite of my handcuffs
I have a million nightingales
On the branches of my heart
Singing the song of liberation.

By Mahmoud Darweesh

Palestine National Front (PNF). The announcement of its formation on August 15, 1973 spread like wildfire throughout the occupied territories. The PNF became part of the PLO, but its function was to represent directly the people under Israeli occupation.

Members of the Front built cell organizations, distributed literature, tried to resolve people's grievances and organized strikes and boycotts. One of the Front's first activities was to organize a boycott of the September 1973 trade union elections held in Jerusalem by Israeli authorities. The Israelis thought that the participation of Palestinian Arabs in the elections would symbolize their acceptance of Israeli annexation of Jerusalem. Largely through the Front's efforts, only about 6 percent of the Palestinian Arab workers voted. The boycott was a success. Such mass demonstrations of support made it increasingly clear that only the PLO could claim to speak for the Palestinians.

In Lebanon, too, the Palestinian Resistance was recovering from the effects of the setback in Jordan. On April 10, 1973, an Israeli commando group moved silently into Beirut. They murdered four top Palestinian leaders, including Kamal Nassar, one of Palestine's foremost poets. One-fifth of Beirut — a quarter of a million people — marched in the funeral procession of the fallen leaders. Lebanese poor and working people shut down the city in a general strike to protest the government's passivity. Government leaders were frightened by the swell of support for the Palestinians. In May they ordered a full-scale army and air force attack on Palestinian refugee camps around Beirut. Again, Lebanese workers and students supported the Palestinians, this time under the slogan, "There will be no new Black September in Lebanon." The Lebanese Army attack was repulsed in several days of heavy fighting.

Despite the setback in Jordan, the repression in the West Bank and Gaza and the Israeli bombing of Lebanon, the Palestinians were able to build new organizations and new alliances. The much-heralded "death" of the Palestinian movement had not occurred. Yasser Arafat, speaking of the Gaza uprisings in 1972, praised this Palestinian resilience:

> Moshe Dayan said, "I have finished off the resistance in Gaza." But today we see the resistance in Gaza breaking out again, although he made the streets 120 meters wide in our camps and though he has deported a third of our people from the Strip. In spite of this, resistance has broken out again — this generous sacrifice! How do trees die? They die standing up so that new trees and flowers may spring up.[5]

The Palestinian people continued to stand in the way of all who would make "peace" in the Middle East at their expense. Among these was the new leader of Egypt, who was trying hard to reach a settlement with Israel.

Footnotes

1. Briefing at San Clemente, California, 26 June 1970, cited by Eqbal Ahmed, "A World Restored Revisited: American Diplomacy in the Middle East," *Race and Class*, vol. 17, no. 3 (Winter 1976), p. 223.
2. Russell Stetler, ed., *Palestine: The Arab-Israeli Conflict* (San Francisco: 1972), pp. 246-57.
3. Sheila Ryan and Joe Stork, "U.S. and Jordan: Thrice-Rescued Throne," *MERIP* no. 7, p. 5.
4. Stetler, p. 275.
5. Interview with Yasser Arafat in *Filastin al-Thawra*, 1 January 1973, reprinted in *Journal of Palestine Studies*, vol. 2, no. 3 (Spring 1973), p. 169.

16: The October War: The Olive Branch and the Gun

Washington is damned lucky to have Egypt, Syria and Saudi Arabia run for once by non-ideological, pragmatic men who've got their ducks in line. . . . They're about as conciliatory a bunch of Arab leaders as Washington could hope to find.
—Aide to U.S. Secretary of State Henry Kissinger

Since the death of Nasser in September of 1970, Anwar al Sadat, the new president of Egypt, had been making strong peace overtures to the United States. He believed that only the United States could pressure Israel to return occupied Egyptian land. At Nasser's funeral, he drew aside the American representative, Elliot Richardson, to assure him that Egypt planned to do all it could to implement the Rogers Plan. But Sadat was afraid that the United States had little inclination to push for a settlement since Hussein had expelled the fedayeen from Jordan and there was now peace on the Suez Canal front. If Sadat didn't recover Egypt's lost territory, he and the landowners and state officials that backed him could not hold power for long. The Egyptian people were demanding that he act.

In his first radio broadcast as president, Sadat pledged to the Egyptian people that

1971 would be "the year of decision" — the year in which Egypt would help get a just settlement for the Palestinians and get back Egyptian land from Israel, hopefully with American help. During that year he tried to please both his own conservative supporters and the U.S. government. He stopped land reform and ordered that all land redistributed to peasants in the past ten years be returned to the big landowners. He opened the country to investment from Western countries and allowed U.S. oil companies to explore for oil and build pipelines. He expelled the left opposition from his government and jailed many socialists, accusing them of an attempted coup.

As Sadat's new policies widened the already massive gap between rich and poor, strikes and demonstrations grew more frequent. Sadat finally turned the silenced guns of Egypt against the poor in late 1971. He sent troops and tanks against a militant strike of ten thousand workers at the giant Helwan Steelworks. The "year of decision" passed with no visible results. In January 1972, Cairo University erupted. Students fought a week-long battle with police and troops. It was the first in a series of demonstrations and strikes demanding fuller democracy, a cut in major government bureaucrats' salaries and the formation of popular militias to fight Israel.

Sadat moved even further to the right. While his troops crushed the student and worker protests, he patched up relations between Egypt and oil-rich Saudi Arabia, the staunchest Arab ally of the United States in the Middle East. He hoped that King Feisal would give him economic aid and urge the U.S. government to push for a peace settlement. But the United States did not respond.

In the summer of 1972, Sadat took a very dramatic step: he expelled the fifteen thousand Soviet military advisers from Egypt. He did not break relations with the Soviets completely, because he knew he would eventually need Soviet military aid if his peaceful overtures failed. But the expulsion was a clear signal to Washington. Sadat was ready to abandon Egypt's relationship with the Soviet Union and throw in his lot with the United States. He sent his diplomats to Washington to test the waters. They got an icy reception. A month later, Prime Minister Golda Meir of Israel paid a visit to the United States. She returned from her successful trip with promises of more Phantom jets for Israel's air force. Sadat concluded that only war could bring the necessary pressure for a settlement. He ordered his generals to prepare for a limited war.

Oil: The Vital Artery

At the same time powerful forces in the United States were pushing for a political settlement in the Middle East. For several years U.S. oil company executives had watched with alarm the growth of radical forces within OPEC, the Organization of Petroleum Exporting Countries. The oil companies could live with, and even profit from, the higher prices that OPEC members demanded. But with the U.S. driven out of Indochina, policy-makers feared that the more radical oil countries would follow Vietnam's example by reclaiming their resources. Some OPEC countries began to talk of nationalizing the oil companies and using the "oil weapon" against Israel and the United States.

King Feisal of Saudi Arabia and his bodyguards

The U.S. government's support of Israeli expansionism was becoming a burden to the oil men. Even King Feisal of Saudi Arabia felt the pressure from the left. He was more and more isolated in his defense of the United States in OPEC meetings. A leading U.S. oil economist, Walter J. Levy, lamented:

These are terrible, dangerous and difficult times. It is no longer just Arab against Israeli, it is Arab government against Arab government and Arab revolutionaries against Arab government.[1]

In May of 1973 an American oil executive gave President Richard Nixon and Henry Kissinger an urgent report from King Feisal: the Saudis could not "go it alone" in defending U.S. interests in the councils of OPEC and the Arab League.[2] Feisal needed Arab allies. He could not get them as long as the United States continued to support Israeli occupation of Arab land. That August, Mobil Oil — a Rockefeller-controlled company — placed a full-page ad in major newspapers in the United States. The text declared, "It is time for the world to insist on a settlement in the Middle East."[3]

Henry Kissinger shared that view. As a long-time adviser to the Rockefellers before he became Nixon's National Security Adviser, Kissinger had learned well the importance of oil to the U.S. empire. As a leading American economist put it, oil was "the vital artery of the capitalist world." U.S. control of Middle Eastern oil was immensely profitable. It also gave the United States important leverage over Western Europe and Japan, countries which depended heavily on that oil. During the Vietnam war, those countries had grown stronger in their competition with the United States for markets. Controlling their economies through the flow of oil was now more important than ever. Henry Kissinger planned to work toward an Arab-Israeli settlement to keep Middle Eastern oil under U.S. control. But it would not be easy.

Kissinger's hands were tied in the early months of 1973. For twenty years one of the ways U.S. policy-makers had guarded oil interests in the Middle East was by backing Israel and encouraging Zionist efforts to build strong emotional support for Israel among the American people and Congress. Kissinger did not want to risk a major collision with Congress by suddenly pressuring Israel to withdraw from the

141

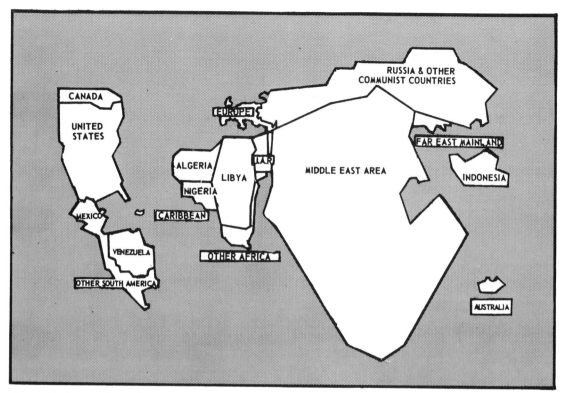

Geographical areas shown in proportion to oil reserves

occupied territories. He reportedly told a confidant, "I can't do anything until I have all the strings in my hand; and I won't have them in my hand until there is a crisis."[4]

Anwar Sadat was, at that moment, preparing the necessary crisis. He was holding urgent meetings with President Hafez Assad of Syria, who was under strong pressure to recover the occupied Golan Heights. The two leaders were making final plans for a limited war against Israel on two fronts.

On October 6, 1973, Egyptian troops launched a massive surprise assault across the Suez Canal, and Syrian tanks and soldiers stormed into the Golan Heights. Well-trained and well-equipped Arab soldiers drove back the Israeli occupiers in the initial fighting. Even the fiercest critics of Sadat in Egypt were caught up for a few days in the elation that swept the Arab capitals. Egypt and Syria were at last fighting for their land — and winning!

Israel mobilized rapidly for the counterattack, expecting a quick victory. Instead, the fighting was intense on both fronts. Israel suffered thousands of casualties and lost large numbers of planes and tanks. As the fighting continued, Israel attacked the Syrian capital of Damascus. To punish the Syrians, Zionist leaders decided to reduce much of the Syrian economy to rubble. The Israeli air force bombed ports, factories, power plants and oil refineries throughout the country and government buildings in the capital. These attacks killed many civilians.[5] As Israeli troops began to drive the Syrians back toward Damascus, the government formed popular militias to defend the city.

142

In Egypt Sadat ruled out mass mobilization. The Egyptian government told volunteers that their help was not needed and turned down offers of support from Algeria and Libya. Once his troops had set up their beachhead across the Canal, Sadat's limited war had served its purpose.

Israeli troops quickly seized the initiative. They drove the Egyptians back toward the Canal and some units crossed the Canal to try to encircle Egypt's Third Army. Even as they did this, Israel was running out of crucial equipment and supplies for its army. Without a quick U.S. re-supply effort, Israel's military would grind to a halt. The United States began a massive airlift to rearm the advancing Israelis.

This action outraged even conservative Arab leaders. From the outbreak of the war, the Palestinians and nationalist forces within OPEC had been calling for the use of the "oil weapon." Iraq had immediately nationalized U.S. oil company holdings. When the United States began to re-supply Israel, even Feisal of Saudi Arabia had to act. Saudi Arabia and the other Arab members of OPEC announced a 25 percent cut in production and an embargo on oil shipments to the United States until it changed its Middle East policy and helped bring about a settlement.

The oil embargo alarmed Kissinger. But worse was yet to come. The Israeli troops were completing their encirclement of Egypt's Third Army and threatening to destroy it. The Soviet Union told Nixon and Kissinger that it would take measures to prevent this. The threat of U.S.-Soviet confrontation was the last straw. On October 22, the United States and the Soviet Union pushed a cease-fire through the UN Security Council. Syria and Egypt accepted it quickly, and U.S. pressure eventually convinced the reluctant Israelis to agree to it. Moshe Dayan commented, "How can you oppose a country that sends you ammunition in the morning that you fire in the afternoon?"[6] The cease-fire agreement stipulated that negotiations toward an overall settlement begin at once.

The U.S. Wins the War

The real victor to emerge from the October War was the U.S. empire. Even the oil embargo and subsequent "energy crisis" had helped the United States government and oil companies in the long run.[7] The American oil companies reaped many of the benefits of the OPEC price hikes at the expense of Europe, Japan and other countries. Exxon's profits went up 59 percent in 1973. Saudi Arabia's income also grew, and it used some of the money to finance conservative forces in Syria and Egypt. American arms sales to the oil-rich countries skyrocketed, especially to Iran, which the United States was building up as policeman for the oil-producing Gulf area.

More importantly, Kissinger had his crisis and could now begin to pull the strings that eluded him before. The expense of the war set off a major economic crisis in Israel. Israel was going to need large amounts of American aid to survive. That aid meant more U.S. leverage on Israeli policy. In the twenty-five years of Israel's existence, the U.S. government had supplied it with $3 billion in grants and credits. Now the United States was considering giving *$8 billion* to the desperate Israelis over the next four years.

Henry Kissinger boarded a plane in December of 1973 for the first of his famous "shuttles" to the Middle East. His immediate goal was to see that Israel, Egypt,

A Palestinian boy registers his rejection of a U.S. settlement. His wall-painting reads 'No to the Peace Resolution'

Syria and Jordan showed up at the U.S. - and Soviet-sponsored Geneva peace talks to begin discussing a settlement. The talks adjourned after only laying the groundwork for mutual troop withdrawals. The adjournment left Kissinger free to pursue his long-term strategy of "step-by-step diplomacy," dividing the Arab countries by holding separate negotiations between each of them and Israel.

Kissinger's strategy had a fatal weakness; it ignored the Palestinians. He and his advisers had worried about them before the Geneva conference. One Washington diplomat warned:

> One thing we can't afford to do is to let the Palestinians come between us and the Arab governments at the peace table.[8]

The Palestinians understood that Kissinger planned to make peace at their expense. While the Arab states fought for limited gains in the October War, Palestinian organizations had called for a people's war against Zionism. They had argued at the OPEC meetings for the use of the "oil weapon." The Palestine National Front had successfully organized a strike among Arabs working in Israeli industries, paralyzing key sectors like construction. Once again the Palestinians alone had stood firmly against Israel and the United States and their long-term plans for the area. The Palestinians were not prepared now to sacrifice their revolution for the narrow interests of the Arab heads of state.

144

A Palestinian National Authority

In the months after the October War, Palestinian organizations had to confront the possibility of a peace settlement that would turn the West Bank and Gaza over to the harsh rule of King Hussein of Jordan. After much struggle and discussion, Fatah, the Democratic Front and other groups developed a strategy to guide the revolution through this difficult period.[9] The PLO would call for the establishment of its own "national authority" — a Palestinian government — on any Palestinian land liberated from Israeli occupation. The PLO rejected Hussein's claim to the occupied territories. At the same time, the PLO would begin a diplomatic offensive to gain recognition as the "sole legitimate representative of the Palestinian people." The PLO could not allow Hussein or other Arab leaders to speak in the name of the Palestinians.

During the winter and spring before the Palestine National Council meeting, Palestinian leaders held meetings in the camps and cities to debate with people the pros and cons of setting up a national authority. The Palestine National Front and most of the people of the occupied territories, whose future was immediately at stake, endorsed the plan. Other Palestinians, especially refugees whose original homes in Palestine were inside Israel, feared that accepting a national authority in the territories might mean abandoning the long-range goal of establishing a democratic secular state in *all* of Palestine. PLO leaders insisted in many stormy debates that the acceptance of a national authority would only be a step in the total liberation of Palestine. But, they argued, it was an absolutely necessary step to take at this point to advance the revolution.

The Popular Front for the Liberation of Palestine emphasized the dangers of accepting the national authority. Its leaders argued that a national authority could only be granted in the context of an imperialist settlement, the kind of settlement likely to emerge from the Geneva Conference. Such a settlement would require the Palestinians to recognize the state of Israel and drop their long-term goal. The national authority might well end up as a demilitarized state, sandwiched between Israel and Jordan, rather than a base for carrying on the revolution. The Popular Front called for the PLO to reject the Geneva Conference and any settlement that might come out of it. In the months ahead it united with other groups to form the "Rejection Front" which opposed the PLO's going to Geneva.

Most PLO leaders argued that the PLO should not refuse in advance to go to a conference to which it was not even invited. Such refusal would just play into the hands of its enemies, who would offer to represent the Palestinians. The task for the movement was to ensure that only the PLO represented the Palestinian people at Geneva or elsewhere. The PLO had to define what kind of national authority it would accept and struggle to win it at any conference. Only in this way could the PLO avoid the traps laid by the enemies of the Palestinian people.

At the twelfth Palestine National Council meeting in June of 1974, all the resistance groups united to pass a ten-point program. It called for the creation of a "fighting national authority" on any Palestinian territory liberated from Israel and emphasized the PLO's commitment to the total liberation of Palestine. The PLO declared that it alone represented the Palestinian people, including those in the West Bank and Gaza.

No sooner had the National Council adjourned, than King Hussein challenged the PLO. He claimed to represent the million Palestinians living in Jordan and the half-million living in the West Bank. He demanded that Israel return the West Bank to Jordan in any peace settlement. Sadat of Egypt and King Feisal of Saudi Arabia backed Hussein. They knew that Israel would accept Jordan as a neighbor, but had sworn never to negotiate with the PLO.

Recognize the PLO!

In October of 1974 an Arab Summit Conference met in Rabat, Morocco. On the agenda was the question of who should represent the Palestinian people in any possible peace negotiations. On the eve of the conference, Yasser Arafat received a manifesto smuggled out of the occupied territories. The manifesto, signed by one hundred eighty leading Palestinian figures, proclaimed that the PLO, not Hussein, was the "sole legitimate representative of the Palestinian people." Given this development, Sadat and Feisal could not make their move to undercut the PLO. The Rabat Conference declared the PLO the "sole legitimate representative" of the Palestinians. Progressive and right-wing Arab leaders combined to present a motion to the United Nations, asking that the PLO be invited to address the UN General Assembly. The General Assembly issued an invitation.

On November 13, 1974, Yasser Arafat stood before the United Nations General Assembly as a representative of the Palestinian people. His speech had been hammered out by all forces in the resistance movement. He carefully reviewed the history of the exile of the Palestinian people and compared it to the histories of other peoples — especially Africans in Rhodesia, Southwest Africa and South Africa — who had fought for so many years against the oppression of their people by European settlers and Western corporations.

In the audience were delegates from many countries which had won their own independence in wars of national liberation. Arafat explained the goal of the democratic secular state and its roots in Palestinian history. He called on all Jews living in the state of Israel to join with the Palestinians in building a just society free of racism and discrimination. He ended by saying:

> I am a rebel and freedom is my cause. I know well that many of you present here today once stood in exactly the same adversary position I now occupy and from which I must fight. You were once obligated by your struggle to convert dreams into reality. Therefore, you must now share my dream .... Today I have come bearing an olive branch and a freedom fighter's gun. Do not let the olive branch fall from my hand.[10]

The countries of the United Nations voted one hundred five to four to recognize the right of the Palestinian people to self-determination and to grant the PLO observer status at the United Nations. Only Israel, the United States, Bolivia and the Dominican Republic voted against the resolution.

In a wave of demonstrations and strikes coordinated by the Palestine National Front to coincide with the UN deliberations, the people of the West Bank poured

146

Yasser Arafat addresses the United Nations, November 1974.

into the streets for ten days of defiance of Israeli occupation. The slogans of the insurrection clearly reflected the desires of Palestinians under occupation: "No to the Zionist occupation! No to the return of the West Bank to Jordan! Yes to the PLO — the sole legitimate representative of the Palestinian people!"

Shortly after the PLO won this diplomatic and political victory, its enemies launched new assaults against it. Smoldering conflict in Lebanon broke out into the open when the Phalangists, a right-wing Lebanese group which opposed the Palestinian presence in Lebanon, attacked a bus full of Palestinians and killed twenty-six people in April of 1975. The resistance organizations fought back against the Phalangists. The battles escalated into a war that soon engulfed all of Lebanon.

While the Palestinians and Syria were preoccupied with the fighting in Lebanon, Kissinger mounted a final, concerted drive for a settlement between Egypt and Israel. In September of 1975 Egypt and Israel signed the Sinai Accords. Under this plan Israel returned part of the Sinai to Egypt. In exchange for its territory, Egypt signed a series of non-aggression pledges. Israel's public reward was a $2.2 billion aid package from the United States, which would be renewed each year. The package included the delivery of F-16 fighter planes which were capable of carrying nuclear warheads. Newspapers later revealed Kissinger's private assurances to Israel: the United States agreed not to pressure Israel to negotiate with Syria or the PLO.

For its part, Egypt received a half-billion dollars from the United States. In signing the accords, Egypt accepted the presence of U.S. "technicians" in the Sinai passes to guarantee the treaty. The Palestinians immediately understood the immensity of Sadat's betrayal. With one stroke of the pen he had withdrawn Egypt from the "confrontation states" with Israel, leaving Syria and the Palestinians isolated. He had allowed American personnel to be stationed on Arab land, and he undermined the Arab unity against Zionism which had been built over the previous thirty years — one of the strongest weapons the Arabs had to offset the immense military might of the United States and Israel.

The PLO broadcast that Egypt had passed the "keys of war and peace" to Israel and the United States. Under attack militarily in Lebanon and politically in Egypt, the Palestinians had to rely increasingly on their own strength. While resistance fighters shouldered their guns in Lebanon, Palestinians in the occupied territories and inside Israel itself took up the struggle with a new intenstiy.

Footnotes

1. *Mid East Report,* 21 June 1970, cited by Freed, *War in the Mid East,* p. 98.
2. MERIP staff, "Open Door in the Middle East," *MERIP* no. 31, p. 5.
3. *Christian Science Monitor,* 20 August 1973, cited by Barry Rubin, "U.S. Policy January - October 1973," *Journal of Palestine Studies,* vol. 3, no. 2 (Winter 1974), p. 102.
4. John Galvani, Peter Johnson and Rene Theberge, "The October War: Egypt, Syria, Israel," *MERIP* no. 22, p. 20.
5. Ibid., p. 14.
6. *New York Times,* 1 November 1973, cited in *MERIP* no. 31, p. 6.
7. For a general source on the effects of the oil embargo see Michael Tanzer, *The Energy Crisis* (New York: 1974).
8. *Washington Post,* 29 October 1973, cited in *MERIP* no. 31, p. 6.
9. For a general source on the debate in the resistance movement see *Palestinian Leaders Discuss: New Challenges for the Resistance* (Beirut: 1973).
10. Yasser Arafat, *Palestine Lives! (San Francisco: 1976), pp. 20-21.*

17: Our Roots Are Still Alive

This village belongs to Palestine, not to Israel!
—Chant of Palestinian demonstrators

Israeli authorities hoped that the West Bank demonstrations during Arafat's visit to the United Nations were isolated events. West Bank Palestinians shattered those hopes throughout 1975. Despite harsh Israeli bans on any kind of demonstration, people took to the streets to protest attacks on Palestinians in Lebanon and to march against the Sinai Accords. In small groups and in large rallies, they showed their support for the PLO before being quickly dispersed by Israeli troops. At night they put up posters and painted pro-PLO slogans on the walls. What Israeli leaders had feared for years was beginning to happen: the Palestine National Front was providing an organized link between Palestinians in exile and Palestinians under occupation.

The Israelis used all the devices of military occupation to stop the Front's activities. They conducted random searches of homes and arrested large numbers of West Bankers on suspicion of being Front members. Harsh questioning gave way to

149

Palestinian women pack Gaza oranges in crates marked 'Product of Israel'.

torture as the occupiers tried to learn about and destroy the cells of the Front. Suspects faced long prison terms and expulsion from the territories if they were just *accused* of hostile acts.[1]

It did not take much to prompt the occupation troops to action. One day in the West Bank town of Bireh, Israeli soldiers stormed into the city hall. They tore an exhibit of Palestinian folklore off the wall and buried it in a cellar. Any resurgence of Palestinian culture was considered threatening to Israel's ability to control its colonies. Moshe Dayan, on reading a poem by Fadwa Toquan, a woman poet from occupied Nablus, exclaimed, "This poem is more dangerous than twenty commandos!"

The Palestine National Front encouraged a wide range of cultural resistance. The poems of Toquan, who was a descendant of the famous poet of the 1936 Rebellion, appeared in the pages of *Falastin,* the underground newspaper of the Front. A nod to an Arab newsboy in Jerusalem got the buyer a copy of this paper stuffed between the pages of an Arabic daily. The Front's theatre groups hastily set up makeshift stages and performed in small villages in the West Bank. On weekend nights in Jerusalem, teenagers gathered for the usual parties, but they sang new songs about the liberation of Palestine. The Israeli repression could not stop all these visible acts of resistance.

Squeezing Blood from a Stone

Israel's economic policies in the occupied territories were generating resistance much faster than Israel's police or military could possibly discover and destroy it. Israel had been extracting wealth from the territories since the first days of occupation. The West Bank and Gaza were already second only to the United States as a market for Israeli goods. Many people in the occupied territories were unemployed or served as cheap labor for Israeli industries. Palestinians got only one-half the wages paid to a Jewish worker and none of the unemployment insurance, health insurance or sick leave that Jewish workers received. By not paying these benefits to Palestinian workers, Israel's industries saved an estimated $260 million between 1968 and 1974.[2]

The jobs that were open to the Palestinians were among the hardest and dirtiest — jobs that many Israelis did not want. Thus, the half of all Palestinian wage-earners in the territories who traveled every day by bus to Israel worked as cooks, factory workers, dishwashers, laborers, construction workers or agricultural workers on the kibbutzim. At the end of the day they returned by bus to the West Bank or Gaza, forbidden by law to remain overnight in Israel.

Palestinians who had received a university education or were professionals or highly skilled found no place to use their training in the territories or inside Israel. The Israelis encouraged such people to emigrate. An average of forty thousand Palestinians left the West Bank and Gaza each year, some as a result of expulsion, others to look for work elsewhere. Many found jobs as engineers and technicians in the oil-producing countries of the Arabian Gulf. From there they sent money back to their familes.

Whether breadwinners went to Israel each day or to another country to earn their wages, by 1973 their incomes could barely match the growing needs of their families. Despite this, the Israeli government tried to squeeze even more from the Palestinians to help Israel survive its post-October War financial crisis. Israel levied new taxes on the already hard-pressed Arab businesses, and increased old taxes at a steady rate. It ended subsidies for basic foods, and raised the price of other Israeli goods. But such moves were like trying to get blood out of a stone. Rising prices put more and more essential items out of the reach of Palestinians, especially those with large families. Lagging Israeli industries began to lay off Palestinian workers. With their husbands laid off, some Palestinian women managed to find even lower-paying jobs in new factories in the Gaza Strip. There they packaged oranges grown by Gaza farmers into cartons marked "Products of Israel."

The Palestine National Front responded to this growing nightmare by calling for an immediate end to the Israeli occupation. Front organizers explained that there could be no stopping the constant economic, military and cultural attacks until the Palestinians had their independence. Neither Israel nor Hussein could solve the Palestinians' problems.

Palestinians answered the Front's call with a series of strikes and demonstrations demanding independence. In November of 1975 demonstrators in the West Bank cities of Hebron, Halhoul and Jerusalem marked the anniversary of the PLO appearance at the United Nations by piling rocks in the road to keep out Israeli patrols. Carrying Palestinian flags and chanting slogans calling for independence and denouncing the Israeli occupation and King Hussein, demonstrators blocked the road to the al-Amari refugee camp in the West Bank. Throughout the West Bank Palestinian flags flew from the top of mosques or hung from windows. Although Israeli troops patrolled Nablus and Ramallah all night, each morning soldiers found new slogans painted on the walls. One slogan appeared again and again: "Long Live the PLO!"

That same month the PLO took the case of the Palestinians to the United Nations once again. The General Assembly passed three resolutions, including one

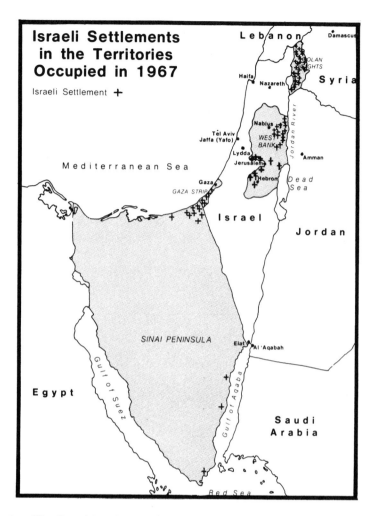

Israeli Settlements in the Territories Occupied in 1967

Israeli Settlement +

Damascus

Lebanon

GOLAN HEIGHTS

Syria

Haifa

Nazareth

Nablus

WEST BANK

Jordan River

Tel Aviv
Jaffa (Yafo)

Lydda

Jerusalem

Amman

Mediterranean Sea

Dead Sea

Gaza

GAZA STRIP

Hebron

Israel

Jordan

SINAI PENINSULA

Elat

Al 'Aqabah

Gulf of Suez

Egypt

Gulf of Aqaba

Saudi Arabia

Red Sea

which insisted that the "inalienable right of the Palestinian people to self-determination" be the basis for any future negotiations on the Middle East. Western media barely mentioned this resolution as they mounted a savage attack on the resolution which rightfully called Zionism a form of racism. Israel responded to these UN resolutions by bombing Palestinian refugee camps in southern Lebanon, killing ninety-two people. The U.S. government stood almost alone in defense of Israel in the United Nations. It cast a lone veto in the Security Council against a resolution affirming the national rights of the Palestinians on January 26, 1976.

No to the Occupation!

As news of the U.S. veto came over West Bank radios, students from three Nablus high schools charged out of their classrooms, chanting slogans in support of the PLO and against the United States. Joined by workers who had received leaflets predicting the veto on their way to work, the demonstrators converged in the casbah, the ancient center of Nablus — largest town in the West Bank. Running

152

through the maze of alleyways, they kept Israeli soldiers at bay. Ramallah, Jerusalem and Bireh followed the lead of Nablus. This wave of demonstrations lasted for three months and shattered all Israeli illusions that the West Bank would not fight occupation.

Major targets of the demonstrations were the new Zionist settlements in the West Bank. Since the beginning of the occupation, the Israeli government had been illegally building new Jewish settlements in the territories. An Israeli official told Terrence Smith in a May 1976 *New York Times* interview:

Look at the chain of settlements on a map and you will see what we intend to be the future borders of Israel.

Palestinians knew that these settlements threatened the future independence of the West Bank.

On March 7 Palestinian students in a Nablus schoolyard held a peaceful demonstration against the nearby settlement of Kadum. Israeli soldiers burst into the courtyard, pursued students into classrooms and beat them brutally. The people of Nablus went out on strike and the entire municipal council resigned. Surrounding villages joined the fighting.

When the demonstrations did not cease, Israeli troops began to shoot to kill. The first casualty was an eleven-year-old boy, Ali Husain al Sana, killed in a suburb of Jerusalem. At his funeral crowds followed his coffin carrying olive branches and flowers. Over and over again the crowd chanted "Abu Ammar," the code name of PLO leader Yasser Arafat. Palestinians in Jerusalem observed a general strike. Israeli tanks moved in to surround the city, but they could not enter the Old City. A leader of the Palestine National Front explained why:

These demonstrations reached their peak with the massive resistance in Jerusalem with students and people throwing stones and firebombs and fire torches at the Israeli soldiers. The Old City was totally controlled by the Palestinian patriots and no Israeli soldiers were able to enter it. When they tried to enter the women and children would throw flower pots and hot water and hot oil on them in the narrow streets.[3]

In the spring of 1976 a new Palestinian force joined the fight against Israel. For the first time since the creation of the Jewish state, the Palestinian population of the Galilee — the Palestinians who live *inside* Israel and are Israeli citizens — responded to their oppression in the same way as Palestinians in the territories, with prolonged strikes and demonstrations.

Trouble had been brewing in the Galilee for some time. Seventy percent of all Palestinians in Israel lived there. David Ben-Gurion once said, "Whoever tours the Galilee gets the feeling that it is not part of Israel."[4] In the eyes of Israeli leaders, it had too many Arabs and not enough Jews. According to a publication of the Ministry of Agriculture:

It is necessary to change the existing situation regarding the demographic ratio between the Jewish population and the non-Jewish, by means of implementing a long-term development program.[5]

A "development program" meant more land confiscation. The state set out to

"Judaize" the area by building new Jewish settlements, like the industrial town of upper Nazareth, on Arab land. Israel's planners assumed that years of repression and the cooperation of local Arab leaders loyal to Israel would prevent any protest by Israel's Arabs. They were wrong. In December of 1975 the people of Nazareth, the largest town in the Galilee, elected Tawfiq Zayyad as their mayor. Zayyad, a member of Rakah, the Israeli Communist Party, ran on a program calling for an end to discrimination against Palestinians and an end to land confiscation.

Israeli government officials went all out to stop his election. They offered the people of Nazareth the return of some land if Zayyad was not elected. They made veiled threats against his life. Moshe Barain, the Minister of the Interior, said, "the people of Nazareth must not imagine that the state of Israel would allow the town administration to fall into the hands of an admitted agent of Arafat."[6] But for most people both the threats and the promises had a hollow ring.

Nazareth had no industries, no public library, no social services. A majority of its inhabitants, like those of the occupied territories, left their town every day to work in menial jobs in Israeli industry. From their windows many could see land they once farmed. Now as "non-Jews" they could not live on, rent, or even be employed on land that had belonged to their families for generations. They were ready to resist. A poem written by Zayyad several years before, called "We Shall Remain," expressed the new spirit of resistance among Palestinians living inside Israel:

> It is a thousand times easier
> For you
> To pass an elephant through the needle's eye
> To catch fried fish in the milky way
> To plow the sea
> To teach the alligator speech
> A thousand times easier
> Than smothering with your oppression
> The spark of an idea.
>
> Here we shall remain
> A wall on your chests.
> We wash dishes in the hotel
> And serve drinks to the masters.
> We mop the floors in the dark kitchens
> To extract a piece of bread
> From your blue teeth
> For the little ones.
>
> Here we shall remain
> A wall on your chests
> We starve,
> Go naked,
> Sing songs
> And fill the streets
> With demonstrations
> And the jails with pride.

154

Palestinians in the Galilee applaud a speech by Tawfiq Zayyad

The Day of the Land

Palestinians in Israel showed their anger and determination in March of 1976. The Committee for the Defense of the Land, in which Zayyad and his party played an important role, organized a one-day general strike called "Land Day" among Palestinians in Israel to protest the continued seizure of Palestinian land for Jewish settlement and industry. Israeli leaders frantically called on loyal Arab notables to oppose the strike. Any who did were confronted by angry villagers. Strikers burned the car of the mayor of Tamra because he opposed the strike.

The strike on Land Day was, according to a British newspaper, "almost 100 percent effective in the Arab towns and villages."[7] Tens of thousands of Palestinians demonstrated. Their slogans were linked to the demands of Palestinians everywhere. In the villages of Sakhnin and Deir Hanna demonstrators surrounded police stations, hurled stones and Molotov cocktails and shouted, "Fatah, Fatah!" In Arraba young demonstrators barricaded the road with burning tires and chanted at the Israeli patrols, "This village belongs to Palestine, not to Israel!" The price for the

155

one-day strike was heavy. Israeli soldiers killed six Palestinians. But at their funeral, people marched with clenched fists, crying, "With spirit and blood we shall liberate the Galilee!"

After the Land Day strike was over, Israel Koenig, the Israeli Commissioner for the Galilee, penned the conclusion to a study entitled "Memorandum — Proposal: Handling the Arabs of Israel."[8] Koenig recognized that the effect of Land Day on Palestinians inside Israel had been to "infuse them with pride and straighten their backs." In a lengthy proposal he argued that Israel should use every method at its disposal to break this new Palestinian resistance. He recommended, among other things, that the Israeli government try to cut off support to large Palestinian families; that admission to college be made harder for Arabs; that new taxes be levied to reduce money available to support political parties; and that Arabs be encouraged to study abroad and stay there. He hoped such measures might reduce Palestinian resistance in the long run and drive even more Arabs from Israel.

As the uprisings in the West Bank and the strike on Land Day clearly showed, such attempts were doomed to failure. The Israelis had been using similar measures against Palestinians in Israel since 1948 and against those in the occupied territories since 1967. Rather than submit to their own slow destruction as a people, the Palestinians had resisted with all the means at their command. Israeli repression of the Palestinians raised a storm of international protest and Israel found itself more and more isolated and condemned. The Palestinians pledged to continue fighting Israel and supporting the PLO as their true representative.

Unable to break the strong ties between Palestinians inside Israel, within the occupied territories and in other Arab countries, Israel's only hope lay in crushing the last stronghold of the Palestinian resistance. Israel and its allies were trying to do just that in neighboring Lebanon, where civil war threatened to destroy the PLO and its last independent base in the Middle East.

Footnotes

1. For eyewitness accounts see Felicia Langer, *With My Own Eyes* (London: 1975).
2. Jamil Hilal, "Class Transformation in the West Bank and Gaza," *MERIP* no. 52, p. 11.
3. Interview with the Palestine National Front, *MERIP* no. 50, p. 20.
4. Cited by Tawfiq Zayyad, "The Fate of the Arabs in Israel," *Journal of Palestine Studies,* vol. 6, no. 1. (Autumn 1976), p. 97.
5. Cited in *MERIP* no. 47, p. 4.
6. Cited in *DFLP Report,* no. 13/14 (1976), p. 14.
7. *Manchester Guardian,* cited in *Palestine!* (New York), vol. 1, no. 2 (10 May 1976), p. 1.
8. Koenig Report excerpts reprinted in *MERIP* no. 51, pp. 11-14.

18: The Battle of Lebanon

We have survived hunger, thirst, and a total lack of medicines with a steadfastness which no one can paralyze or break. For we know that in defending our camp, we are defending our very existence — the life of our people, their will to exist, and their determination to struggle for their return to their homeland.

—Message from Tal al Zaatar

Palestinian fighters based in southern Lebanon had been staging raids into Israel since 1969. When Jordan expelled the fedayeen after Black September, Lebanon became the major base for the armed struggle against Israeli occupation. The Israelis dubbed the hilly border area of southern Lebanon "Fatahland" and launched hundreds of "punitive operations" against it in the early 1970s. A visiting journalist described the repeated bombings of one Lebanese village:

Rashaya Fuqhar, once a prosperous little village of two thousand Christian Arabs, is now nearly a ghost town. Known for its simple but striking brown and tan pottery, its kilns are now cold. In the past year, five villagers have been killed and over thirty wounded by Israeli air and artillery bombardment.

The pottery factory has been smashed by bombs. Scores of others have been damaged by shelling .... Only a hundred residents remain. A few of the villagers still farm, but most are afraid to because the fields are strafed.[1]

The Israelis thought their attacks would drive a wedge of hatred between the Lebanese and Palestinians. They were mistaken. The Lebanese peasants knew that Israel had designs on their land. Since the early days of the Zionist movement, its leaders had wanted to include southern Lebanon up to the Litani River inside the borders of a "Greater Israel." Rather than turn against the Palestinians, most Lebanese peasants demanded that the Lebanese army fight back against Israeli raids. The army never did. Only the fedayeen stood up to Israel. French journalist Eric Rouleau described the result:

Faced with the Lebanese army's failure, [Lebanese and Palestinians] see no choice but to unite in defense of their homes, their children, their lives. Through the years, the collective resistance has taken an organic form. Citizens have organized to defend the borders and population centers. The fedayeen, whose duty is to protect the refugee camps and the exclusively Palestinian quarters, also furnish arms and military instructors to the Lebanese militia ... [B]oth Lebanese and Palestinians consider themselves part of the "community of misery" ... [T]hey live in hatred of the Lebanese state, the army, the Maronite middle class, who are perceived as enemies.[2]

The Maronite middle class — bankers, businessmen, nightclub owners and professionals of the Maronite Catholic sect — had run the government and army of Lebanon for years. Groomed by the French, who took their fellow Christians under "protection" in the time of the Ottoman Empire, the Maronites gained their position of privilege during the French mandate in Lebanon. They served Europe loyally as traders and middlemen for French capital. They considered Moslem Arabs inferior and thought of themselves as more French than Arab. France rewarded them when Lebanon became independent in 1943 by setting up a political system based on "confessionalism" or religious differences. The Maronite Christians, who were half the population, received a majority of seats in the parliament and control of the army. The remaining seats and other positions in the government went to other religious sects, primarily Moslems, who made up the other half of the population.

A Society Divided

The creation of Israel in 1948 had a profound effect on Lebanon. When the Arab states organized the trade boycott against Israel, Lebanon suddenly received Palestine's historic shipping and banking business. It also gained more than a hundred thousand Palestinian refugees. The Maronites wanted the new business but despised the new immigrants, who threatened to upset the delicate balance between Christian and Moslem. Throughout the 1950s and 1960s Beirut's skyline became dominated by American business. Chase Manhattan, Bank of America, Holiday Inn, the oil companies and other corporations set up shop in this "neutral" financial oasis on the border of the Arab-Israeli conflict. The Maronites prospered in their role as middlemen. The government looked after their interests and kept the army out of the conflict with Israel.

Some of the first Palestinians to flee the Israeli attacks in 1948 settled in Beirut. Soon Palestinian refugee camps and slums ringed the city in what became known as the "belt of misery." Starting in the late 1960s, thousands of Lebanese poor joined them. Refugees from Israeli bombing in the south, farmers who had lost their land and unemployed workers from neglected and declining industries crowded into Beirut in search of work. There were few jobs for them except as maids, janitors and shoeshine boys. The government had done little to create jobs in the city, just as it had built few new roads or irrigation projects in the countryside to help the largely Moslem peasants. By 1975, six hundred thousand people were trying to survive in the belt of misery. The French journalist Rouleau described one slum:

> A nauseous stench rises from the numerous garbage heaps lining the narrow alley. Children with fly-covered faces wade in the muddy puddles .... [A] hut of rusted sheet-metal houses children, parents and grandparents. The squatters in this shanty town in the heart of Beirut are painfully aware of their abandonment. They have but to raise their eyes to contemplate the proud buildings with flower-painted verandas where wealthy Christians live.[3]

The belt of misery was quickly becoming a "belt of anger" directed at the Lebanese rich and their self-serving control of the Lebanese government. That anger was expressed in waves of strikes and demonstrations by Lebanese workers and students that began in the early 1970s and grew stronger by the year. They protested the failure of the Lebanese government to serve all the people of Lebanon, and they demanded an end to the privileges of the Maronites and the Western corporations.

The Palestinians acted as a sort of shield to protect the growing Lebanese movement from the army and began training militias of the progressive organizations to defend themselves. Such self-defense was an absolute necessity. For several years the right-wing businessmen and politicians had been organizing large private militias to use against the poor, in case the army did not prove strong enough. The journalist Rouleau described the training of one right-wing militia by a French mercenary who was so used to fighting guerrillas in Africa that he ordered his men into battle with the cry, "Let's go men, the niggers are over here."[4]

The growth of the progressive movement in Lebanon posed a serious threat to the power and privilege of the reactionaries who ruled Lebanon. By 1975, with the American and Arab drive for a general peace settlement in the Middle East, the Lebanese government and its supporters could count on U.S. backing for an offensive against the Palestinians. In January 1975, Pierre Gemayel, head of the right-wing Phalangists, demanded that the Lebanese army take action against the Palestinians in the south and in the cities. The Cedars Defense Front, called the "Lebanese Ku Klux Klan" by the left, covered Beirut walls with its racist slogans: "No to the Palestinian Resistance! No to the Arabs! No to foreigners! No to Communism!"[5]

In February fishermen in the port city of Sidon went out on strike. They had learned that the government had granted all fishing rights off Sidon to a company controlled by Christian rightists who reportedly had connections to the CIA. The government ordered the army into Sidon, where soldiers killed eleven strikers. Palestinians joined Lebanese in building barricades against the army and in blockading Beirut harbor in solidarity with the workers of Sidon. That same week,

Gemayel's right-wing Phalangists marched through Beirut chanting their praise of the army's actions and calling for the expulsion of the Palestinians from Lebanon.

After the Sidon demonstrations a slogan appeared all over the walls of Beirut: "Gemayel = Rabin = CIA." The Palestinians and Lebanese progressives knew that the Phalangists were acting in the interests of U.S. imperialism and the Zionists. The United States and Israel understood this too. As the conflicts between the Phalangists and the Lebanese-Palestinian alliance grew sharper, the United States sent G. McMurtrie Godley as its new ambassador to Lebanon. He was notorious for his CIA connections, having directed covert operations in Zaire, Cambodia and Laos. Godley's mission was to work with Lebanon's upper-class and right-wing militias to protect U.S. corporate interests in Lebanon.

Israel had been secretly supplying weapons and military training to the Lebanese rightists for several years. Israel, like the United States, wanted to see the Palestinians defeated in Lebanon — their last open stronghold. Israeli Prime Minister Yitzhak Rabin was frank about his strategy. When a reporter asked him why Israel failed to retaliate for a Fatah attack on a Tel Aviv hotel in April, Rabin replied, "We have chosen not to reply to this operation because we are planning on and waiting for a confessional [religious] war in Lebanon which would have the same result."[6]

Civil War: The Rich Against the Poor

The "confessional war" broke out a few days later when the Phalangists fired on a busload of Palestinians who were returning from a demonstration. Twenty-six Palestinians were killed. Fighting between Phalangists and Palestinians escalated. Soon a full-scale civil war between the Lebanese rightists and the newly formed Front of Progressive and Patriotic Parties and Forces engulfed Lebanon.

Although the Western media ignored the underlying class conflict and tried to portray the fighting as a "religious war," it clearly was not. The Lebanese Front, which included Moslems and Christians in its ranks, fought for an end to a government organized along religious lines. It wanted to create a democratic and secular state in Lebanon. It also demanded reforms in the army, better social services for the poor, more jobs and a living wage for all work. It firmly supported the Palestinians' presence in Lebanon. These demands horrified the rightists and their international backers. Besides the CIA, one of the major suppliers of arms to the largely Christian right wing was Saudi Arabia, the bastion of Moslem orthodoxy, which sent $200 million worth of aid. The Saudis understood that the war in Lebanon was not between religions, but between classes.

The fighting raged throughout 1975. Many thousands died from malaria and TB epidemics as well as from bullet wounds. The year ended without decisive victory for either side. Beirut was a burned-out city, its port and office buildings destroyed. The Lebanese Front and the Palestinians controlled western Beirut, and the rightists had the eastern half of the city. The Palestinian camps in the belt of misery blocked the right-wing forces from joining east Beirut to their mountain strongholds beyond the camps. Each side held parts of the rest of the country.

In January of 1976 the rightists launched a new offensive. They blockaded the

Destruction from rightist artillery in downtown Beirut.

Palestinian camp of Tal al Zaatar and overran the smaller camp of Dabaye, home of two hundred Christian Palestinians. Up to this point, the Palestinians had not thrown their full weight into the fighting. Now they did. By the spring, the forces of the Lebanese Front and the Palestinians controlled 80 percent of the country.

The prospect of a victory for the Palestinians and their Lebanese allies spurred Israel and the United States to more direct action. In March of 1976, Israeli ships began a blockade of the leftist-controlled ports of Sidon and Tyre, stopping ships bound for Lebanon with arms and supplies. Israel shipped massive amounts of its own U.S.-supplied ammunition and supplies, including heavy weapons like rockets and tanks, to the rightists.[7] The United States sent the helicopter carrier *Guadalcanal,* six other ships and seventeen hundred Marines to cruise off the Lebanese coast in April. They served as a grim reminder of the American Marine landing in Lebanon in 1958 on the side of the rightist government.

But none of these moves stopped the Palestinians and Lebanese. Both Israel and the United States were alarmed, and Israel threatened to intervene directly. However, neither Israel nor the United States could invade Lebanon without risking a wider war and a massive international outcry. Only another Arab country could get away with sending its troops into Lebanon. Hafez Assad, the President of Syria, was ready to do just that.

Assad had feared from the beginning of the war that Israel was going to use the threat of a Palestinian-Lebanese nationalist victory as an excuse to invade Lebanon and Syria. Assad did not want to see a strong and independent Palestinian movement or a radical Lebanon on his western border. He had never supported the

161

Syrian troops invade Lebanon, May 1976.

existence of an independent Palestinian movement outside the control of Arab governments. An independent PLO might block the chances of a peace settlement with Israel and the return of Syria's occupied Golan Heights. As commander of the Syrian Air Force in 1970, he had refused to give air cover to the Syrian tank column moving into Jordan to support the Palestinians during Black September.

A power struggle had followed, in which Assad staged a successful coup against his leftist opponents in Syria who strongly supported the Palestinians. He jailed his opponents and purged Saiqa, the Palestinian guerrilla organization sponsored by Syria, of its most independent members. Like Sadat of Egypt, once he was in power, Assad reversed many of the progressive economic policies and social reforms of his predecessors. In Lebanon, he wanted to see a "moderate" government and a humbled Palestinian movement that he could control.

When the Palestinian-Lebanese offensive was on the brink of victory in the spring of 1976, Assad decided to send his army into Lebanon — once he had American permission. In March King Hussein of Jordan visited Washington, D.C., and told Ford and Kissinger that Assad was ready to intervene on the side of the

162

rightists in Lebanon. This solved the American dilemma, and the United States agreed to restrain Israel from any counterattack. On May 31, tens of thousands of Syrian troops and hundreds of tanks crossed the border into Lebanon. The Syrian government, which had once been the consistent supporter of the Palestinian people, was now the powerful ally of the Lebanese rightists.

Assad expected an easy advance. But at Sidon, Aley and Sofar, united Lebanese and Palestinian troops stopped the Syrian tanks and drove back the infantry. The battles were fierce and bloody. One captured Syrian soldier who had fought against Israel in the October War said:

> Even on the Golan, I never experienced such fighting. Here, in Sidon, it was street fighting, very difficult. The war on the Golan was very much easier.[8]

Assad had not counted on such determined resistance. Palestinians encouraged the Syrian soldiers to mutiny. In the next months, most members of Saiqa — the Syrian-supported Palestinian guerrilla group — defected to other organizations in the PLO. With his troops stalled and Saiqa weakened, Assad sanctioned increasingly brutal attacks on Palestinian camps by the rightists. The Syrians themselves began shelling camps in June.

Tal al Zaatar Fought for the Revolution

Finally Syria approved an all-out rightist assault on the refugee camp of Tal al Zaatar. Located in the rightist section of Beirut, Tal al Zaatar had withstood months of attacks and a blockade of food and supplies. The Syrians and rightists thought the destruction of the camp would weaken and demoralize the Palestinian and Lebanese movements. The rightists laid siege to the camp on June 21, 1976. During the next fifty-three days, they poured thousands of artillery shells and rockets into Tal al Zaatar. They mounted over seventy attacks on the camp. They blocked all food and medical supplies from going in and refused to allow the Red Cross to carry away the wounded. Yet the people of Tal al Zaatar stood firm.

On July 13, the inhabitants of Tal al Zaatar smuggled out of the camp an open letter "to the people of the world." It was sent to a meeting in Cairo of Arab heads of state. In it, they described their situation, criticized Syria's role and asked for medical supplies:

> [W]e speak to you now ... not to obtain sympathy but from a position of heroic steadfastness which this camp has maintained for every moment of this long siege ....
>
> Our camp — which is now inhabited by around thirty thousand men, women, children and old people, about 40 percent of whom are poor Lebanese and the rest Palestinians — is today a scene of utter destruction. There is no water except the very little we can carry from the wells amidst the danger of shelling and death; no food except what we have been able to salvage from the wreckage of our homes; no electricity whatsoever, no medicines and no medical treatment ....
>
> Syrian weapons are being used — most unfortunately — against our camp, while the rulers of Damascus continue to repeat that they are here in Lebanon in order to defend our camp. This is a murderous lie, a lie which pains us more than anyone else....But we wish to inform you that we will fight in defense of

Refugees flee Tal al Zaatar.

this camp with our bare hands if all our ammunition is spent and all our weapons are gone, and that we will tighten our belts so that hunger will not kill us. For we have taken a decision not to surrender and we shall not surrender . . . .

We have survived hunger, thirst and a total lack of medicines, with a potential for steadfastness which no one can paralyze or break. For we know that in defending our camp, we are in fact defending our very existence, the life of our people, their will to exist, and their determination to struggle for their return to their homeland.[9]

The Arab states did not help the people of Tal al Zaatar, nor did they restrain Syria. Iraq and Algeria condemned the Syrian invasion, but Saudi Arabia sent more aid to the Assad government. International help for the Palestinians and Lebanese was blocked at the ports. The Soviet Union condemned the invasion, but took no steps to break the naval blockade or to pressure Syria, which it supplied with arms. Most arms and food for the Palestinian and Lebanese fighters came from PLO stockpiles in the south or were smuggled into Lebanon on small ships from Cyprus. Although only small amounts of it got into Lebanon, the aid that meant the most to Palestinians came from their brothers and sisters under Israeli occupation. West Bank Palestinians had demonstrated in June against the Syrian intervention in Lebanon. In July they managed to send several planeloads of medical supplies to Lebanon. But none of these desperately needed supplies could get through the blockade of Tal al Zaatar.

On August 13, after fifty-three days of unrelenting siege, the defenders of the camp let down their guard as the first Red Cross vehicles approached Tal al Zaatar with the permission of the rightists. The people of the camp believed that a final agreement between the Arab League and the International Red Cross to evacuate the camp had been reached. As the inhabitants of the camp began to leave their

164

shelters, they saw they had been betrayed: behind the Red Cross vehicles were the rightist troops! As soldiers overran the camp, they unleashed a bloody massacre, gunning down defenseless civilians, including medical personnel. The rightists deliberately killed every Palestinian male between the ages of fourteen and forty. Before the camp was totally overwhelmed by the attackers, thousands of people were forced to flee; over two thousand people were killed. The rightists razed Tal al Zaatar to the ground.

Rightists, Syrians and the American press all proclaimed that the fall of the camp signaled the beginning of the end for the Palestinians. But to every Palestinian and Lebanese fighting against the Syrian occupation and the rightist forces, Tal al Zaatar stood for something very different. One Fatah leader said, "It has become a torch for all those struggling for freedom in the Arab world."[10] The people of Tal al Zaatar, like Palestinians and Lebanese in the rest of the country, were determined to fight to the end. Fatah leader Abu Eyad explained why:

> We have nothing left to lose. We have burned our ships behind us. There is nothing but the sea in back of us. We have no choice. We cannot retreat, but they cannot exterminate us.[11]

The Syrian army encountered this grim determination wherever it fought. The Syrians were failing in their offensive to capture Sidon and Western Beirut. The war was now costing Syria a million dollars a day. Israel was taking advantage of the drawn-out war to encroach on southern Lebanon. And the PLO refused to replace Arafat with a pro-Syrian leadership as Assad demanded.

Finally, the Arab states decided they had to intervene. At the Riyadh Conference called by Saudi Arabia, Yasser Arafat and Hafez Assad sat down with delegates from the other countries in the Arab League to work out an agreement. The resulting "peace plan" gave the beleaguered Palestinians and their Lebanese allies a breathing spell. It reaffirmed the 1969 Cairo Accords which gave the Palestinians freedom of movement and their right to bear arms in Lebanon. Syria, on the other hand, expanded its occupation of Lebanon, under the cover of an "Arab peace-keeping force" which was paid for by the Arab states. The uneasy "peace" that settled on Lebanon brought Syrian troops into western Beirut. They oversaw the installation of a pro-Syrian Lebanese government led by Elias Sarkis. This government began censoring all pro-Palestinian and anti-government publications and closed down guerrilla offices.

Despite this repression, Lebanon had not become the graveyard of the Palestinian movement. Although twenty thousand Palestinians had died in the fighting, the PLO remained intact and independent of Syrian control. Palestinians were in control of the camps and held on to their heavy weapons. With the major fighting over, the PLO was able to hold the first meeting in three years of the Palestine National Council in Cairo. The Council reaffirmed the unity of the Palestinian and Lebanese peoples. Despite strong pressure from the Arab governments to change its position of non-recognition of Israel, the Council stated once again its opposition to the Zionist state and its commitment to building a democratic secular state in all of Palestine.

In the meantime, the Palestinians and Lebanese went about the difficult task of healing the many wounds of war and preparing for the likely battles ahead. A poster tacked on a wall in Damour, the village where the inhabitants of Tal al Zaatar had resettled, expressed the spirit in which the Palestinians and their allies would move forward. It read simply: "Tal al Zaatar is in our hearts until victory."

Footnotes

1. Judith Coburn, "Israel's Ugly Little War," *New Times*, 7 March 1975.
2. Eric Rouleau, "Civil War in Lebanon," *Le Monde* (Paris), 20-25 September 1975, reprinted in translation in SWASIA, Vol. 2, no. 41 (17 October 1975), pp. 5-6.
3. Ibid., p. 4.
4. Ibid., p. 2.
5. Ibid.
6. Al-Sha'ab, 12 April 1975, cited in DFLP Reports (Spring 1975), pp. 3-4.
7. *Time*, 13 September 1976, cited in "Why Syria Invaded Lebanon," *MERIP* no. 51, p. 5.
8. *Le Monde*, 15 June 1976, cited in *MERIP* no. 51, p. 4.
9. *Tal al Zaatar: The Fight Against Fascism* (Washington, D.C.: 1977), p. 7.
10. *SWASIA*, vol. 3, no. 32 (13 August 1976), p. 7.
11. *San Francisco Examiner*, This World, 25 July 1976.

Conclusion: Revolution Until Victory

You may take the last strip of our land
Feed my youth to prison cells
You may plunder my heritage
You may burn my books, my poems,
Or feed my flesh to the dogs
You may spread a web of terror
On the roofs of my village
O ENEMY OF THE SUN
But
I shall not compromise
And to the last pulse in my veins
I shall resist.

Throughout their history, the Palestinian people have endured countless attacks on their land and their lives, and they have resisted the many enemies who sought to conquer them. In this century, the Palestinians, like other Arab peoples, have fought for the right to nationhood—the right to determine their own future in

Palestine. In this era of national liberation, the fight of the Palestinians for their homeland is both just and irreversible. There can be no other solution to the problems facing the Palestinians. They are at the heart of the whole crisis in the Middle East. Until they gain their national rights, there will be no peace in the area.

The empires of the world have never accepted this fact. The British came to the Middle East at the close of the nineteenth century, looking for oil, stable colonies and a garrison near the Suez Canal. They deceived and betrayed the Arabs, especially the Palestinians. The British thought they could ignore or destroy the force of Palestinian nationalism. But despite betrayals by their traditional leaders, the Palestinian people continually fought for independence.

After World War II, the United States emerged as the most powerful imperialist country. It captured the lion's share of Middle Eastern oil—a vital resource for its expanding empire. The United States too opposed Palestinian nationalism, and used direct military intervention, massive arms aid and CIA-style covert activities to shore up conservative Arab governments and to protect American investments.

Both Britain and the United States supported the creation of a Zionist settler colony in Palestine as one way to extend their control in the Middle East and to safeguard their interests. The European Jewish settlers who came to colonize Palestine identified with their imperialist sponsors, and rapidly became enemies of the Palestinians. Zionism refused to admit the existence of the Palestinian people, let alone recognize the validity of their fight for nationhood.

In 1948, 1956 and 1967, Israel—with the support of Western powers—went to war against the Palestinian and Arab peoples. But these declared wars were only part of a larger war to crush the Palestinian nation. In the last thirty years, Israel destroyed several hundred Arab villages and expelled over one million Palestinian people Israeli and Western leaders were convinced that Israel's superior military power would easily crush the Palestinian movement and force the Arab states to recognize Israel's existence.

But Palestinian resistance has shattered the illusions of these twentieth century conquerors. The freedom fighters and demonstrators of today are part of an unbroken chain of resistance that reaches back to the beginning of the century and the Arab Revolt. The 1936-39 Palestinian rebellion shocked both British and Zionists with its strength and tenacity. The refusal of the Palestinians to forget and renounce their homeland after their expulsion in the 1948 War sabotaged the plans of Israel and the U.S. for the area. Today Palestinians who have never seen their homeland have joined with Palestinians under Israeli occupation in a massive resistance. They have also become a leading force in every Arab nationalist movement. Homeless, the Palestinians have been the fiercest advocates of independence and self-determination for all peoples in the Middle East.

In the early years of exile, Palestinians hoped that the Arab states would help them return to Palestine. But as the conservative nature of the Arab regimes became clear, these hopes soon faded. The struggles of Algeria, Vietnam and other African, Asian and Latin American nations taught them that success came through self-reliance and a total mobilization of all the people in the fight for victory. By the mid-1960s, the independent, armed Palestinian movement emerged, convinced that only the Palestinians themselves could lead their people out of exile, to return to the land that Israel occupied.

In their drive to return to their homeland, the Palestinians have seen Zionism and the state of Israel, not the Jewish people, as their enemy. The Palestinians and their representative organization, the PLO, recognize that any solution to the homelessness of their people has to include Israel's Jews. Only the creation of a democratic secular state in all of Palestine can provide a just and lasting solution for both Palestinians and Jews in the area. The PLO has pledged itself to the fight against all forms of racism and religious discrimination, including anti-Semitism and Zionism. It has made the crucial distinction between *anti-Zionism* and *anti-Semitism,* between opposition to the Zionist movement and racism against Jews—a distinction which the state of Israel has consistently tried to blur among its supporters.

Both the United States and Israel have opposed every step the Palestinians have taken toward their goal of a democratic secular state. Since the emergence of the fedayeen in the 1960s, the United States and Israel have been trying to either destroy the PLO or weaken it so much that it can be excluded from any role in U.S.-sponsored negotiations. In Israel's 1967 offensive against the Palestinians and the Arab states, in Jordan's Black September attack in 1970 and in the 1973 rightist attacks on the Palestinians in Lebanon, the allies of the United States tried to destroy the guerrilla movement. But each time they failed.

169

The U.S. Settlement

When Henry Kissinger launched the U.S. "peace offensive"—an attempt to impose a settlement on the area that would safeguard U.S. oil interests, protect Arab regimes friendly to the United States, give Israel secure borders and exclude the Palestinians—it floundered on the rock of Palestinian resistance. Once more the United States and its allies tried to destroy the Palestinian movement, this time in Lebanon—its last and strongest base outside the occupied territories. Once again they failed because ordinary people, like the inhabitants of Tal al Zaatar, performed extraordinary deeds, refusing to surrender even against impossible odds. They failed also because Lebanese and Palestinians stood together in an alliance that could not be shattered—the kind of alliance that will continue to be forged between the Palestinians and other Arab peoples who have a common interest in fighting imperialist domination.

The latest U.S. proposals for a Middle East settlement that excludes the Palestinians or by-passes the PLO are also doomed to failure. President Carter endorses the vague notion of a Palestinian "homeland" federated with Jordan, on condition that the PLO renounce its goal of a democratic secular state in Palestine. In seeming contradiction, the new rightist Israeli government of Menahem Begin refuses outright to consider any negotiation with the PLO under any circumstances. Yet in essence, the United States and Israel agree: neither is willing to recognize the right of the Palestinian people to self-determination in their homeland, free of the racism and religious discrimination of the Jewish state. In fact, neither the Israeli nor the U.S. government wants a just and lasting peace in the area. In this intransigence lie the seeds of the fifth Arab-Israeli war.

History has shown us that there cannot be a stalemate in the Middle East for long. In the absence of genuine peace, the pressures build for war. Expansionist Israel threatens intervention in southern Lebanon and the new Begin government calls the occupied West Bank "liberated" Israeli land. The governments of Egypt and Syria are under tremendous popular pressure to recover their lands which Israel occupies. If the Arab countries cannot regain these through settlement, war will be their only option. A new Arab-Israeli war, once begun, could easily lead to U.S. military intervention and a confrontation between the United States and the Soviet Union, with dangerous consequences for the whole world.

The only real alternative to another war is the political solution of the underlying conflict that has beset the region for decades. Since the early days of the mandate period, the Palestinian people have fought for the right to self-determination in their homeland. In the last decade the PLO—the representative voice of the Palestinian people—has had great success in gaining recognition and support from progressive people around the world, winning them to the goal of a democratic secular state. Each year the Palestinians have found new friends and allies, while Israel has become increasingly isolated.

A graphic example of this process is now unfolding in southern Africa. While the PLO builds stronger ties with the African guerrillas fighting for majority rule, Israel strengthens its links through trade and arms sales with the apartheid regime of South Africa. Israel's growing isolation and increasing economic and political crises force it to rely more and more on the United States for political and economic support. But U.S. imperialism has itself been weakened around the world, following its defeat in Indochina and setbacks to its allies in southern Africa. As a result, more people in the United States are opposing their government's support of racist and reactionary regimes. A growing number of Americans are coming to understand that the state of Israel is such a regime.

The PLO has called on the people of the world, and the American people in particular, to examine for themselves the history of the Palestinians and Israel—a history that has been distorted and buried in this country. The Palestinians believe that people who learn their story will understand that only an end to religious and racial discrimination and the establishment of a democratic secular state in Palestine can provide a long-term solution to this bitter conflict. The PLO asks the American people to insist that their government recognize the PLO as the representative of the Palestinian people, and urges all Americans to take action against U.S. support of Israel and the right-wing Arab states.

In his 1974 address to the United Nations, Yasser Arafat called on the American people and the international community to join with the Palestinian people in their struggle for a just and lasting peace in the Middle East. He knew that the road would be long and hard, and that it would not be simple to heal the divisions that have plagued Palestine in this century. But he appealed to all those who have fought for freedom and against bigotry and discrimination to share with him and his people the dream of a peaceful future. Describing the harassment and imprisonment of a

Children in New York demonstrate in solidarity with Palestine, 1976.

Christian priest and a Jewish revolutionary inside Israel who had supported the Palestinians, he said:

> Why therefore should I not dream and hope? For is not revolution the making real of dreams and hopes? So let us work together that my dream may be fulfilled, that I should return with my people out of exile, there in Palestine to live with this Jewish freedom fighter and his partners, with this Arab priest and his brothers, in one democratic state where Christian, Jew and Moslem live in justice, equality and fraternity."

Postscript: "We Shall Never Forget Palestine"

In May 1977, one of the authors traveled with a small group of Americans to Lebanon and the occupied territories. One purpose of the trip was to see the effect of the Lebanese civil war on the strength and morale of the Palestinian people. As the following excerpts from her journal indicate, the Palestinians emerged from the fighting more determined than ever to create a democratic secular state in their homeland.

Damour, Lebanon

A tattered banner hangs over the main street of Damour, the temporary home of eighteen thousand refugees from Tal al Zaatar. It reads: "Karameh taught us courage." To the survivors of Tal al Zaatar, the meaning is clear—the defense of their camp was, like the battle of Karameh in 1968, a turning point, an event that strengthened and deepened the roots of the Palestinian revolution. Such an understanding helps people face their bitter memories and their personal losses.

Most people in Damour lost more than one family member at Tal al Zaatar. Zeinah Qassem, for example, lost her father and two brothers. She is seventeen years old and fought at Tal al Zaatar in the bloody battles on the outskirts of the camp. On the last day, she escaped into the mountains, living for six days without food or water before she reached Damour. Her eyes flashing, Zeinah explains the lesson of Tal al Zaatar: "The enemy won't destroy the people. We will never forget Palestine! The revolution did not begin in Tal al Zaatar to end in Tal al Zaatar."

Zeinah today is chief of military training in Damour for the Ashbals, children between the ages of seven and fourteen. She is typical of the teenagers who have shouldered many responsibilities in Damour—since many of the older men died in the massacre on the last day. Zeinah belongs to a generation of Palestinians that has emerged from the harsh fighting in Lebanon determined to build a peaceful future in Palestine for its children.

We hesitate at first to probe the grim memories of the siege and massacre of Tal al Zaatar. But people dispel our awkwardness quickly, telling us affectionately of the special heroisms or sufferings of their friends. At a party, Zeinah disappears to return with a special food from Zaatar—a dip of oil and thyme. Tal al Zaatar means "hill of thyme." Ahmed, a slender twelve-year-old boy with large brown eyes, who was born in Tal al Zaatar, spends an hour drawing an exact picture of the camp in my notebook. He exclaims, "Next to Palestine, I love Tal al Zaatar!" In these small ways, people continue to affirm that they have not forgotten their homes. For these children and thousands of other Palestinians, Tal al Zaatar has become not a painful memory, but a symbol of revolution.

Southern Lebanon

According to the Palestinian fighters, Israel's involvement in southern Lebanon has increased dramatically since the end of the civil war. As we walk through the almost deserted Lebanese village of Taibe—deserted because of heavy shelling from

Palestinian guerrillas in southern Lebanon. The youngest, 13-year-old Ahmed, lost all his family at Tal al Zaatar.

the Lebanese rightists—we see the remnants of the recent rightist occupation of Taibe, including Israeli ammunition, food tins and weapons. All supplies for the rightists come across the Israeli border, but Israeli help extends beyond supplies. At a Palestinian artillery position along the main supply road from Israel, we watch as shells are fired from Metulla, an Israeli settlement in the upper Galilee.

Abu Jihad, the head of Fatah's military operations, analyzes Israeli involvement as an attempt to keep Lebanon unstable and to accomplish what the rightists failed to do in the civil war—the destruction of the Palestinians in their last base of operations. He tells us of continued warnings from Israeli sources that Israel will invade southern Lebanon if the Palestinian presence remains strong.

But among Palestinians fighting in the south, despite the grim threat of all-out war and the obvious military superiority of the Israelis, we find an optimism about

174

the strength of the revolution that matches the spirit of Damour. Sitting in a bunker, safe from the shelling going on outside, we talk to the fighters in one battalion stationed only a few miles from the Israeli border. "From up there, I can see Palestine!" an eighteen-year-old guerrilla tells us excitedly. Most of the battalion participated in the war in Lebanon and feel that it was "a war to destroy us, a dirty war." The youngest member, thirteen-year-old Amid, lost his entire family at Tal al Zaatar. They explain that the situation is different in the south from the way it was during the civil war. Here they are directly facing their real enemy—Zionism—and they are succeeding in their objectives. They have stopped many supplies from Israel and recently re-captured a series of strategic towns from the rightists. "Here we are on the frontlines," said the head of the unit, who had survived six years of prison and torture in Jordan after Black September. "We will never leave our position unless Abu Ammar [Yasser Arafat] personally tells us to go."

The dangers of this frontline position are made real to us when Abu Harb, another fighter, shows us a picture of his best friend who was killed only three weeks ago in the battle of Taibe. But Abu Harb too becomes happy as his friends urge him to lead the singing. He is the battalion poet, quick to compose heroic and humorous verse to suit the occasion. One of his refrains is very popular with everyone: "We are the liberation army. We don't kill by the identity card." The song refers to the rightists' practice of killing people who possess either a Palestinian "green card" or an identity card identifying them as Moslem. This song leads into an animated discussion of the democratic secular state. The religious discrimination of the Lebanese right has added a particular intensity to the fighters' desire to establish in Palestine a state free of racism and religious conflict.

When the fighters learn that we are going to the occupied territories, they besiege us with requests and sightseeing tips. There are shy individual requests to go to a certain street in Nablus, a certain orchard in Jaffa, or to watch the sun set on the Jerusalem hills. All of them join in sending their courage and love to their "brothers and sisters in occupied Palestine." "For you know," these frontline troops tell us, "it is they who have the hardest struggle."

The West Bank

We are standing in a Ramallah street, watching Palestinian schoolgirls in blue-checkered pinafores build a roadblock to halt the Israeli soldiers who constantly patrol the troubled West Bank. The schoolgirls are eleven and twelve years old. It is common for children to participate in and even lead demonstrations, and they will be arrested and fined heavily if caught.

The election of the rightist Menahem Begin as Prime Minister of Israel, and his pledge to increase Israeli settlements around population centers like Ramallah, can only lead to an upsurge in both resistance and the already harsh repression. In talking with West Bank Palestinians, we hear again and again of a pattern of constant Israeli harassment of Palestinians in the West Bank and Gaza—a man forced to sit in the rain for two hours; a young teacher tortured for two months and then released without trial. Abu Saleh, a forty-five-year-old shoe repairman from Jerusalem, tells us a typical story of Palestinian resistance. He spent two years in prison after Israeli soldiers arrested him at a friend's house where they had found literature from the Palestine National Front. Abu Saleh was tortured—forced to stand naked between two space heaters during questioning until his flesh blistered.

Fatima, 18 year old fighter, in Nabatiye, Lebanon.

But in fact, he readily gave his "confession" without any torture when the Israelis first asked him if he belonged to the Palestine National Front. "No," Abu Saleh replied to his questioners, "I do not formally belong to the Front. But I am a Palestinian and therefore I do belong to the Front."

Arriving in Nazareth, the largest Arab town in Israel, we ask in broken Arabic at the gas station for Tawfiq Zayyad, the mayor of Nazareth, and a member of Rakah, the Israeli Communist Party. Our question brings a flood of excited conversation. We understand a few words—Tawfiq Zayyad has been shot during the night!

When we finally find him unharmed at his home, he tells us the real story. Thirty bullets from an Uzi machine gun raked his bedroom in the early hours of the morning. The shots, we speculate, are the outgrowth of a bitter campaign in the Galilee to persuade Palestinians in Israel, whether by threat or promise, not to vote for the Front—a coalition of Rakah, the Black Panthers (a group based among Oriental Jews) and independent Arab and Jewish figures. The Front stands for peace and for an end to Israeli occupation of Arab lands captured in 1967; it opposes annexation and confiscation of Arab land and fights racism in Israel. With these positions, it challenges all the other major political parties in Israel.

176

At a night rally in a small village outside Nazareth, we listen to Zayyad, joined by a Black Panther leader, addressing a large crowd which has gathered to show support for his campaign. Children press at the edge of the crowd; old people listen from their balconies. Zayyad's speech is not an electoral pep talk. Instead, for almost two hours, he traces a detailed and moving history of the Palestinian people "from the beginning to last night," as a man from the village tells us. Zayyad dwells on the same theme that has struck us so sharply in Lebanon and the West Bank: the endurance and determination of the Palestinian people. He reviews the many attempts of the Israelis to erase the Palestinian identity, and their clear failure to do so. A Rakah member who has lived in the village since 1948 tells us, "In 1956 four people voted for Rakah. In 1960 that number doubled. Today, we expect 1250 from our 1500 voters." Judging from the reaction of the crowd to Zayyad's speech, Palestinian resistance to Zionism is stronger than ever inside Israel.

Beirut, Lebanon

On the last day of our trip, we stand in the ruins of Tal al Zaatar, now in an area controlled and patrolled by rightists and Syrians. We can barely trace from Ahmed's careful drawing the location of his house or of the school. The physical reality of Tal al Zaatar has been bulldozed by the rightists into miles of concrete rubble. We begin to talk of one of the first families we met in Damour. For us, they represent the continuity and the spirit of the Palestinian revolution.

Ammar, the seventy-year-old grandfather who wears traditional Arab dress, fought with a World War I rifle in the 1936 revolt against the British. Mustafa, the stocky, barrel-chested father of the family, fought in the 1948 war and was driven out of Palestine with his family. They settled in southern Lebanon, but were forced to the north by the Israeli bombings in the 1960s. Mustafa lost his leg when the Lebanese army attacked the Palestinian camps in 1973. They moved to Tal al Zaatar, where Amina, the twenty-four-year-old daughter, became a nurse and militia member during the siege. The family survived the massacre and came to Damour. They tell us that the only acceptable and possible solution for them is to return to Palestine.

The United States government and the state of Israel oppose their return, as they have opposed it for almost forty years. Amina directs many pointed questions to us about the United States. She wants to know how we felt about the war in Vietnam, asking us if we would have fought in the war. We explain that we opposed the war. When we describe the American people's resistance to U.S. policy, the whole family listens eagerly. Amina smiles and claps her hands. "Down, down with the U.S. government!" she teaches us in Arabic. Mulling over what we said about American opposition to the war in Vietnam, Mustafa finally asks, "Why, then, do you elect presidents that support Israel?" We try to explain how the rich and the corporations and the Zionist movement—all with their interests in the Middle East—influence the American people and elections. Our explanations are received well, but we are left feeling the human reality that grows from these political facts.

After seeing the destruction of Palestinian camps in southern Lebanon by U.S.-supplied Phantom jets or the devastation of the civil war, it is a painful experience to face a people—and a family—which your government has tried to destroy. Yet these survivors of Tal al Zaatar do not blame us, saying clearly, "We do not find fault with the American people." Warda, Amina's fifteen-year-old neighbor, also

from Tal al Zaatar, touches my arm and tells me, "Probably the Americans do not know enough about our revolution. When you tell them, they will change their minds." We realize that simply telling the story of the Palestinians will not be enough. But we know that it is an important step.

Recommended Reading

Ibrahim Abu-Lughod, ed., *The Transformation of Palestine*. Contains the best article available in English on the 1948 war, "The Wordless Wish: From Citizens to Refugees," by Erskine Childers. Also contains excellent articles on the mandate period. Some of the better essays are reprinted in pamphlet form and are available from MERIP (see RESOURCES).

———, and Baha Abu-Laban, ed., *Settler Regimes in Africa and the Arab World*. Contains good articles on Zionism and Palestinian nationalism before and during the mandate.

Yasser Arafat, *Palestine Lives!*. Arafat's famous speech at the United Nations outlines the history of the Palestinians and their fight against Zionism. It projects a vision of their goal of a democratic secular state in Palestine. Available from Peoples Press.

Arie Bober, ed., *The Other Israel: The Radical Case Against Zionism*. Contains unique criticisms of Zionism as well as articles on the class nature of Israeli society from the perspective of a small anti-Zionist socialist organization in Israel.

Fuad Faris, "A Palestinian State," *MERIP* No. 33. Strong argument for the PLO's transitional program.

Samih Farsoun and Walter Carroll, "The Civil War in Lebanon," *Monthly Review* (June 1976). Good account of contradictions leading up to the war in Lebanon.

Fred Halliday, *Arabia Without Sultans*. Excellent introduction to the economies and political developments of countries in the oil-rich Persian-Arabian Gulf. Also information on the national liberation movements in the area.

Mahmoud Hussein, *Class Conflict in Egypt 1945-1970*. Excellent analysis of the structure of Egyptian society and its transformation under Nasser. Also contains good appendix on the structure of Israeli society.

——— ,"The Lebanese Impasse," *Monthly Review* (November 1976). Good analysis of role of Arab states in the Lebanese civil war.

Sabri Jiryis, *The Arabs in Israel*. Best statistical, legal and historical description of the conditions of Palestinians living in Israel.

Ghassan Kanafani, "The 1936 Revolt: Details, Analysis and Background," *PFLP Bulletins*. Best analysis of the Palestinian Revolt of 1936-39. Unfortunately this has not been reprinted and issues of *PFLP Bulletins* are hard to find.

Leila Khaled, *My People Shall Live*. An important and moving autobiography of a dedicated Palestinian woman revolutionary.

Ahmed al Kodsy and Eli Lobel, *The Arab World and Israel*. Two essays on Arab nationalism and on Zionism and imperialism.

Felicia Langer, *With My Own Eyes*. Eyewitness accounts of Israeli violations of human and civil rights of Palestinians by a prominent Israeli lawyer.

V.I. Lenin, *Imperialism, The Highest Stage of Capitalism*. The classic Marxist text on imperialism.

Abraham Leon, *The Jewish Question*. An excellent class analysis and history of anti-Semitism.

Zachary Lockman, "The Left in Israel," *MERIP* No. 49. A good historical summary of the effects of Zionist ideology and the material benefits of settler-colonialism on movements for social change within Israel. Issue also contains documents on the movements of Oriental Jews within Israel.

MERIP Staff, "Open Door in the Middle East," *MERIP* No. 31. A good summary of the economic and political developments in the Middle Eastern countries and movements since the 1973 war. Issue also contains an interview with leaders of the Palestine National Front.

MERIP Staff, "The Syrian Invasion of Lebanon," *MERIP* No. 51. Good background on Syria's role, the United States and other international forces in the Lebanese conflict.

Abdul Waheb al-Messiri, ed., *A Lover From Palestine and Other Poems*. Anthology of Palestinian poetry of the Resistance and exile. Also contains line drawings by a Palestinian artist.

Palestine Research Center, *Palestinian Leaders Discuss: The New Challenges for the Resistance*. A debate between leaders of different Resistance organizations over the proposed transitional program for the PLO.

Maxime Rodinson, *Israel: A Colonial-Settler State?*. Good exposition of the colonial and imperialist nature of Israel with clear refutations of Zionist arguments.

_____, *Israel and the Arabs*. Good overview of Arab, Israeli, United States and Soviet policy in the region up to 1967.

Sheila Ryan, "Israeli Economic Policy in the Occupied Areas: Foundations for a New Imperialism," *MERIP* No. 24. Excellent description of the effects of Israeli occupation on the economy of the occupied territories.

Qais Salim, "The Palestinian Resistance," *MERIP* No. 28. Good short essay on major political questions confronted by the Resistance throughout its history.

Amal Samed, "The Proletarianization of Palestinian Women in Israel," *MERIP* No. 50. Good analysis of effects of entering the Israeli workforce on Palestinian women from the occupied areas and from Israel. Issue also contains a long interview with a leader of the Palestine National Front.

Abdullah Schleifer, *The Fall of Jerusalem*. Best English-language account of the 1967 war and the events leading up to it, with special emphasis on the fighting in Jerusalem. Also contains a good overview of Zionism and Palestinian history.

Ronald Segal, *Whose Jerusalem? The Conflicts of Israel*. The main value of this book lies in its description of the internal class and national conflicts within Israel and the short and accurate descriptions of the class and national contradictions of Egypt, Syria, Jordan and Lebanon.

Russell Stetler, ed., *Palestine: The Arab-Israeli Conflict.* Contains many important political documents of the Resistance movement as well as articles about the class nature of Israel and its foreign policy. Also contains the remarkable "Diary of a Resistance Fighter" from September 1970.

Joe Stork, *Middle East Oil and the Energy Crisis.* Excellent, detailed study of the oil industry, U.S. oil politics, OPEC and the energy crisis.

Fawaz Turki, *The Disinherited: Journal of a Palestinian Exile.* Moving autobiography of a Palestinian refugee and the story of his and other Palestinians' growth into political consciousness.

Resources

Publications

To understand the Palestinian struggle and continuing developments in the Middle East, it is essential to have access to sources of information outside of the regular media. We suggest seven regular publications which contain accurate reporting on the Palestinian movement, other liberation struggles and political movements in the Middle Eastern countries and reports of solidarity activities in the United States.

Palestine! focuses on news about the Palestinian movement. Published monthly by the Palestine Solidarity Committee, Box 1757, Manhattanville Station, New York, New York 10027. Subscriptions $5/year. Also distributes books, pamphlets and periodicals which may not be available in your area.

Arab Student Bulletin contains news and analysis on the Middle East. Published bi-monthly in the U.S. and Canada by the Organization of Arab Students, P.O. Box 8437, Portland, Oregon 97207. Subscriptions $1/year.

Gulf Solidarity Newsletter is a source of news about the Arabian Gulf. Published by Gulf Solidarity, P.O. Box 4155, Station C, San Francisco, California 94140. Subscriptions $2/year.

MERIP Reports gives in-depth coverage and analysis of the Middle East. Published monthly by Middle East Research and Information Project, P.O. Box 3122, Columbia Heights Station, Washington, D.C. 20010. Subscriptions $10/year. Also distributes books, pamphlets and other periodicals.

Journal of Palestine Studies provides a scholarly treatment of different aspects of the Palestinian and Middle Eastern situation. Published quarterly by the Institute for Palestine Studies, P.O. Box 19449, Washington, D.C. 20036. Subscriptions $15/year; students $9/year.

International Bulletin is a source of international news and analysis. Published weekly by Internews, P.O. Box 4400, Berkeley, CA 94704. Subscriptions $8/year.

SWASIA covers major events in the Middle East and includes translations from the Hebrew and Arabic press. Available from 3631 39th St., N.W., Washington, D.C. 20016. Subscriptions $15/year; students $9/year.

Study Guide

Peoples Press Middle East Project has produced a short study guide for groups or individuals interested in pursuing some of the subjects covered in *Our Roots Are Still Alive* in greater depth. It provides systematically arranged further readings on the topics of Palestine and Israel, oil, U.S. Policy and the Arabian Gulf, with short descriptions of each suggested reading, its strengths and weaknesses and how to obtain the books. It also contains several useful maps. Order from Peoples Press, P.O. Box 40130, San Francisco, California 94110. Price 25¢.

Solidarity and Educational Organizations

Increasingly, throughout the United States and other countries, organizations are forming to educate people about the Palestinian struggle and to build solidarity with the Palestinian and other Middle Eastern liberation movements. Their demands include: recognition of the PLO and of the Palestinian people's right to self-determination in their homeland; an end to U.S. involvement in the Middle East; an end to arms sales and military and economic aid to Israel; and an end to U.S. tax exemptions on donations to Israel. Their activities range from organizing demonstrations to educational forums and publications. This list is necessarily incomplete, as the number of such organizations is constantly growing. You may obtain the address of an organization near you by writing to one of the solidarity organizations listed below.

Palestine Solidarity Committees:
New York - P.O. Box 1757, Manhattanville Station, New York City, 10027
Pennsylvania - P.O. Box 312, Schenley Hall, University of Pittsburgh, Pittsburgh, 15760
Ohio - P.O. Box 2203, Youngstown, 44504
Colorado - P.O. Box 2072, Denver, 80201
California - P.O. Box 6123, Albany, 94706

Committee on Palestine and the Middle East (COPME)
P.O. Box 40561, San Francisco, California 94140

Bibliography

Ali Ibrahim Abdo and Kairieh Kasmieh, *Jews of the Arab Countries* (1971). Source for Chapter 10.

Ibrahim Abu-Lughod, ed., *The Arab-Israeli Confrontation of June 1967: An Arab Perspective* (1970). Source for Chapter 13.

-----, *The Transformation of Palestine* (1971). Source for Chapters 1, 3, 4, 5, 8 and 9.

----- and Baha Abu-Laban, eds., *Settler Regimes in Africa and the Arab World* (1974). Source for Chapters 1, 2, 4, 5 and 14.

----- and Edward Said, *Two Studies on the Palestinians Today and American Policy* (1976). Source for Chapter 14.

Michael Adams, *Chaos and Birth: The Arab Outlook* (1968). Source for Chapters 13 and 15.

George Antonius, *The Arab Awakening* (1946). Source for Chapters 1 and 3.

Yasser Arafat, *Palestine Lives!* (1974). Source for Chapter 16.

Hannah Arendt, *Eichmann in Jerusalem* (1963). Source for Chapter 6.

Nasser Aruri and Edmund Gareed, eds., *Enemy of the Sun* (1970). Source for poems.

Uri Avnery, *Israel Without Zionism* (1971). Source for Chapters 2 and 6.

Michael Bar-Zohar, *Ben-Gurion: The Armed Prophet* (1968). Source for Chapters 6 and 10.

Menahem Begin, *The Revolt: Story of the Irgun* (1951). Source for Chapter 8.

David Ben-Gurion, *Israel, Years of Challenge* (1963). Source for Chapter 10.

Amity Ben-Yona, "What Israel Does to its Palestinians: A Letter from Israel to Jews of the American Left," *Arab American University Graduate Bulletin* No. 2. Source for Chapter 14.

Arie Bober, ed., *The Other Israel: The Radical Case Against Zionism* (1972). Source for Chapters 2, 6, 10, 12 and 14.

Gerard Chaliand, *The Palestinian Resistance* (1972). Source for Chapters 9 and 14.

Judith Coburn, "Interview with Palestine National Front," *MERIP* No. 32. Source for Chapters 15 and 16.

-----, "Israel's Ugly Little War," *New Times,* 7 March 1975. Source for Chapter 18.

John Cooley, *Green March, Black September* (1973). Source for Chapters 11, 14 and 15.

Uri Davis, Andrew Mack, and Nira Yuval-Davis, eds., *Israel and the Palestinians* (1975). Source for Chapters 2, 4, 11, 14, 16 and 17.

Democratic Popular Front for the Liberation of Palestine, *Historical Development of the Palestinian Struggle* (1971). Source for Chapters 4, 5 and 8.

-----, *September Counter-Revolution in Jordan* (1971). Source for Chapter 15.

-----, *Terrorism; Leninism vs. Zionism; The Party* (1971). Source for Chapter 15.

-----, *Towards a Democratic Solution to the Palestinian Problem* (1970). Source for Chapter 14.

-----, *D.F.L.P. Reports* (1974-75). Source for Chapters 16, 17 and 18.

Isaac Deutscher, *The Non-Jewish Jew and Other Essays* (1968). Source for Chapters 2 and 6.

Esco Foundation for Palestine, Inc., *Palestine: A Study of Jewish, Arab and British Politics* (1947). Two volumes. Source for Chapters 2, 4, 5 and 6.

Fuad Faris, "A Palestinian State," *MERIP* No. 33. Source for Chapter 16.

Samih Farsoun, "Student Protests and the Coming Crisis in Lebanon," *MERIP* No. 19. Source for Chapters 15 and 18.

----- and Walter Carroll, "The Civil War in Lebanon," *Monthly Review,* June 1976. Source for Chapter 18.

Fatah, *Towards a Democratic State in Palestine for Moslems, Christians and Jews* (1970). Source for Chapter 14.

Feingold, *The Politics of Rescue: The Roosevelt Administration and the Holocaust 1938-45* (1970). Source for Chapter 6.

A.C. Forrest, *The Unholy Land* (1972). Source for Chapters 13 and 14.

Free Palestine, *Zionist-Israeli Acts of Terrorism 1938-1974* (1975). Source for Chapters 8, 15 and 16.

Rita Freed (Committee to Support Middle East Liberation), *War in the Mid East* (1972). Source for Chapters 12, 13 and 15.

John Galvani, Peter Johnson and Rene Theberge, "The October War," *MERIP* No. 22. Source for Chapter 16.

George Habash, *Liberation Not Negotiation* (1974). Source for Chapter 16.

Jamil Halil, "Class Transformation in the West Bank and Gaza," *MERIP* No. 52. Source for Chapter 17.

Fred Halliday, *Arabia Without Sultans* (1975). Source for Chapters 7, 12 and 15.

Samuel Halpern, *The Political World of American Zionism* (1961). Source for Chapters 6 and 7.

Arthur Herzberg, *The Zionist Idea* (1959). Source for Chapters 2 and 4.

Theodore Herzl, *Complete Diaries* (1960). Source for Chapter 2.

-----, *The Jewish State* (1960). Source for Chapter 2.

Raul Hilberg, *The Destruction of the European Jews* (1961). Source for Chapter 6.

Mahmoud Hussein, *Class Conflict in Egypt 1945-1970* (1973). Source for Chapters 12, 13 and 15.

-----, "The Lebanese Impasse," *Monthly Review,* November 1976. Source for Chapter 18.

Hatem I. Husseini and Fathalla El-Boghdady, eds., *The Palestinians, Selected Essays* (1976). Source for Chapter 14.

George Jabbour, *Settler Colonialism in Southern Africa and the Middle East* (1970). Source for Chapters 1 and 2.

Sabri Jiryis, *The Arabs in Israel* (1976). Source for Chapter 10.

-----, "The Land Question in Israel," *MERIP* No. 47. Source for Chapters 10 and 17.

Robert John and Sami Hadawi, *Palestine Diary* (1970). Two volumes. Source for Chapters 3, 4, 5, 6, 7 and 8.

Leila Kadi, ed., *Basic Political Documents of the Armed Palestinian Resistance* (1969). Source for Chapters 9, 11 and 14.

Sharif Kanaana, "Survival Strategies of Arabs in Israel," *MERIP* No. 41. Source for Chapters 10 and 17.

Anni Kanafani, *Ghassan Kanafani* (1972). Source for Chapter 8.

Ghassan Kanafani, "The 1936 Revolt: Details, Analysis and Background," *PFLP Bulletins* (1974-75). Source for Chapters 4 and 5.

Leila Khaled, *My People Shall Live* (1973). Source for Chapters 9, 11, 14, 15 and 16.

Walid Khalidi, ed., *From Haven to Conquest: Readings in Zionism and the Palestine Problem Until 1948* (1971). Source for Chapters 4, 5, 6, 7 and 8.

Ahmed al Kodsy and Eli Lobel, *The Arab World and Israel* (1970). Source for Chapters 1, 2 and 4.

Joyce and Gabriel Kolko, *The Limits of Power: The World and United States Foreign Policy; 1945-1954* (1972). Source for Chapters 7 and 10.

Felicia Langer, *With My Own Eyes* (1973). Source for Chapters 15 and 17.

Walter Laquer, ed., *The Israel-Arab Reader* (1971). Source for Chapters 3, 4, 5, 7 and 12.

V.I. Lenin, *Imperialism, The Highest Stage of Capitalism* (1973). Source for Chapter 2.

-----, *The Jewish Question* (1972). Source for Chapter 2.

Abraham Leon, *The Jewish Question* (1970). Source for Chapter 2.

Ann Mosely Lesch, unpublished dissertation. Source for Chapter 1.

Alfred M. Lilientahl, *The Other Side of the Coin* (1955). Source for Chapter 10.

-----, *What Price Israel?* (1969). Source for Chapter 7.

Zachary Lockman, "The Left in Israel," *MERIP* No. 49. Source for Chapters 4 and 17.

Nathaniel Lorch, *The Edge of the Sword* (1961). Source for Chapter 8.

Kenneth Love, *Suez: The Twice-Fought War* (1969). Source for Chapters 10 and 11.

Neville J. Mandell, *The Arabs and Zionism Before World War I* (1976). Source for Chapter 1.

MERIP, "Lebanon Explodes," *MERIP* No. 44. Source for Chapter 18.

-----, "Open Door in the Middle East," *MERIP* No. 31. Source for Chapter 16.

-----, "The Syrian Invasion of Lebanon," *MERIP* No. 51. Source for Chapter 18.

Abdul Waheb al-Messiri, ed., *A Lover From Palestine and Other Poems* (1970). Source for poems.

Edgar O'Ballance, *Arab Guerrilla Power* (1973). Source for Chapters 14 and 15.

-----, *The Arab-Israeli War 1948* (1956). Source for Chapter 8.

-----, *The Third Arab-Israeli War* (1972). Source for Chapter 13.

Organization of Arab Students, *Arab Student Bulletin* (1975-77). Source for Chapters 6, 16, 17 and 18.

-----, *The Kissinger Mid-East Peace Trap* (1976). Source for Chapter 16.

-----, *Lebanon, The Price of Blood* (1976). Source for Chapter 18.

Ibrahim M. Oweiss, *The Israeli Economy, A War Economy* (1974). Source for Chapter 12.

Chris Paine, "The Political Economy of Arms Transfers to the Middle East," *MERIP* No. 30. Source for Chapters 13 and 15.

Palestine Liberation Organization, *Palestine* (1975-76). Source for Chapters 6, 14, 15, 16, 17 and 18.

-----, *Palestine Lives!* (1975-76). Source for Chapters 4, 5, 11, 14, 16, 17 and 18.

Palestine Research Center, *Palestinian Leaders Discuss: The New Challenges for the Resistance* (1974). Source for Chapter 16.

Palestine Solidarity Committee (New York), *Zionism: The Colonial Process* (1976). Source for Chapters 2, 4, 6, 7, 8, 12 and 15.

-----, *Palestine!* (1976-1977). Source for Chapters 2, 8, 9, 10, 17 and 18.

Amos Perlmutter, *Military and Politics in Israel* (1969). Source for Chapters 4 and 5.

Tabitha Petran, *Zionism, a Political Critique* (1973). Source for Chapters 6, 8, 12 and 13.

-----, *Syria* (1972). Source for Chapter 12.

William Polk, *Backdrop to Tragedy* (1957). Source for Chapter 1.

Popular Front for the Liberation of Palestine, *A Strategy for the Liberation of Palestine* (1969). Source for Chapter 14.

-----, *PFLP Bulletin* (1974-77). Source for Chapters 4, 5, 16, 17 and 18.

Terence Prittie, *Israel; Miracle in the Desert* (1967). Source for Chapter 10.

William Quandt, Fuad Jabber and Ann Mosely Lesch, *The Politics of Palestinian Nationalism* (1973). Source for Chapters 4, 5, 11, 14 and 15.

Maxime Rodinson, *Israel: A Colonial-Settler State?* (1973). Source for Chapters 2 and 4.

-----, *Israel and the Arabs* (1970). Source for Chapters 9, 10, 11 and 12.

Sharon Rose and Joe Stork, "Zionism and American Jews," *MERIP* No. 29. Source for Chapters 6 and 7.

Barry Rubin, "U.S. Policy and the October War," *MERIP* No. 23. Source for Chapter 16.

Sheila Ryan, "Israeli Economic Policy in the Occupied Areas: Foundations for a New Imperialism," *MERIP* No. 24. Source for Chapters 14 and 17.

----- and George Cavelleto, "Palestine on the Brink of People's War," unpublished article (1970). Source for Chapter 14.

----- and Joe Stork, "The U.S. and Jordan: Thrice Rescued Throne," *MERIP* No. 7. Source for Chapter 15.

Howard Sacher, *The Course of Modern Jewish History* (1958). Source for Chapters 2 and 6.

Isam Sakhnini, *PLO, The Representative of the Palestinians* (1974). Source for Chapter 14.

Qais Salim, "The Palestinian Resistance," *MERIP* No. 28. Source for Chapters 4, 5, 11, 14, 15 and 16.

Amal Samed, "The Proletarianization of Palestinian Women in Israel," *MERIP* No. 50. Source for Chapter 17.

Joseph Schectman, *On Wings of Eagles: The Plight, Exodus and Homecoming of Oriental Jewry* (1961). Source for Chapter 10.

Abdullah Schleifer, *The Fall of Jerusalem* (1973). Source for Chapters 2, 6, 7, 8, 9, 11, 12 and 13.

Dana Adams Schmidt, *Armageddon in the Middle East* (1974). Source for Chapter 8.

Erica Schoenberger, "Soviet Policy in the Middle East," *MERIP* No. 9. Source for Chapter 2.

Ronald Segal, *Whose Jerusalem? The Conflicts of Israel* (1973). Source for Chapters 10, 15, 16 and 18.

Peter Seidman, *Socialists and the Fight Against Anti-Semitism* (1973). Source for Chapter 6.

Israel Shahak, *The Shahak Report* (1973). Source for Chapter 17.

Robert Silverberg, *If I Forget Thee, O Jerusalem: American Jews and the State of Israel* (1970). Source for Chapters 6 and 7.

Leonard Stein, *The Balfour Declaration* (1937). Source for Chapter 3.

Russell Stetler, ed., *Palestine: The Arab-Israeli Conflict* (1972). Source for Chapters 12, 13, 14 and 15.

Joe Stork, *Middle East Oil and the Energy Crisis* (1976). Source for Chapters 7, 12 and 16.

SWASIA (weekly news service). Source for Chapters 16, 17 and 18.

Christopher Sykes, *Crossroads to Israel* (1968). Source for Chapters 3, 4, 5, 6, 7 and 8.

Alan Taylor, *Prelude to Israel 1897-1947* (1959). Source for Chapters 2 and 3.

Arlette Tessier, *Gaza* (1971). Source for Chapter 14.

Henry J. Tobias, *The Jewish Bund in Russia* (1972). Source for Chapter 2.

Tricontinental, *Palestine: Crisis and Liberation* (1970). Source for Chapters 2 and 14.

Fawaz Turki, *The Disinherited: Journal of a Palestinian Exile* (1972). Source for Chapters 9, 11 and 14.

Ehud Yaari, *Strike Terror, The Story of Fatah* (1970). Source for Chapters 11 and 14.

Tawfiq Zayyad, "The Fate of the Arabs in Israel," *Journal of Palestine Studies,* Autumn 1976. Source for Chapter 17.

OTHER PUBLICATIONS AVAILABLE FROM PEOPLES PRESS

Puerto Rico: The Flame of Resistance
With Freedom in Their Eyes: A photo-essay of Angola
From Slavery to Freedom: A Story From Angola
Women of Viet Nam
The Earth Belongs to the People: Ecology and Power
Cuba for Beginners

Please write Peoples Press for a complete list of its books, pamphlets and posters:

Peoples Press
P.O. Box 40130
San Francisco, Ca.
94110